# WHOSE IDEAS MATTER?

A VOLUME IN THE SERIES

CORNELL STUDIES IN POLITICAL ECONOMY

*edited by* Peter J. Katzenstein

A list of titles in this series is available at www.cornellpress.cornell.edu.

# Whose Ideas Matter? AGENCY AND POWER IN ASIAN REGIONALISM

**Amitav Acharya**

Cornell University Press ITHACA AND LONDON

First published 2009 by Cornell University Press
First printing, Cornell Paperbacks, 2011

Printed in the United States of America

Library of Congress Cataloging-in-Publication Data

Acharya, Amitav.
   Whose ideas matter? : agency and power in Asian regionalism /
by Amitav Acharya.
      p. cm. — (Cornell studies in political economy)
   Includes bibliographical references and index.
   ISBN 978-0-8014-4751-8 (cloth : alk. paper)
   ISBN 978-0-8014-7708-9 (pbk. : alk. paper)
      1. Regionalism—Asia.   2. International agencies—Asia.
3. Asian cooperation.   4. Asia—Foreign relations.
5. Asia—Politics and government—1945-   I. Title.
II. Series: Cornell studies in political economy.
   JZ5333.A27 2009
   327.5—dc22
2008047453

Cloth printing      10  9  8  7  6  5  4  3  2  1
Paperback printing  10  9  8  7  6  5  4  3  2  1

# Contents

# Illustrations and Tables

## Illustrations

## Tables

# Acknowledgments

This book owes its origin and inspiration to my three research fellowships at Harvard University—with the Harvard Asia Center (2000–2001), with the Center for Business and Government at the John F. Kennedy School of Government (2000–2002), and with the Weatherhead Center for International Affairs (2004–5). I am grateful to Ezra Vogel and Bill Kirby at the Asia Center, Joe Nye and Dennis Encarnation at the Kennedy School, and Iain Johnston and Jorge Dominguez at the Weatherhead Center for their help and advice as well as arranging institutional support that made the research and writing of this book possible. Portions of this book have been presented as seminars at the Belfer Center for Science and International Affairs, Harvard University (April 2001); the Modern Asia Seminar Series at the Harvard Asia Center (May 2001); the Fellows program of the Center for Business and Government at the Kennedy School (May 2001); and the Weatherhead Center for International Affairs (November 2004). Other seminars on the theme of the book have been presented at the Department of International Relations, Australian National University (September 2001); and the Institute of International Relations, University of British Columbia (April 2002 and May 2005). I am grateful to these institutions for arranging a vibrant, engaging, and critical audience to test the arguments of the book.

Peter Katzenstein has been a major inspiration behind this project, and his own work on Asian regionalism has been a central influence on my work. Roger Haydon of Cornell University Press took interest in the project from the moment I discussed it with him and offered invaluable comments and guidance through the review process. I am grateful to Jack Snyder, Chris Reus-Smit, Brian Job, Paul Evans, Anthony Milner, John Hobson, Etel Solingen, Michael Barnett, Richard Price, and Martha Finnemore, all of whom commented on earlier drafts of chapters 2 and 5 (which appeared as an article in *International Organization*). Parts of chapters 2 and 3 were published as a Weatherhead Center working paper and benefited from comments by Barry Buzan, Michael Barnett, Jeffrey Herbst, Andrew Hurrell, Jorge Dominguez, Elizabeth Kier, Steve Walt, Jack Snyder, Leszek Buszynski, Robert O. Keohane, Sumit Ganguly, Scott Snyder, T.V. Paul, Lawrence Prabhakar, Iain Johnston, Andrew Kydd, and participants at a seminar organized by the Weatherhead Center on 22 November 2004.

I am also grateful to Muthiah Alagappa, Victor Cha, Iain Johnston, and Itty Abraham for their feedback on the outline of the book project. Helen Nesadurai and John Ravenhill generously shared their expertise on the political economy of Asian regionalism. A good deal of the research for the book was conducted at the Institute of Defense and Strategic Studies (IDSS) in Singapore, whose research program I headed for five and a half years (2001–2006). The Department of Politics at the University of Bristol provided a very encouraging scholarly environment to bring closure to the book. Hiro Katsumata's suggestions were important in developing the final structure of the book, and Tang Shiping provided valuable comments on several chapters. I thank IDSS-Singapore for its generous support, particularly to Tan Ban Seng, Deborah Lee, Karyn Wang, Morten Hansen, Marguerite Luong, Herbert Lin, Jack Kwon, and Yolanda Chin, all of them IDSS staff who provided invaluable research or editing assistance. Susan Specter at Cornell University Press offered numerous helpful editorial suggestions.

I thank Priyanka Gandhi Vadra of the Jawaharlal Nehru Memorial Fund, New Delhi, for giving permission to reproduce Nehru's reflections on intervention at Bandung (figure 3.2), and the National Archives of the UK for permission to reproduce extracts from the official British documents included in "Colombo powers' reaction to SEATO" (figure 3.1). Hugh Alexander, Deputy Manager of the Image Library of the National Archives, helped with obtaining images of the documents. M. V. Malla Prasad greatly assisted my research into archival documents in India, while Jingchun Zhang worked closely with me in conducting archival research in China. I will never forget the incomparable generosity of Roselan Abdulghani, the Secretary-General of the 1955 Bandung Conference, for giving me two interviews despite his advanced age, shortly before his death in 2005. And special thanks go to Yang Shanhou for translating the Chinese documents and Matthew Hope of the University of Bristol for preparing the index.

# 1  Why Study the Norm Dynamics of Asian Regionalism?

Why didn't a regional multilateral security organization take root in Asia in the aftermath of World War II?[1] Why do Asia's regional institutions remain "soft," and resist demands for reform and change since the end of the Cold War? As Peter Katzenstein observes, while "Europe is undergoing fundamental institutional change, with far-reaching efforts to redefine state prerogatives . . . Asia is characterized by marginal adjustments, insistence on state sovereignty and a preference for bilateralism."[2]

## Empirical Puzzles

This book investigates these two puzzles about Asia's post-war regional institutional architecture, which have attracted growing interest from academics (table 1.1) and policymakers.[3] Realists seeking to explain the first

1. The major Cold War era exception to this, the South East Asia Treaty Organization (SEATO), is widely regarded as ineffectual and moribund almost from the start—it was "no Asian NATO." Christopher Hemmer and Peter J. Katzenstein, "Why Is There No NATO in Asia: Collective Identity, Regionalism, and the Origins of Multilateralism," *International Organization* 56, no. 3 (Summer 2002): 575–607. The Association of Southeast Asian Nations (ASEAN) Regional Forum (ARF), established in 1994, is not only a latecomer but is also wedded to a softer "cooperative security," rather than collective security or collective defense approach. For distinctions among "cooperative security," "collective security," and "collective defense," see appendix of this book; Charles A. Kupchan, "Regionalizing Europe's Security: The Case for a New Mitteleuropa," in *The Political Economy of Regionalism*, ed. Edward Mansfield and Helen Milner (New York: Columbia University Press, 1997), 220–21.

2. Peter J. Katzenstein, *A World of Regions: Asia and Europe in the American Imperium* (Ithaca: Cornell University Press, 2005), 103, 148.

3. The soft institutionalism of Asia prevails in both economic and security institutions, such as Asia Pacific Economic Cooperation (APEC) and the ARF. Realist and functionalist explanations of this feature that are focused on economic institutions can also apply to soft institutionalism in multipurpose or security institutions such as ASEAN and the ARF.

**Table 1.1.** Selected Perspectives on Asian Regionalism

| Author | Explanation[a] |
|---|---|
| Crone (mainly neorealist) | U.S. "extreme hegemony" inhibited institution-building after World War II; its decline created powerful incentives for cooperation.[b] |
| Grieco (mainly neorealist) | U.S. grand strategy in Asia after World War II constrained Japan's regional role, thereby affecting the prospects for Asian multilateralism.[c] |
| Kahler (neoliberal) | Rational calculation and pursuit of self-interest linked to growing economic interdependence in the 1990s encouraged institution-building by fostering a shared commitment to growth and performance legitimacy among regional actors and increasing the costs of non-cooperative behavior; market-driven economic interactions rendered the tasks to be performed by institutions (e.g., monitoring and enforcement) less demanding, thereby reducing the cost of institution-building.[d] |
| Katzenstein (constructivist and domestic politics) | Identity dissonance between U.S. policymakers and their Asian allies prevented NATO-like security multilateralism in Asia; "non-Weberian" statehood and "rule by law," as opposed to "rule of law," limited regional institutionalization; the international norm of "open regionalism" shaped Asian avoidance of EU-style economic institutions.[e] |
| Duffield (mixed) | "Regional structural factors," i.e., the number, relative size, relative capabilities and geographic dispersion of states determined Asian security institutionalization.[f] |

[a] Crone and Katzenstein explain both economic and security institution-building. Kahler is concerned mainly with economic institutions (e.g., why APEC emerged when it did). See Miles Kahler, "Institution-Building in the Pacific," in *Pacific Cooperation: Building Economic and Security Regimes in the Asia-Pacific Region*, ed. Andrew Mack and John Ravenhill (St. Leonards, NSW: Allen & Unwin, 1994), 27–43. But his perspective can be used to explain why there was no economic or security institution before APEC. For a discussion of liberal and functionalist views on the relationship between economic interdependence and security, see Hadi Soesastro, "Economic Integration and Interdependence in the Asia Pacific: Implications for Security," paper presented at the Eighth Asia Pacific Roundtable, Kuala Lumpur, Malaysia, 5–8 June 1994.

[b] Donald Crone, "Does Hegemony Matter? The Reorganization of the Pacific Political Economy," *World Politics* 45, no. 4 (July 1993): 501–525.

[c] Joseph M. Grieco, "Realism and Regionalism: American Power and German and Japanese Institutional Strategies During and After the Cold War," in *Unipolar Politics: Realism and State Strategies After the Cold War*, ed. Ethan B. Kapstein and Michael Mastanduno (New York: Columbia University Press, 1999), 107–131.

[d] Kahler, "Institution-Building in the Pacific," 16–39; Miles Kahler, "Legalization as Strategy: The Asia-Pacific Case," *International Organization* 54, no. 3 (2000): 549–71.

[e] Peter Katzenstein, "Introduction: Asian Regionalism in Comparative Perspective," in *Network Power: Japan and Asia*, ed. Peter Katzenstein and Takashi Shiraishi (Ithaca: Cornell University Press, 1997), 1–46; Katzenstein, *A World of Regions*.

[f] John S. Duffield, "Why Is There no APTO? Why Is There no OSCAP? Asia-Pacific Security Institutions in Comparative Perspective," *Contemporary Security Policy*, 22, no. 2 (August 2001): 69–95.

puzzle argue that U.S. strategic policies and power differential relative to Asian actors hold the clue to the absence of an Asian NATO. Functional perspectives explain Asia's late and weak regional institutionalism by stressing the role of rational calculations and the pursuit of self-interest linked to levels of regional economic interdependence.[4] One constructivist perspective

4. Apart from Kahler (see table 1.1), other functionalist, interest-based neo-liberal explanations of Asian regionalism include Peter Drysdale, *International Economic Pluralism: Economic*

finds U.S. perceptions of its "collective identity," whereby U.S. policymakers saw their potential Asian allies as inferior to their potential European ones, to have been the critical reason why there could be no NATO in Asia. Analysts have also offered "mixed" explanations that include domestic political structures, the "structural" features of the region, and the influence of *international* norms.

I offer a different explanation. While accepting the constructivist view that ideational forces mattered, I argue that these forces were generated from *within* the region. Take, for example, the power gap and identity-dissonance explanations of why there is no Asian NATO. These are primarily arguments about why the United States did not pursue a multilateral approach in Asia, rather than why Asian actors did not want it. It was either *U.S.* power or *U.S.* perceptions of collective identity that mattered. Missing here is any serious consideration of intra-regional interactions and norms developed by Asians themselves. This is a major gap.

Challenging this top-down constructionist view, this book argues that after the end of World War II, but especially after the outbreak of the Korean War, U.S. policymakers were not strategically averse to, or culturally predisposed against, an Asian multilateral security organization. However, their ability to create such an organization was challenged by strong normative opposition from an influential segment of Asia's nationalist leaders. At a series of regional gatherings, these leaders framed the idea of a regional collective defense organization as a new form of Western dominance damaging to their newfound national sovereignty and regional autonomy. The normative outcome of this contestation was the delegitimation of collective defense as a regional security framework.

This argument leads to the second question raised in the opening paragraph: What explains the institutional features of Asian regionalism such as its aversion to legalization and bureaucratization? The answer is that early postwar interactions, while expanding the scope of the non-intervention norm also predisposed the region toward a softer form of multilateralism. They constituted elements of a regional "cognitive prior," conditioning subsequent

---

*Policy in East Asia and the Pacific* (Sydney: Allen and Unwin, 1988); Wendy Dobson and Lee Tsao Yuan, "APEC: Cooperation Amidst Diversity," *ASEAN Economic Bulletin* 10, no.3 (1994): 231–44; Andrew Elek, "APEC Beyond Bogor: An Open Economic Association in the Asian-Pacific Region," *Asia-Pacific Economic Literature* 9, no. 1 (1995): 183–223; Peter Drysdale, "The APEC Initiative: Maintaining the Momentum in Manila," *Asia-Pacific Magazine*, May 1996, 44–46; and Peter Drysdale and Ross Garnut, "The Pacific: An Application of a General Theory of Economic Integration," in *Pacific Economic Dynamism and the International Economic System*, ed. C. Fred Bergsten and Marcus Nolan (Washington, DC: Institute for International Economics, 1993), 183–223.

regional institution-building efforts, including those inspired by new ideas about multilateralism and institutional strengthening.

## Theoretical Arguments

The theoretical purpose of this book is to contribute to our understanding of how ideas and norms spread in world politics. Despite much recent work on norms, the literature on international relations remains "underspecified with regard to the causal mechanisms and processes by which . . . ideas spread."[5] It offers little systematic investigation of a key question: Why do some emerging ideas and norms find acceptance in a particular locale while others do not?[6]

Scholarship on normative change is biased in favor of a "moral cosmopolitanism." It concentrates on moral struggles in which *good* global norms (championed by mainly Western norm entrepreneurs) displace *bad* local beliefs and practices (mainly in the non-Western areas). It overlooks local beliefs and practices which, as part of a legitimate normative order, determine the fate of new norms.

This book focuses on the agency role of norm-takers. Central to the norm dynamic is contestation between emerging norms and existing local beliefs and practices. The outcome is shaped by the ideas and initiative of local actors. This is not simply a question of the existential fit between local norms and external norms. Rather, it is a dynamic process of "constitutive localization" that enables norm-takers to build congruence between the local (including norms previously institutionalized in a region) and external norms. In this process, external norms, which may not initially cohere with existing local beliefs and practices, are incorporated after undergoing modifications to their meaning and scope. This book identifies several conditions that facilitate this process. The evidence shows that a strategy of norm diffusion that provides opportunities for localization is more likely to succeed than one that does not.

5. Thomas Risse and Kathryn Sikkink, "The Socialization of International Human Rights Norms into Domestic Practices: Introduction," in *The Power of Human Rights: International Norms and Domestic Change*, ed. Thomas Risse, Stephen C. Ropp, and Kathryn Sikkink (New York: Cambridge University Press, 1999), 4.

6. The terms "norm-maker" and "norm-taker" are taken from Jeffrey Checkel, "Norms, Institutions and National Identity in Contemporary Europe," *ARENA Working Papers*, 98/16 (Oslo: Advanced Research on the Europeanization of the Nation-State, University of Oslo, 1998), 2.

The idea of constitutive localization, outlined in detail in chapter 2, can be summarily presented with the help of the following propositions:

1. New international norms do not enter into a local normative vacuum. Local norms, including norms previously borrowed from the global arena, may enjoy a robust legitimacy and therefore influence the reception of new international norms.

2. The global prominence of a norm and the reputational power of transnational norm entrepreneurs are necessary but not sufficient conditions for successful norm diffusion. The congruence between outside norms and local norms also matters.

3. "Congruence" between emerging and existing ideas is to be understood not as a static fit, but as a dynamic process. Local actors do not passively accept new international ideas and simply adjust their beliefs to fit with them. Instead, they assess outside ideas in terms of their suitability for local reconstruction. Norms that can be made to fit local conditions and traditions spread more easily than those that cannot. Normative change occurs because of the successful fusion of foreign ideas with local ones.

4. The localization of new ideas and norms does not extinguish existing local beliefs and practices, but may instead universalize and amplify the latter. The borrowing and reconstructing of new ideas could enhance the prestige of local beliefs, identities, and practices before a larger stage or a wider community.

The constitutive localization perspective accepts that ideas and norms matter in international relations. However, it seeks to remedy the neglect of *legitimate resistance* to outside norms by local actors. It pays special attention to local historical and institutional contexts often ignored by both rationalist and constructivist explanations of norm diffusion.

Moreover, the constitutive localization perspective goes beyond constructivists who tend to pick out successful or dramatic cases of moral transformation and avoid "the dog who didn't bark."[7] Challenging this tendency, Ted Hopf argues that constructivism should be "agnostic about change in world politics. . . . What [it] does offer is an account of how and where change may occur."[8] The constitutive localization perspective accounts for a range of responses to new norms that fall in between outright compliance and total rejection. It highlights path-dependent forms of acceptance—an

7. Checkel, "Norms, Institutions and National Identity in Contemporary Europe," 4.
8. Ted Hopf, "The Promise of Constructivism in International Relations Theory," *International Security* 23, no. 1 (1998): 180.

evolutionary form of norm diffusion that produces everyday forms of normative change in world politics.

## Structure of the Book

The normative explanation of Asian regionalism presented in this book can be traced through two stages of constitutive localization. (See figure 1.1 for illustration of this framework.) During the first phase, described in chapter 3 and covering the immediate post–World War II period, Asia's leaders faced two ideas about how to promote regional security and order: nonintervention and collective defense. These ideas interacted with their prior beliefs about anti-colonialism and aversion to great power sphere of influences. After a period of contestation and compromises, non-intervention found broad acceptance. It was even enhanced to include an injunction against superpower-led military pacts. In contrast, collective defense, promoted by the United States and represented by the South East Asian Treaty Organization, failed.

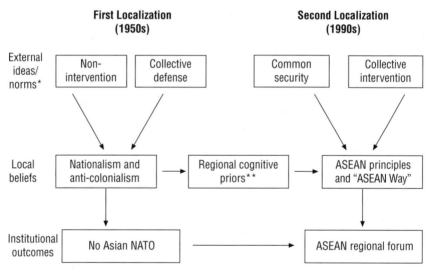

**Figure 1.1.** Constitutive localization in Asian regionalism.
 * The presentation and discussion of these norms follows the historical sequence of their appearance in the Asian regionalist context. Thus in the 1950s, non-intervention was prior to collective defense, whereas in the 1990s, common security predated the prominence in Asia of collective intervention. For definitions and interpretations of these concepts, see the appendix.
 ** Regional cognitive priors include enhanced non-intervention, soft institutionalism, defense bilateralism, and security proto multilateralism.

This outcome, and attendant ones such as a framework of soft institutionalism and principles and mechanisms of cooperative security, created a regionalist cognitive prior, which is the subject of chapter 4. This cognitive prior not only diffused through subsequent institution-building processes (especially through the Association of Southeast Asian Nations established in 1967), but also shaped post–Cold War era institutional change. Then, it became the receptacle for new international norms through a second post–Cold War phase of constitutive localization. During this phase, traced in chapter 5, Asia's leaders considering a new regional security architecture were faced with two sets of norms: common security and collective intervention. The outcome of this second phase was the acceptance and institutionalization of the former, and the rejection (at least for the immediate future) of the latter.

NEITHER power politics nor functional imperative adequately explains the institutional trajectory and outcomes of Asian regionalism. Normative contestations and compromises through which local ideas and cognitive priors shaped the borrowing of international norms of sovereignty and cooperation are crucial to understanding and explaining institution building in Asian regionalism.

In developing this argument, I hold that the diffusion of ideas and normative change in world politics is not produced by universal moral entrepreneurs whereas local actors remain "passive targets." Local actors also condition the reception of global norms by acting out of a historically constructed normative base. The constitutive localization dynamic explains the successes, limitations, and prospects for Asian regionalism. Instead of expecting it to replicate the European institutional purpose and design, normative change and institution-building in Asia are better viewed as evolutionary processes contingent upon prior regional norms and processes.

A broader implication is that contestations over seemingly incompatible "universal" values and ideas on the one hand, and local ones on the other hand, often result in compromises imbued with moral purpose and defined by mutual adaptations. As ideational or civilizational entities, regions do not always clash, but learn and borrow from each other.[9] The ideational

---

9. Samuel Huntington offers a contrary perspective in *The Clash of Civilizations and the Remaking of World Order* (New York: Simon and Schuster, 1996). Huntington sees the tendency of elites in developing countries to retreat into their local religious or cultural values (a phenomenon he calls "de-Westernization and indigenization of elites") as a major reason behind the clash of civilizations, whereas I see the localization of ideas by such elites as being motivated by a desire to achieve an incremental and progressive promotion of universal ideas and norms (whether it be Gandhi's localization of nationalism and passive resistance in India or more recent efforts to introduce cooperative security and collective intervention norms in Asia).

foundation of world politics is formed by a continuous process of constitutive localization, which does not result in instant or comprehensive wins and defeats of one set of ideas over another. Rather, it rests on gradual, evolutionary, and everyday forms of normative and institutional change and a progressive blending of local and universal norms and values.

# 2 Perspectives on Norm Diffusion

Why do some ideas and norms find acceptance in a particular locale and others do not? For some time, rationalists and constructivists have debated the causal and transformative impact of ideas and norms. However, questions about normative change in world politics are not only about *whether* ideas matter, but also *whose* ideas matter.

## Perspectives on Norm Diffusion

### Moral Cosmopolitanism

The "first wave" of norm scholarship in the constructivist literature can be termed as a "moral cosmopolitanism" perspective with four distinctive features. First, the norms that are being propagated are *cosmopolitan*, or *universal*, such as campaigns against land mines, bans on chemical weapons, the protection of endangered species, struggles against racism, interventions against genocide, and the promotion of human rights.[1] Second, the

1. See, for example, Richard Price, "Reversing the Gun Sights: Transnational Civil Society Targets Land Mines," *International Organization* 52, no. 3 (1988): 613–44 and *The Chemical Weapons Taboo* (Ithaca: Cornell University Press, 1997); Kathryn Sikkink, "Human Rights, Principled Issue-Networks, and Sovereignty in Latin America," *International Organization* 47, no. 3 (1993): 411–14; M.J. Peterson, "Whales, Cetologists, Environmentalists, and the International Management of Whaling," *International Organization* 46, no. 1 (1992): 147–86; Karen Litfin, *Ozone Discourses: Science and Politics in Global Environmental Cooperation* (New York: Columbia University Press, 1994); Audie Klotz, *Norms in International Relations: The Struggle Against Apartheid* (Ithaca: Cornell University Press, 1995); Audie Klotz, "Norms Reconstituting Interests: Global Racial Equality and the U.S. Sanctions Against South Africa," *International Organization* 3, no. 49 (1995): 451–78. Summarizing the literature on norms, Keith Krause points out the overwhelming dominance of "environmental or human rights issues, with case studies of such topics as international whaling, human rights in Latin America and Western Europe, the abolition of apartheid, protection of the Ozone Layer or the world's

key actors who spread these norms are transnational agents, whether individual "moral entrepreneurs" or social movements.[2] Third, despite recognizing the role of persuasion in norm diffusion, this literature focuses heavily on "proselytism" and pressure: what Ethan Nadelman has described as the "moral proselytism of transnational moral entrepreneurs."[3] Influenced by sociological institutionalism, many norm scholars tend to reproduce its underlying assumptions of a global social structure that acts as a wellspring of *good* normative ideas and standards.[4] The social movement perspective on norm diffusion stresses shaming over framing, and sanctions over "saving face," thereby according little space to positive action or voluntary initiative by the norm-takers.[5] Finally, this perspective is generally more concerned with conversion rather than contestation, although the latter is acknowledged,[6] viewing resistance to cosmopolitan norms as illegitimate or immoral.[7]

Despite pioneering the study of norm diffusion, moral cosmopolitanism has contributed to two unfortunate tendencies. First, many moral cosmopolitanists view norm diffusion as *teaching* by transnational agents, which tends to overlook the agency role of local actors.[8] Second, and closely

---

forests, or the creation and activities of international institutions such as the ICRC or UNESCO." Studies of norms in "high" security issues have been far fewer and that too from a "peace research perspective"; these include the International Campaign to Ban Land Mines and the more recent work on the proliferation of small arms and light weapons (Keith Krause, *Culture and Security: Multilateralism, Arms Control, and Security Building* [Portland, Oregon: Frank Cass, 1998], 6–7).

2. Ethan Nadelmann, "Global Prohibition Regimes: The Evolution of Norms in International Society," *International Organization* 44, no. 4 (1990): 483; Thomas Risse, Stephen C. Ropp, and Kathryn Sikkink, *The Power of Human Rights: International Norms and Domestic Change* (Cambridge: Cambridge University Press, 1999); Margaret Keck and Kathryn Sikkink, *Activists Beyond Borders: Advocacy Networks in International Politics* (Ithaca: Cornell University Press, 1998).

3. Nadelman, "Global Prohibition Regimes."

4. Martha Finnemore, "Norms, Culture and World Politics: Insights from Sociology's Institutionalism (A Review Essay)," *International Organization* 50, no. 2 (1996): 341. On sociological institutionalism, see John W. Meyer, "The World Polity and the Authority of the Nation-State," in *Studies of the Modern World-System*, ed. A. Bergesen (New York: Academic Press, 1980), 109–37; John W. Meyer, John Boli, George M. Thomas, and Francisco O. Ramirez, "World Society and the Nation-State," *American Journal of Sociology* 103, no. 1 (July 1997) 144–48; John Meyer, John Boli, and George Thomas, *Institutional Structure: Constituting State, Society, and the Individual* (Newbury Park, CA: Sage, 1987).

5. Risse, Ropp, and Sikkink, *The Power of Human Rights*.

6. Martha Finnemore and Kathryn Sikkink, "International Norm Dynamics and Political Change," in *Exploration and Contestation in the Study of World Politics*, ed. Peter Katzenstein, Robert Keohane, and Stephen Krasner (Cambridge: MIT Press, 1999), 257.

7. Risse, Ropp, and Sikkink, *The Power of Human Rights*.

8. Martha Finnemore, "International Organizations as Teachers of Norms: The United Nations Educational, Scientific, and Cultural Organization and Science Policy," *International*

related, by assigning causal primacy to "international prescriptions," it ignores the appeal and feedback potential of norms that are rooted in regional, national, or subnational groups.[9] The strong ethos of normative
universalism predisposes constructivist norm theorists to view regional or
local norms as morally deficient. Moreover, it sets up an implicit dichotomy
between *good* global/universal norms and *bad* regional/local norms.[10] This
view is misleading. Some universal norms can have negative consequences;
for example, self-determination, a supposedly *good* cosmopolitan norm,
can result in narrow nationalism and violent ethnic conflict. In contrast,
there are many examples of local norms that successfully promote pacific
management of disputes; for example, the cultural norms of Japan discussed
by Katzenstein, or the norms of consensus in some Asian societies.[11] Yet, for
moral cosmopolitans, norms that make a universalistic claim about what
is good are considered more desirable and more likely to prevail than norms
that are localized or particularistic.[12]

### Domestic Fit

The "second wave" of norm scholarship centers on the role of domestic
political structures and agents in shaping normative change.[13] It looks beyond

*Organization* 47, no. 4 (1993): 565–97; Michael N. Barnett and Martha Finnemore, "The
Politics, Power, and Pathologies of International Organizations," *International Organization*
53, no. 4, (1999): 699–732.

9. Jeffrey W. Legro, "Which Norms Matter? Revisiting the 'Failure' of Internationalism,"
*International Organization* 51, no. 1 (1997): 32.

10. Jeffrey Checkel, "Norms, Institutions, and National Identity in Contemporary Europe," *ARENA Working Papers* 98/16 (Oslo: Advanced Research on Europeanization of the
Nation-State, University of Oslo, 1998).

11. Peter Katzenstein, *Cultural Norms and National Security: Police and Military in Post-
war Japan* (Ithaca: Cornell University Press, 1996).

12. Finnemore, "Norms, Culture and World Politics"; Finnemore and Sikkink, "International Norm Dynamics and Political Change," 267.

13. Andrew P. Cortell and James W. Davis, "Understanding the Domestic Impact of International Norms: A Research Agenda," *International Studies Review* 2, no. 1 (2000): 65–87. The
"first wave" focused on the level of the international system, leading examples being Finnemore,
"International Organizations as Teachers of Norms" and Finnemore and Sikkink, "International
Norm Dynamics and Political Change." On the "second wave," see Amy Gurowitz, "Mobilizing
International Norms: Domestic Actors, Immigrants, and the Japanese State," *World Politics* 51,
no. 3 (1999): 413–45; and Theo Farrell, "Transnational Norms and Military Development:
Constructing Ireland's Professional Army," *European Journal of International Relations* 7, no. 1
(2001): 63–102. Powerful domestic level explanations are also offered by Klotz, *Norms in Inter-
national Relations*; Klotz, "Norms Reconstituting Interests"; Andrew P. Cortell and James W.
Davis, Jr., "How Do International Institutions Matter? The Domestic Impact of International
Rules and Norms," *International Studies Quarterly* 40, no. 4 (1996): 451–78; and Legro,
"Which Norms Matter?" For a comprehensive review of the "second wave" literature, see Cortell and Davis, "Understanding the Domestic Impact of International Norms."

international prescriptions and stresses the role of domestic political, organizational, and cultural variables in conditioning the reception of new global norms.[14] Legro's notion of organizational culture refers to the "pattern of assumptions, ideas, and beliefs," which acts "as a heuristic filter for perceptions and calculation" employed by actors in responding to outside norms.[15] Checkel's notion of *cultural match* describes "a situation where the prescriptions embodied in an international norm are convergent with domestic norms, as reflected in discourse, the legal system (constitutions, judicial codes and laws), and bureaucratic agencies (organizational ethos and administrative agencies)."[16] Norm diffusion is therefore "more rapid when a cultural match exists between a systemic norm and a target country, in other words, when it resonates with historically constructed domestic norms."[17]

Domestic politics perspectives can be unduly static, however. They explain how "historically constructed domestic identity norms create barriers to agent learning from systemic norms"[18] rather than a dynamic process of *matchmaking*. Moreover, congruence is often conceptualized as a fit with domestic "institutional and historical contexts."[19] One finds echoes of historical institutionalism, which offers an essentially static perspective on the importance of prior choices.[20] Prior action or agreement is a constraining

14. Thomas Risse-Kappen, "Ideas Do Not Flow Freely: Transnational Coalitions, Domestic Structures, and the End of the Cold War," *International Organization* 48, no. 2 (1994): 185–214; Cortell and Davis, "How Do International Institutions Matter?"; Legro, "Which Norms Matter?"; Checkel, "The Constructivist Turn in International Relations Theory"; Jeffrey Checkel, "Why Comply? Social Learning and European Identity Change," *International Organization* 55, no. 3 (2001): 553–88.

15. Legro, "Which Norms Matter?" 33, 36.

16. Checkel, "Norms, Institutions," 4.

17. Checkel, "Norms, Institutions," 6.

18. Checkel, "Norms, Institutions."

19. Checkel, "Norms, Institutions"; idem, *Ideas and International Political Change: Soviet/Russian Behavior and the End of the Cold War* (New Haven: Yale University Press, 1997); idem, "Why Comply"; Cortell and Davis, "How Do International Institutions Matter?"

20. Historical institutionalism sees norms and institutions not just as products of "self-consciousness, voluntarism, deliberate intentionality." Rather, normative change proceeds "organically, over time, by custom, habit, tradition" (Peter A. Gourevitch, "The Governance Problem in International Relations," in *Strategic Choice and International Relations*, ed. David A. Lake and Robert Powell [Princeton: Princeton University Press, 1999], 142). See also Karol Soltan, Eric M. Uslaner, and Virginia Haufler, eds., *Institutions and Social Order* (Ann Arbor: University of Michigan Press, 1998), 3, 8. On historical institutionalism, see Elinor Ostrom, *Governing the Commons: The Evolution of Institutions for Collective Action* (Cambridge and New York: Cambridge University Press, 1990); Sven Steinmo, Kathleen Thelen, and Frank Longstreth, eds., *Structuring Politics: Historical Institutionalism in Comparative Analysis* (Cambridge: Cambridge University Press, 1992); Peter A. Hall and Rosemary C.R. Taylor, "Political Science and the Three New Institutionalisms," in *Institutions and Social*

device that conditions the reception of emerging ideas, but we know little about how local actors use prior choices to localize and reconstruct ideas in order to make them fit their circumstances and preferences.[21]

The constructivist notions of "framing" and "grafting," offer a more dynamic view of congruence between emerging and existing norms. Framing is necessary for norm diffusion because "the linkages between existing and emergent norms are not often obvious and must be actively constructed by proponents of new norms." Through framing, norm advocates highlight and "create" issues "by using language that names, interprets, and dramatizes them."[22] Audie Klotz's study of the anti-apartheid campaign shows the critical role the framing of the global norm of racial equality and the global anti-apartheid campaign played in the context of the prevailing civil rights discourse in the United States. Framing can thus make a global norm appear local.[23]

"Grafting" is a tactic employed by norm entrepreneurs to institutionalize a new norm by associating it with an existing one, resulting in a similar prohibition or injunction. Richard Price has shown how invoking the prior norm against poison helped the campaign to develop a norm against chemical weapons.[24] However both framing and grafting are largely acts of reinterpretation or representation rather than reconstruction. Neither is necessarily a local act; outsiders usually perform them. Moreover, framing and grafting are undertaken with a view to produce change at the "receiving end" without altering the persuader's beliefs.

---

*Order*, ed. Karol Soltan, Eric M. Uslaner, and Virginia Haufler (Ann Arbor: University of Michigan Press, 1998); Stephen Krasner, "Sovereignty: An Institutional Perspective," *Comparative Political Studies* 21, no. 1 (1988): 86; Brian M. Downing, *The Military Revolution and Political Change: Origins of Democracy and Autocracy in Early Modern Europe* (Princeton: Princeton University Press, 1992); Ruth Berins Collier and David Collier, *Shaping the Political Arena: Critical Junctures, the Labor Movement, and Regime Dynamics in Latin America* (Princeton: Princeton University Press, 1991); Paul Pierson and Theda Skocpol, "Historical Institutionalism in Contemporary Political Science"; available at http://www.polisci.berkeley.edu/faculty/bio/permanent/Pierson,P/Discipline.pdf.

21. The literature on historical institutionalism treats prior action or agreement as a static constraining device or a fixed prism that conditions the reception of emerging ideas. It tells us little about how local actors dynamically use prior actions or agreements as a device to localize and reconstruct ideas so as to make them fit their circumstances and preferences. Institutionalist approaches in general "have been better at explaining what is not possible in a given institutional context than what is." Steinmo, Thelen, and Longstreth, *Structuring Politics*, 14; John G. Ikenberry, David A. Lake, and Michael Mastanduno, eds., *The State and American Foreign Economic Policy* (Ithaca: Cornell University Press, 1988), 242.

22. Finnemore and Sikkink, "International Norm Dynamics and Political Change," 268.

23. Klotz, *Norms in International Relations*; and Klotz, "Norms Reconstituting Interests."

24. Price, *The Chemical Weapons Taboo*.

Constitutive Localization

In this book I conceptualize and test a different process, termed "constitutive localization." It may start with the reinterpretation and rerepresentation of the external norm, but may also extend into more complex processes of reconstitution to make an external norm congruent with an existing local normative order. The role of local actors, the "persuadee's choice," is more crucial than that of external actors in producing norm diffusion. Instead of treating framing, grafting, and other adaptive processes as distinct and unrelated phenomena, I use localization to bring them together under a single conceptual framework that stresses the role of local agents.

In developing the concept of constitutive localization, I draw on Southeast Asian historiographical arguments claiming that Southeast Asian societies were not passive recipients of foreign (Indian and Chinese) cultural and political ideas, but active borrowers and localizers.[25] To localize some-

25. By Southeast Asian historiography I mean a body of writings by historians of Southeast Asia about the region's past. An important element of this literature, which this book draws upon, covers the precolonial states of the region, which emerged and perished roughly between the fourth and the fourteenth century AD. They include Funan, Champa, Sri Vijaya, Pagan, Angkor, Ayutthia, and Majapahit. George Coedès refers to them collectively as the "Indianized states of Southeast Asia" (*The Indianized States of Southeast Asia* [Honolulu: University of Hawaii Press, 1968]). For an excellent and insightful summary of these debates, see I.W. Mabbett, "The 'Indianization' of Southeast Asia: Reflections on the Prehistoric Sources," *Journal of Southeast Asian Studies* 8, no. 1: (1976): 1–14 and "The 'Indianization' of Southeast Asia: Reflections on the Historical Sources," *Journal of Southeast Asian Studies* 8, no. 2 (1976): 143–61. The specific historiographical debate that this book refers to is about how Indian (and Chinese ideas that were particularly influential in Dai Viet or modern northern Vietnam) ideas came into these states, and the sort of impact they had on the indigenous societies and politics. Until about World War II, as John Legge put it, "most . . . studies . . . of Southeast Asian history" were marked by "a tendency of scholars to see that history as shaped by influences external to the region rather than as the product of an internal dynamic" ("The Writing of Southeast Asian History," in *The Cambridge History of Southeast Asia*, ed. Nicholas Tarling [Cambridge: Cambridge University Press, 1992], 6.) Following World War II, this view came under attack because of new research, archeological discoveries, and debates, which resulted in a growing tendency to stress the region's distinctive and "autonomous" past. Historians recognized Southeast Asia's claim to be a "culturally independent region" from both India and China. Not only did they point to Southeast Asia's distinctive civilizational past predating the advent of Indian and Chinese influences, but also to the resilience of its cultural, social, and political features that had survived the coming of foreign influences. Moreover, the emphasis of the new scholarship was less on how Southeast Asians adopted Indic, or Sinic, art religion, political concepts and practices, and more on how they "adapted these foreign ideas to suit their own needs and values" (Milton Osborne, *Southeast Asia: An Introductory History* ([Sydney: Allen and Unwin, 1979], 5–6). The region's "symbolic and organizational patterns" that were once regarded as being of Indian origin were now seen to be "merely redefinitions of indigenous institutions" (Paul Wheatley, "Presidential Address: India Beyond the Ganges—Desultory Reflections on the Origins of civilization in Southeast Asia," *Journal of Asian Studies* 42, no. 1 (1982): 27). The argument was that Southeast Asians were not to be "regarded as

thing is to "invest [it] with the characteristics of a particular place."[26] I define localization as the active construction (through discourse, framing, grafting, and cultural selection) of foreign ideas by local actors, which results in the latter developing significant congruence with local beliefs and practices.[27]

A key aspect of localization is the agency role of local actors. Constructivist argue that the task of transnational moral entrepreneurs is to "mobilize popular opinion and political support both within their host country and abroad"; "stimulate and assist in the creation of likeminded organizations *in other countries*'" and "play a significant role in elevating their objectives beyond its identification with the national interests of their government." Much of their effort is "directed toward persuading foreign audiences, especially foreign elites."[28] The constitutive localization perspective shifts the understanding of norm entrepreneurship from "outsider proponents" committed to a transnational or universal moral agenda toward "insider proponents" committed to a localized normative order, albeit one that can be legitimized by building congruence with universal norms.[29]

Norm diffusion strategies that accommodate local sensitivities and contexts are more likely to succeed than those seeking to dismiss or supplant the latter. As an example, Wiseman shows how supporters of the non-provocative defense norm within the Soviet defense community facilitated its acceptance "by resurrecting a defensive 'tradition' in Soviet history," thereby reassuring "domestic critics that they were operating historically within the Soviet paradigm and [avoiding] ... the impression that they were simply borrowing Western ideas."[30]

---

recipients (or victims) of history, but as makers of it" (G. Carter Bentley, "Indigenous States of Southeast Asia," *Annual Review of Anthropology* 15 [1986]: 299). Localization describes a process of idea transmission in which Southeast Asians borrowed foreign ideas about authority and legitimacy and fitted them into indigenous traditions and practices. In this process, ideas that could be constructed to fit indigenous traditions were better received than those that did not have such potential.

26. *The Concise Oxford Dictionary*, 1976, 638.

27. O.W. Wolters, *History, Culture, and Region in Southeast Asian Perspectives* (Singapore: Institute of Southeast Asian Studies, 1982), 57.

28. Nadelmann, "Global Prohibition Regimes," 482 (emphasis added).

29. The theory of entrepreneurship acknowledges that there has been inadequate attention to the adaptive role of entrepreneurs as they adjust to their environment and to their learning experience. Some of this learning experience may relate to the attitude of consumers or norm-takers. David Deakins, *Entrepreneurship and Small Firms*, 2nd ed. (London: McGraw-Hill, 1999), 23. See also Peter Drucker, *Innovation and Entrepreneurship: Practice and Principles* (New York: HarperBusiness, 1993); and John G. Burch, *Entrepreneurship* (New York: John Wiley & Sons, 1986).

30. Geoffrey Wiseman, *Concepts of Non-Provocative Defence: Ideas and Practices in International Security* (London: Palgrave, 2002), 104.

Why do norm-takers want to localize international norms, and what conditions affect the likelihood that localization would occur due to their actions? Cottrell and Davis argue that actors borrow international rules to justify their actions and call into question the legitimacy of others.[31] Keck and Sikkink's study of the anti-foot binding campaign in China at the turn of the nineteenth century and the anti-circumcision campaign in Kenya in the 1930s shows that the success of these campaigns was contingent on whether the norm being propagated by foreign missionaries encouraged or conflicted with the local nationalists' agenda. The anti-foot binding campaign succeeded because it reinforced the Chinese national reform movement that sought to improve women's status as a "necessary part of their program for *national self-strengthening*."[32] However, attempts to ban female circumcision in Kenya failed because it conflicted with the existing nationalist agenda that perceived female circumcision as an integral part of local culture and identity.[33] Hence, norm diffusion succeeds when a foreign norm seeks to replace a local norm that embodies a moral claim or function that has already been challenged from within, but fails when it competes with a strong local norm.[34]

Why localization? There are several generic forces behind the demand for new norms. First, a major security or economic crisis (war or depression) can generate demands for norm borrowing by calling into question "existing rules of the game."[35] Shifts in the distribution of power or the great powers' interests and interactions can also generate pressures for normative change.[36] Decolonization and the end of the Cold War brought to fore a set of European security cooperation norms, which in turn attracted the attention of regional actors outside of Europe.[37] Domestic political changes on the norm-taker's side can also effect change.[38] For example, newly democratic regimes may seek to import ideas about human rights to solidify their own foreign policy and legitimize their new identity. Finally, international or regional

---

31. Cottrell and Davis, "How Do International Institutions Matter?" 453.

32. Keck and Sikkink, *Activists Beyond Borders*, 63.

33. Keck and Sikkink, *Activists Beyond Borders*, 63.

34. This also explains the popularity of Gandhian non-violence in Tanganyika (Tanzania), following the failure of earlier ideas about resistance that had produced violent struggles. Julius K. Nyerere, *Freedom and Unity* (Dar es Salam: Oxford University Press, 1966), 2–3.

35. John G. Ikenberry, "Conclusion: An Institutional Approach to American Foreign Economic Policy," in *The State and American Foreign Economic Policy*, ed. Ikenberry, Lake, and Mastanduno, 234.

36. Klotz, *Norms in International Relations*, 23.

37. Krause, *Culture and Security*.

38. Cortell and Davis, "Understanding the Domestic Impact of International Norms."

demonstration effect could prompt norm borrowing through emulation, imitation, contagion, and so on.[39]

Beyond these general triggers of demand-driven norm diffusion, one must also explain why the demand for new norms leads to their *localization* whereby some characteristics of the existing normative order are retained; local beliefs and practices are therefore not necessarily displaced. Localization is simply more practical, especially when prior norms are embedded in strong local institutions. Institutionalist scholars hold that it is "easier to maintain and adapt existing institutions than to create new ones."[40] This tendency would be further strengthened if recipients of ideas believed that existing beliefs and approaches are not dysfunctional, but merely inadequate, (i.e., not geared to addressing newer challenges) and therefore have to be broadened and strengthened. The tendency to localize is thus a by-product of the desire of the idea-recipient to exploit a new idea for power, efficiency, and status without admitting to cultural or knowledge inferiority or compromising its existing identity.

A *sense of uniqueness* of the actors' values and identities creates a desire and tendency to localize. Scholars have spoken of a deeply engrained habit in Southeast Asian societies to "[adapt] . . . foreign ideas to suit their own needs and values."[41] In his study of Indonesian politics, Benedict Anderson explores the "whole trend to absorb and transform the Western concepts of modern politics within Indonesian-Javanese mental structures."[42] Similarly, looking at modern political institutions in Southeast Asia, McCloud concludes, "At national and popular levels, Western political and social institutions have been rejected, not out of hand and categorically but with the qualification—as old as the region itself—that externally derived concepts and institutions will be

39. Finnemore and Sikkink, "International Norm Dynamics and Political Change," 262.

40. Robert Keohane and Joseph Nye, "The United States and International Institutions in Europe After the Cold War," in *After the Cold War: International Institutions and State Strategies in Europe, 1989–1991*, ed. Robert Keohane, Joseph Nye, and Stanley Hoffmann (Cambridge: Harvard University Press, 1993), 19. See also Vinod Aggarwal, "Analyzing Institutional Transformation in the Asia-Pacific," in *Asia-Pacific Crossroads: Regime Creation and the Future of APEC*, ed. Vinod Aggarwal and Charles E. Morrison (London: MacMillan, 1998), 53.

41. Milton Osborne, *Southeast Asia: An Illustrated Introductory History*, 5th ed. (St. Leonards, Australia: Allen & Unwin, 1990), 5–6.

42. Describing the dynamics of ideational contestation involving ideas such as democracy and socialism, Anderson writes, "In any such cross-cultural confrontation, the inevitable thrust is to 'appropriate' the foreign concept and try to anchor it safely to given or traditional ways of thinking and modes of behavior. Depending on the conceptions of the elite and its determination, either the imported ideas and modalities or the traditional ones assume general ascendancy: in most large and non-communist societies it is almost invariable that at least in the short run, the traditional modalities tend to prevail" (Benedict Anderson, "The Languages of Indonesian Politics," *Indonesia*, no. 1 [1966]: 113).

**Table 2.1.** The Trajectory of Localization and Conditions for Progress

| Trajectory of Localization | Conditions for Progress |
| --- | --- |
| Indifference and/or resistance | Most local actors remain indifferent, or offer resistance, to a new external norm because of uncertainty or doubts about its utility and applicability and fears that it might undermine existing ideas, beliefs and practices. |
| | *Condition 1:* Some aspects of the existing normative order remains strong and legitimate, although other aspects may be already discredited from within or found inadequate to meet with new and unforeseen challenges. |
| Local initiative and prelocalization | Some insider proponents recognize the potential of an external norm to contribute to the legitimacy and efficacy of extant institutions without undermining them significantly. They may prelocalize the norm by framing[a] it in such a way that establishes its value and appeal to the local audience, and grafting it onto some extant local norms and practices. |
| | *Condition 2:* There must be willing and credible local actors (insider proponents). The tendency to localize is especially salient if local agents are not seen as "stooges" of outside forces and if their local audience has developed a reputation for being unique. |
| Localization | Insider proponents persuade the local audience to accept the norm through argument and peer pressure. The process may involve pruning[a] those elements that do not fit the pre-existing normative structure and keeping those that do, and/or extension of its meaning to demonstrate its congruence with local interests and identities. |
| | *Condition 3:* Norm-takers as a group must be convinced of the local value of the norm. There must be scope for selection and extension of elements of the external norm. |
| Institutionalization and amplification | New instruments and practices are developed from the syncretic normative framework in which local influences remain highly visible. |
| | *Condition 4:* Association with the external norm must afford opportunities to local actors to enhance their greater domestic and international legitimacy. |

[a] "Framing" is mainly a discursive act, whereas pruning involves actual modifications to the norm with policy consequences. Norm entrepreneurs at the prelocalization stage would not be in a position to make an authoritative modification to the norm; hence they can only frame.

blended with the indigenous (much of which was also previously imported) and fitted to local sensibilities and needs."[43] (Table 2.1 outlines a trajectory of localization, specifying the conditions of progress.)

What kind of change does localization produce? In some respects, localization is akin to adaptation.[44] However, adaptation is a generic term that

---

43. Donald G. McCloud, *Southeast Asia: Tradition and Modernity in the Contemporary World* (Boulder, Colorado: Westview Press, 1995), 338.

44. Alastair I. Johnston, "Learning Versus Adaptation: Explaining Change in Chinese Arms Control Policy in the 1980s and 1990s," *China Journal*, no. 35 (1996): 27–61.

can subsume all kinds of behaviors and outcomes., whereas localization has more specific features. As Wolters points out, "adaptation shirk[s] the crucial question of where, how and why foreign elements began to fit into a local culture" and obscures "the initiative of local elements responsible for the process and the end product."[45] In localization, the initiative to seek change belongs to the local agent. Moreover, although adaptation may involve an "endless elaboration of new local-foreign cultural 'wholes,'" in localization, the "local beliefs . . . were always responsible for the initial form the new 'wholes' took."[46] Moreover, localization is a long-term and evolutionary assimilation of foreign ideas, whereas some forms of adaptation in the rationalist international relations literature are seen as "short run policy of accommodation."[47] Thus, whereas adaptation may be tactical and to some extent forced on the target audience, localization is voluntary and the resulting change is likely to be more enduring.

Localization does not extinguish the cognitive prior or identity of the norm-takers but leads to its mutual inflection with external norms. In constructivist perspectives on socialization, norm diffusion is the result of adaptive behavior in which local practices are made consistent with an external idea. Localization, by contrast, describes a process in which external ideas are adapted to meet local practices.[48] The resulting behavior of the recipient can be understood more in terms of the former than the latter, although it can only be fully understood in terms of both.

This aspect of localization renders it *constitutive*. Constructivists have used the term "constitutive" to mean *fundamental* change, implying the displacement of the key attributes of agents. Thus, the "constitutive impact" of norms means the impact of norms "reach deeper; they constitute actor identities and interests and not simply regulate behavior."[49] However, the term "constitutive" need not mean the total displacement of the identities of norm-takers. As Wendt notes, "to say that 'X' [for example, a social structure] constitutes 'Y' [for example, an agent] is to say that the properties of those agents are made possible by, and would not exist in the absence of, the

45. Wolters, *History, Culture, and Region in Southeast Asian Perspectives*, 56.
46. Wolters, *History, Culture, and Region*, 56.
47. Johnston, "Learning Versus Adaptation," 8.
48. I am grateful to an *International Organization* anonymous referee for suggesting this formulation to distinguish adaptation from localization.
49. Checkel, "The Constructivist Turn in International Relations Theory," *World Politics* 50, no. 2 (1998): 325, 328; See also James Fearon and Alexander Wendt, "Rationalism vs. Constructivism: A Skeptical View," in *Handbook of International Relations*, ed. Walter Carlsnaes, Thomas Risse, and Beth A. Simmons (London: Sage, 2002).

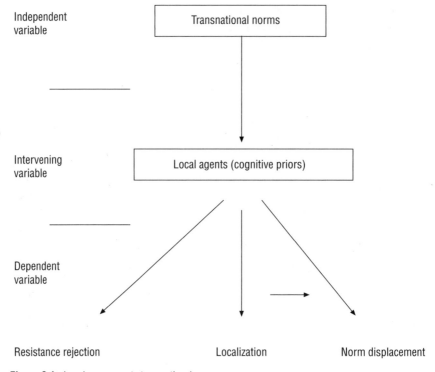

Independent variable

Transnational norms

Intervening variable

Local agents (cognitive priors)

Dependent variable

Resistance rejection            Localization            Norm displacement

**Figure 2.1.** Local responses to transnational norms.

*Resistance*: Limited new tasks and weak policy instruments may be created; the local target norm, the "norm hierarchy," and extant institutions remain largely intact. Too much and sustained resistance leads to the failure of norm diffusion. A *target norm* refers to any specific prior norm that entrepreneurs, both outsider and insider, want to dilute or displace; *norm hierarchy* refers to the ordering of norms in terms of their relative importance to a group or institution.

*Localization:* Visible new tasks and policy instruments are created. The local target norm is modified, but not abandoned. Prior institutions, if any, remain in place, although they may change and spawn new "add-on" institutions that are grafted onto the existing institutional design/model. Sans prior institutions, new institutions or institutional designs emerge and serve as the cognitive priors for future norm diffusion and institution-building efforts. *Institutional design* refers to the "formal and informal rules and organizational features of an existing or proposed institution (including those that may be envisaged for the future), which function as either the constraints on actor choice or the bare bones of the social environment within which agents interact, or both."

*Norm Displacement:* Major new tasks and instruments are created. The target norm is severely weakened and possibly abandoned. A new institution appears or the old institution is significantly modified.

On norm hierarchy, see Theo Farrell, "Transnational Norms and Military Development: Constructing Ireland's Professional Army," *European Journal of International Relations* 7, no. 1 (2001): 81. The definition of institutional design is taken from Amitav Acharya and Alastair Iain Johnston, "Comparing Regional Institutions: An Introduction," in *Crafting Cooperation: Regional International Institutions in Comparative Perspective*, ed. Amitav Acharya and Alastair Iain Johnston (Cambridge: Cambridge University Press, 2007).

structure by which they are constituted."[50] But to say that structure affects agents' attributes is not to say that the latter does not play a role in modifying the former. In a truly constitutive situation, agents and structure *mutually constitute* each other. This means the agent's original identity or belief systems would not be totally displaced, but would play a role in modifying the structure.

Localization is seldom a *final* act or *terminal condition,* but a dynamic and continuous process. The occurrence and outcome of localization is subject to shifting conditions, especially the conditions described in table 2.1. Conditions absent at a given time (t-1) may present themselves at a future juncture (t-2), thereby reversing an earlier resistance to external norms and facilitating their localization. New developments, such as a crisis discrediting existing norms and practices, the arrival of more prominent and persuasive insider proponents, and more creative ideas about and scope for pruning and grafting, may turn failed attempts at norm localization into successful efforts. Similarly, there cannot be a permanent and rigid boundary between localization and norm displacement. After local actors have developed greater familiarity and experience with the new ideas, functions, and instruments, resistance to new norms may weaken, opening the door to fundamental changes, including an incremental shift toward norm displacement. This may come at the very end of a localization process, which occurs and defines normative interactions in the interim. Localization provides an initial response to new norms pending norm displacement, which may or may not occur. But at least localization gives such change a decent chance.

Finally, localization is progressive, not regressive or static. It reshapes both existing beliefs and practices and foreign ideas in their local context. Localization is an evolutionary or everyday form of progressive norm diffusion.

### Localization and the "Cognitive Prior"

Constitutive localization assumes an existing normative framework, or a "cognitive prior." A cognitive prior may be defined as an existing set of ideas, belief systems, and norms, which determine and condition an individual or social group's receptivity to new norms. From where do cognitive priors originate?

The sources of cognitive priors may be culture, or cultural norms, "the shared, sanctioned, and integrated systems of beliefs and practices that char-

---

50. Alexander Wendt, *Social Theory of International Politics* (Cambridge: Cambridge University Press, 1999), 72.

acterize a cultural group."[51] Such norms may reflect ethnicity, religion, group
social belief systems, historical memory, and domestic political rhythms and
peculiarities of societies. The cognitive priors of nations or regions in the
realm of international relations could be built primarily around traditional
culture[52] or historical practices of statecraft and diplomatic interaction patterns. Another source of cognitive priors is ideas, including the worldviews
and the principled and causal beliefs of leaders and elite of a social group,
state, or states in a given region.[53] Of significance here are the ideas of a

51. I have adapted this definition of cultural norms from the *Encyclopedia of Public
Health*. Such norms "foster reliable guides for daily living, [and] lend meaning and coherence
to life, as well as the means to achieve a sense of integrity, safety and belonging. [T]together
with related values and rituals, confer a sense of order and control upon aspects of life that
might otherwise appear chaotic or unpredictable." Cultural norms shape interpretations of
threats and mediate the relationship between the group and environmental exposures, including to outside ideas ("Cultural Norms," *Encyclopedia of Public Health*, [New York: Macmillan, 2002], available at http://www.enotes.com/public-health-encyclopedia/cultural-norms.
On the usage of cultural norms by international relations scholars, see Katzenstein, *Cultural
Norms and National Security*; idem, *The Culture of National Security: Norms and Identity in
World Politics* (New York: Columbia University Press, 1996); Thomas Berger, "From Sword to
Chrysanthemum: Japan's Culture of Anti-militarism," *International Security* 17, no. 4 (Spring
1993): 119–50. I have used the term "socio-cultural norms" elsewhere (Amitav Acharya, *Constructing a Security Community in Southeast Asia: ASEAN and the Problem of Regional Order* [London: Routledge, 2001], 25).
52. The Gandhian idea of non-violence is a good example of this type of cultural cognitive
prior. In developing his concept of non-violent struggle, Gandhi blended a foreign idea "passive resistance" with indigenous traditions. In his view, the struggle against British rule could
hardly be carried out by a movement identified by a "foreign" (English) phrase. (In Gandhi's
own words, "it appeared shameful to permit this great struggle to be known only by an English name.") Hence, he coined the phrase *satyagraha*, connoting a "force which is born of
Truth and Love or non-violence" that was eventually used to capture the essence of the resistance movement. In so doing, Gandhi was not only influenced by the forms of protest in his
native region of Kathiawar, including fasting and *hartals* (strikes), but also the religious traditions of nonviolence represented by the Jain Acharyas—sages known for disallowing any
form of violence, including killing of dangerous animals). These composed the repertoire of
the resistance that Gandhi would employ in the nationwide struggle. Martin Green, *The Origins of Nonviolence: Tolstoy and Gandhi in Their Historical Setting* (New Dehli: HarperCol-
lins, 1998), 134.
53. The distinction among worldview, causal belief, and principled belief comes from
Goldstein and Keohane. Worldviews "define the universe of possibilities for action." The
world's religions constitute a major source of such ideas, another example is the concept of
sovereignty. Principled beliefs are "normative ideas that specify criteria for distinguishing
right from the wrong and just from unjust." Such ideas are represented by the anti-slavery
movement, or the anti-land mines movement in recent decades. Causal beliefs are "beliefs
about cause-effect relationships which derive authority from the shared consensus of recognized elites, whether they are village elders or scientists at elite institutions." Such beliefs include scientific discoveries about the causes of disease, or the link between shared beliefs and
revolutionary political change. Judith Goldstein and Robert Keohane, eds., *Ideas and Foreign Policy: Beliefs, Institutions and Political Change* (Ithaca: Cornell University Press,
1993), 8–11.

country's founding leaders, and for regional orders, the ideas about regional identity and cooperation held by the leaders of key states in the region. Thus, the ideas and beliefs of the nationalist elite were especially important as elements of the cognitive prior of the foreign policy of Third World countries, forming the basis of their international conduct.

Yet another type of cognitive prior are norms that are accepted and institutionalized from outside because of prior choices, including acts of borrowing and localization.[54] This process was especially important in the Third World, where the postcolonial states would seek to translate their newfound sovereign status into foreign policy behavior. In so doing, they could not just rely on traditional cultural norms or historical notions of statecraft. Although these did matter, the newly independent countries had to cope with an international political environment dominated by essentially European norms of sovereignty, which had no prior equivalent in their traditional indigenous setting. Hence, they had to borrow, adapt, and localize Westphalian principles to develop their foreign relations, including non-intervention, sovereign equality of states, and diplomatic recognition.

## International Institutions and the Spread of Norms

International institutions act as an important source of cognitive priors and more generally as sites of the constitutive localization of ideas and norms in world politics. As Andrew Hurrell observes:

> Institutions act as platforms for normative debate, for the mobilization of concern, and for debating and revisiting ideas about how international society should be organized. However much social scientists insist on analyzing international institutions solely in terms of the provision of international public

54. Here I rely heavily on historical institutionalism (note 20), especially its notion of "path dependence." See Paul Pierson, "Increasing Returns, Path Dependence, and the Study of Politics," *American Political Science Review* 94, no. 2 (June 2000): 251–67. But the notion of "cognitive prior" is not the same as path dependence, which "identifies a specific sequence of events in which the mechanisms that produce a given set of institutions are replaced by different mechanisms that reproduce those institutions" (Herman Schwartz, "Down the Wrong Path: Path Dependence, Increasing Returns, and Historical Institutionalism," available at www.people.virginia.edu/~hms2f/Path.pdf (accessed 11 August 2008). My notion of cognitive prior is ideational; it may or may not be institutionalized. Although I describe an institutional path dependence in Asian regionalism (chapter 4), I use the notion of cognitive prior as an ideational framework to explain from where the original models of these institutions came. Moreover, unlike some notions of path dependence, I take cognitive prior to be a more dynamic, agent-driven process of congruence building.

goods, normative issues cannot be kept out of the actual practices of those institutions.[55]

However, international institutions do not function simply as *teachers* of norms.[56] They also serve as *rule-makers* and *innovators*. "Regional organizations . . . play a role in interpreting and coordinating implementation of global conventions, which, by political necessity, must be abstractly defined."[57] They initiate the demand for new norms and provide an initial crucial setting within which norm entrepreneurs persuade others to accept them. Regional organizations in the developing world—Organization of American States (OAS), Organization for African Unity (OAU, recently renamed the African Union), and the Arab League—played an important role in articulating the Third World's demand for self-determination and sovereign equality.[58] Latin American regionalists were major innovators of the non-intervention and *uti possicetis juris* (honoring inherited boundaries) norms.[59] International institutions are also the arena for judging the success and failure of norm diffusion, which can be ascertained from changes to their own institutional design and apparatus, which is indeed the main dependent variable of this study.

The literature on norm diffusion has ignored the ideational role of non-Western regional institutions. The post–Cold War constructivist literature on the role of ideas and norms in world politics is largely inspired by European personalities (Mikhail Gorbachev in particular) and institutions. Both the Organization for Security and Cooperation in Europe (OSCE) and the notion of common security received credit for bringing the Cold War to an end. Subsequent theoretical work on the role of regional institutions as frameworks of socialization and of normative change has focused on Western

55. Andrew Hurrell, "Norms and Ethics in International Relations," in *Handbook of International Relations*, ed. Walter Carlsnaes, Thomas Risse, and Beth A Simmons (London: Sage, 2003), 147.

56. Finnemore, "International Organizations as Teachers of Norms."

57. "A Fork in the Road: Conversations on the Work of the High Level Panel on Threats, Challenges and Change," IPA Report (New York: International Peace Academy, 2005).

58. Lynn H. Miller, "The Prospect for Order Through Regional Security," in *Regional Politics and World Order*, ed. Richard A. Falk and Saul H. Mendlovitz (San Francisco: W.H. Freeman, 1973).

59. Jorge I. Dominguez, "Latin America's Long March Toward International Cooperation: The Jigsaw-Puzzle Approach to the Design of Regional Institutions," in *Crafting Cooperation: Regional International Institutions in Comparative Perspective*, ed. Amitav Acharya and Alastair Iain Johnston (Cambridge: Cambridge University Press, 2007), 126; Ann Van Wynen Thomas and A.J. Thomas, Jr., *Non-Intervention: The Law and Its Import in the Americas* (Dallas: Southern Methodist University Press, 1956).

Europe.[60] Regional institution in other parts of the world and how they developed and internalized global norms of peaceful change received little attention. Nonetheless, Third World regional organizations act as a source of cognitive prior. They develop regional norms to guide the conduct of foreign and security policy of their members.

There are three reasons why the normative role of regional groups included both the regional statement of global norms as well as extension and expansion of global norms at the regional level. First, Third World countries saw regional organizations as an important arena for developing principles of conduct because of their initial lack of representation at global institutions such as the United Nations (UN). The United Nations Conference on International Organization (UNCIO), which drafted the UN Charter in 1945 out of the Dumbarton Oaks proposals, was attended by fifty countries, with scant representation from Third World countries (except Latin American). The Indian delegation was actually chosen by the British and "played a subordinate role" to the British delegation.[61] Lacking membership and voice in the universal organization, many Third World states saw regional organizations as an important instrument in the initial conduct of their foreign policy and international relations.

A second reason for the normative role of regional meetings in the Third World had to do with the global superpower competition and intervention during the Cold War. The violation of non-intervention at the global level by the superpowers created the imperative for regional principles against intervention to safeguard regional security and autonomy. Third, regional adoption and expansion of non-intervention also occurred when Third World countries found global institutions like the UN incapable of preventing the violations of this norm because of the perception that the violators themselves controlled the UN.

Regional institutions and interactions provide indicators of constitutive localization, which can be conceptualized as a form of institutional change. Localization is indicated when an extant institution responds to a foreign idea by functional and/or geographic extension, and creates new workable policy instruments to pursue its new goals without supplanting its original goals and *institutional* structures (defined as "organizational characteristics of groups and . . . the rules and norms that guide the relationships

---

60. See Jeffrey Checkel, "International Institutions and Socialization in Europe," Special Issue of *International Organization* 59, no. 4 (Fall 2005). The conclusion by Alastair Iain Johnston discusses Asia comparatively.
61. V.S. Mani, "An Indian Perspective on the Evolution of International Law," *Asian Yearbook of International Law, 2000,* vol. 9 (Netherlands: Brill, 2004), 66.

between actors").[62] It is possible to draw parallels between what Wheatley calls "mere redefinitions of indigenous institutions" and historical institution-alism's notion of "path dependence" (the claim that the design of new institutions are shaped by the existing choices),[63] and Aggarwal's notion of "nested institutions."[64] Whatever the type of institutional change, its key purpose is to enhance the authority and legitimacy of the local actors.[65] (Figure 2.1 illustrates three main forms of local responses to transnational norms.)

## Theorizing Asian Regionalism

Since the end of the Cold War, Asia has witnessed one of the most active developments of regional institution building. But Asian regional institution-building remains undertheorized. As Mack and Ravenhill note, "most of the theoretically-oriented research on cooperative institutions [in Asia] has been undertaken in North America or Europe. This research has been, and remains, mostly US and Euro-centric in outlook."[66] While there has been a growing body of scholarly writings on Asian regionalism, what Richard Higgott calls "*the* paradigmatic" status of European regional institutions "against which all other regional projects are judged"[67] has not changed.

Indeed, many assessments of Asian regionalism (and non-Western regionalism in general) begin by employing, implicitly if not explicitly, European-style institutionalization as a yardstick for judging effectiveness. "[T]here is

62. Ikenberry, "Conclusion: An Institutional Approach to American Foreign Economic Policy," 223.

63. Ikenberry, "Conclusion," 223.

64. Aggarwal argues that institutional change can lead either to the modification of existing institutions or the creation of new ones. If new ones are created, then they could take two forms: nested institutions and parallel institutions ("Analyzing Institutional Transformation in the Asia-Pacific," 42, 44).

65. By having institutional change as the dependent variable, I separate the question of norm diffusion from norm compliance. I do not hold that diffusion must involve compliance; just because norms are violated does not invalidate them as norms. Although there have been many violations of non-intervention, it remains a powerful norm. Stephen D. Krasner refers to this apparent puzzle, "the presence of long-standing norms that are frequently violated" as "organized hypocrisy" (*Sovereignty: Organized Hypocrisy* [Princeton: Princeton University Press, 1999]), back cover.

66. Andrew Mack and John Ravenhill, "Economic and Security Regimes in the Asia-Pacific Region," in *Pacific Cooperation: Building Economic and Security Regimes in the Asia-Pacific Region*, ed. Andrew Mack and John Ravenhill (St Leonards, Australia: Allen and Unwin, 1994), 2.

67. Richard Higgott, "The Theory and Practice of Region," in *Regional Integration in East Asia and Europe: Convergence or Divergence*, ed. Bertrand Fort and Douglas Webber (London: Routledge, 2006), 23.

a widespread assumption . . . that in order to be 'proper' regionalism, a degree of EU-style institutionalism should be in place."[68] This inevitably leads to the conclusions pointing to the failures and limitations of Asian regionalism. Yet, as Katzenstein notes, "Theories based on Western, and especially West European experience, have been of little use in making sense of Asian regionalism." He warns that "[I]t would . . . be a great mistake to compare European 'success' with Asian 'failure.' Such a Eurocentric view invites the unwarranted assumption that the European experience sets the standard by which Asian regionalism should be measured." Katzenstein suggests instead that the "scope, depth, and character" of regionalism should acknowledge variations across "numerous dimensions and among world regions."[69]

Moreover, the literature on Asian regionalism has paid little attention to the role of ideas and norms in shaping institutional design, change, and performance.[70] This is in contrast to the literature on European and Atlantic regional institutions, which considered the role of "collective identities and norms of appropriate behavior," especially those of republican liberalism, in shaping their evolution as well as performance.[71] Power-based and functionalist explanations of Asian regionalism were equally silent on the effects of changes in the international normative environment on Asian institution-building efforts. Conversely, constructivist explanations focused more on either domestic or international norms of cooperation that have shaped regional institution building in Asia.[72] Such approach ignored regional

68. Shaun Breslin, Richard Higgott, and Ben Rosamond, "Regions in Comparative Perspective," in *New Regionalisms in the Global Political Economy*, ed. Shaun Breslin et al. (London: Routledge, 2002), 13.

69. Peter Katzenstein, "Introduction: Asian Regionalism in Comparative Perspective," in *Network Power: Japan and Asia*, ed. Peter Katzenstein and Takashi Shiraishi (Ithaca: Cornell University Press, 1997), 3, 5.

70. An earlier attempt to generalize Asian norms and identity, well before constructivism became a fashionable label, was Michael Haas's work, *The Asian Way to Peace: A Story of Regional Cooperation* (New York: Praeger, 1989). Geoffrey Wiseman and Kevin Clements were among the first to examine the impact of the "common security" norm to describe the logic and rationale of Asian institutions. But these studies were historically discontinuous, starting their investigation after 1990s and ignoring regional norm setting and identity building before the end of the Cold War. Geoffrey Wiseman, "NOD and the Asia Pacific Region," in *Non-Offensive Defence for the Twenty-First Century*, ed. Bjørn Møller and Hakan Wiberg (Boulder: Westview Press, 1994); Kevin Clements, ed., *Peace and Security in the Asia Pacific Region: Post-Cold War Problems and Prospects* (Tokyo: United Nations University Press, 1993). See also David Dewitt, "Common, Comprehensive and Cooperative Security," *Pacific Review* 7, no. 1 (1994): 1–15; Amitav Acharya, "Ideas, Identity, and Institution-Building: From the ASEAN Way to the Asia-Pacific Way?" *Pacific Review* 10, no. 3 (1997): 319–46.

71. Risse-Kappen, "Collective Identity in a Democratic Community."

72. Katzenstein showed how domestically produced social norms affect inter-state conduct and reinforce the preference for soft institutionalism in Asia. Because Asian domestic structures

normative structures, including norms produced through regional interactions and the regional contextualization and application of international norms. A historically grounded discussion of how international and local norms shape Asian regional institution building is yet to be offered, providing a major rationale for this volume.

Norms developed in Asia were powerful forces behind the design and building of institutions in post-war Asia. Asian leaders, especially those who fought against colonialism, wished to develop cooperation through a series of conferences, beginning with the Asian Relations Conference in New Delhi in 1947 and ending with the Asia-Africa Bandung Conference in 1955.[73] Although these gatherings did not produce a viable regional institution per se, they articulated and legitimized norms that were to have a lasting impact on Asian approaches to institution building for the coming decades, including the 1990s. Yet, no study investigates the normative links among early Cold War pan-Asianism and Afro-Asianism, mid-Cold War ASEAN regionalism, and post–Cold War Asia-Pacific multilateralism. Moreover, these early post-war Asian conferences and their normative impact have received almost no attention in the theoretical literature on international relations.[74]

---

tend to be informal and assimilative, rather than formal and legal-rationalistic, Asian regional organizations tend to be likewise. Katzenstein also points to the influence of General Agreement on Tariffs and Trade norms on the development of APEC (Katzenstein, "Introduction: Asian Regionalism in Comparative Perspective").

73. These conferences include the Asian Relations Conference, New Delhi, 1947; the Second Asian Relations Conference (on Indonesia), New Delhi, 1949; the First Colombo Powers Conference, Colombo, April 1954; the Second Colombo Powers Conference, Bogor, Indonesia, December 1954; and the Asia-Africa Conference, Bandung, Indonesia, 1955. The Colombo Powers were India, Pakistan, Ceylon, Burma, and Indonesia. See Godfrey H. Jansen, *Afro-Asia and Non-Alignment* (London: Faber, 1966); Amitav Acharya, *The Quest for Identity: International Relations of Southeast Asia* (Oxford: Oxford University Press, 2000), 43–77; *Asian Relations: Proceedings of the Asian Relations Conference* (New Delhi: Asian Relations Organization, 1948), 4; Russell Fifield, *The Diplomacy of Southeast Asia: 1945–1958* (New York: Harper, 1958); George McTurnan Kahin, *The Asian-African Conference, Bandung, Indonesia, April 1955* (Ithaca: Cornell University Press, 1956); Guy J. Pauker, *The Bandung Conference* (Cambridge, MA: Center for International Studies, MIT, 1955).

74. See for example, Robert H. Jackson, *Quasi-States: Sovereignty, International Relations and the Third World* (Cambridge: Cambridge University Press, 1991); Thomas J. Biersteker and Cynthia Weber, eds., *State Sovereignty as a Social Construct* (Cambridge: Cambridge University Press, 1996); Krasner, *Sovereignty: Organized Hypocrisy*; Daniel Philpott, *Revolutions in Sovereignty: How Ideas Shaped Modern International Relations* (Princeton: Princeton University Press, 2001); Jens Bartelson, *A Genealogy of Sovereignty* (Cambridge: Cambridge University Press, 1995); F.H. Hinsley, *Sovereignty*, 2nd ed. (Cambridge: Cambridge University Press, 1986); Alan James, *Sovereign Statehood: The Basis of International Society* (London: Allen and Unwin, 1986); Nicholas Onuf, "Sovereignty: Outline of a Conceptual History," *Alternatives* 16, no. 4 (1991): 425–46; Gene M. Lyons and Michael Mastanduno, eds., *Beyond Westphalia: State Sovereignty and International Intervention* (Baltimore and London: Johns

Yet, this was a crucial period in the evolution of the sovereign state-system in international relations. Post-war Asia was where and when two of the largest non-European nations of the world, India and Indonesia, achieved independence. Together with China, the world's most populous country, they began to grapple with Westphalian sovereignty. In translating the idea of sovereignty into foreign policy postures and instruments, they became active contenders, interpreters, and extenders of global norms. To investigate and present how this process of normative action unfolded through early regionalist interactions in Asia is the primary concern of chapter 3, and constitutes one of its major empirical contributions.

There is now a growing recognition of the role of ideational forces in Asian regional institution building. The earlier literature from this perspective focused on the development of knowledge-based epistemic communities.[75] However, these writings paid little attention to the role of values, norms, and issues of collective identity. Recent work has been mostly concerned with the norms of ASEAN,[76] supplemented by analytical and empirical work on Southeast Asian conflict management and dispute settlement styles and processes.[77]

In general, the literature on Asian regionalism offers little insight on some of the key issues in normative change, namely how norms are selected, why some norms are chosen and others are rejected, and the processes through which norms are adapted and diffused within the regional environment. Moreover, the underlying historical continuities and discontinuities in norm diffusion and

---

Hopkins University Press, 1995). An important exception to the neglect of sovereignty norms in the literature on Asian security is Allen Carlson, *Unifying China, Integrating the World* (Stanford: Stanford University Press, 2005).

75. The best early work on this is Lawrence T. Woods, *Asia-Pacific Diplomacy: Nongovernmental Organizations and International Relations* (Vancouver: UBC Press, 1993).

76. See Noordin Sopiee, "ASEAN and Regional Order," in *Regional Security in the Third World: Case Studies from Southeast Asia and the Middle East*, ed. Mohammed Ayoob (London: Croom Helm, 1986); Acharya, *The Quest for Identity*; idem, "Collective Identity and Conflict Management in Southeast Asia," in *Security Communities*, ed. Emanuel Adler and Michael Barnett (Cambridge and New York: Cambridge University Press, 1998); idem, *Constructing a Security Community in Southeast Asia*; Jurgen Haacke, *ASEAN's Diplomatic and Security Culture: Origins, Development and Prospects* (London: Routledge Curzon, 2003); Nikolas Busse, "Constructivism and Southeast Asian Security," *The Pacific Review* 12, no. 1 (1999): 39–60; Tobias Nischalke, "Does ASEAN Measure Up? Post-Cold War Diplomacy and the Idea of Regional Community," *The Pacific Review* 15, no. 1 (2002): 89–117; Amitav Acharya, "Will Asia's Past Be Its Future," *International Security* 28, no. 3 (2003): 149–80.

77. Some of the best empirical work on this subject comes from Southeast Asian scholars. See Tuan Hoang Anh, "ASEAN Dispute Management: Implications for Vietnam and an Expanded ASEAN," *Contemporary Southeast Asia* 18, no. 1 (June 1996): 61–81; Kamarulzaman Askandar, "ASEAN and Conflict Management: The Formative Years of 1967–1976," *The Pacific Review* 6, no.2 (1994): 57–69; Mely Caballero-Anthony, *Regional Security in Southeast Asia: Beyond the ASEAN Way* (Singapore: ISEAS, 2005).

the tensions and adaptations involving global and regional norms and their impact on regional institution building remain understudied.

INSTITUTION-BUILDING interactions in Asia have provided a major platform for the diffusion of norms of international relations. They have functioned as a site of normative contestation and localization involving global and regional norms. Neglecting this aspect in evaluating Asian regionalism misses a major part of their contribution and a major reason for their persistence. By bringing the process of normative contestation and change to the center stage, this book goes beyond traditional realist and liberal theories and offers a broader yardstick for judging the impact of Asian regional institutions. By identifying the evolution and effects of a regional cognitive prior, it offers a historical and inside-out understanding of the prospects and limits of transformation in Asian regional order, in contrast to the top-down perspectives that focus on U.S. power and purpose.

In international relations theory, the dominant perspective on norm diffusion, "moral cosmopolitanism," should be reconciled with a constitutive localization framework. This corrects a widespread tendency among norm scholars to privilege global transnational agents as teachers of norms while treating local actors (states and regional institutions) as learners. Local actors operating out of a historically formed normative context often redefine and reconstruct international norms in accordance with their beliefs and needs. Their ideas matter as much, and often more, in norm diffusion and institutional change in world politics.

# 3 Ideas and Power
## NON-INTERVENTION AND COLLECTIVE DEFENSE

This chapter addresses the first puzzle investigated in this book—why post-war Asia "failed" to develop a multilateral security institution, especially of the collective defense variety. Using the constitutive localization framework, I explain this outcome in terms of a regional contestation staged in post-war Asia over two prominent global security ideas of the period: non-intervention and collective defense. I argue that responses to these ideas from the Asian regionalist actors were shaped by their prior normative beliefs and practices, namely anti-colonialism and nationalism, and led to differing outcomes: collective defense was delegitimized whereas non-intervention was amplified.

## Non-Intervention, 1947–1955

As Stephen Krasner pointed out, the norm of non-intervention was not a direct outcome of the 1648 Treaty of Westphalia. Rather, it emerged from the writings of eighteenth-century European legal scholars.[1] Latin American leaders and jurists (such as Carlos Calvo and Luis Drago of Argentina) and regional meetings of Latin American states in the nineteenth and early twentieth centuries played an important role in extending the non-intervention principle beyond Europe. Originally a response to their fear of a Spanish re-conquest and European meddling, Latin American attention in promoting this norm shifted in the early part of the twentieth century to countering the Monroe Doctrine,[2] finally succeeding in getting the United States to

1. Stephen D. Krasner, *Sovereignty: Organized Hypocrisy* (Princeton: Princeton University Press, 1999), 20.
2. The Monroe Doctrine evolved through two stages. The nineteenth-century version was to exclude European powers from hemispheric affairs. It was not only aimed against further

accept this principle in 1933. During this process, Latin America developed an extensive legal framework for peaceful settlement of disputes, which helped to embed the norms of equality and non-intervention in the inter-American context, both bilaterally and through regional institutions such as the Pan-American Union and the OAS.[3]

But it was the UN that made the doctrine of non-intervention a universal principle.[4] The 1945 United Nations Conferences on International Organization held in San Francisco to draft the Charter of the organization enshrined the norm of non-intervention by giving an expansive meaning to the scope of domestic jurisdiction. In the October 1944 Dumbarton Oaks Proposals which provided the blueprint for the UN's Charter, the so-called "domestic jurisdiction" principle forbidding intervention in matters within the domestic jurisdiction of any state was contained in Chapter VIII which dealt specifically with the role of the Security Council in the maintenance of international peace and security. At the San Francisco Conference, the five sponsoring powers moved this domestic jurisdiction principle to Chapter II ("Purposes and Principles") in the UN Charter, thereby making it "a governing principle for the whole Organization and its members."[5] This move ensured that non-intervention applied not just to the UN's role in the maintenance of international peace and security, but also to the whole gamut of the organization's functions in social, economic, and cultural matters. In the

European conquest of the Americas, but was also an ideological effort to prevent European powers from exporting their political systems—monarchy—into the Americas. The twentieth-century extension was to sanction U.S. intervention in the internal affairs of Latin American nations to stop instability and alleged injustice toward foreigners.

3. Ann Van Wynen Thomas and A.J. Thomas Jr., *Non-Intervention: The Law and Its Import in the Americas* (Dallas, TX: Southern Methodist University Press, 1956); Jorge I. Dominguez, "Latin America's Long March Toward International Cooperation: The Jigsaw-Puzzle Approach to the Design of Regional Institutions," in *Crafting Cooperation: Regional International Institutions in Comparative Perspective,* ed. Amitav Acharya and Alastair Iain Johnston (Cambridge: Cambridge University Press, 2007), 83–128.

4. Hence, the UN may be regarded here as the norm entrepreneur. This is consistent with the view that international organizations often act as a "teacher of norms" (Martha Finnemore, "International Organizations as Teachers of Norms: The United Nations Educational, Scientific, and Cultural Organization and Science Policy," *International Organization* 47, no. 4 [1993]: 565–97). As Ruggie reminds us, "the earliest multilateral arrangements instituted in the modern era were designed to cope with the international consequences of the novel principle of state sovereignty" (John G. Ruggie, "Multilateralism: The Anatomy of an Institution," in *Multilateralism Matters*, ed. John G. Ruggie [New York: Columbia University Press], 15). See also John G. Ruggie, "International Regimes, Transactions and Change: Embedded Liberalism in the Postwar Economic Order," *International Organization* 36, (Spring 1982), 379–415.

5. *Documents of the United Nations Conference on International Organization, San Francisco, 1945* (henceforth *UNCIO Documents)* (London and New York: United Nations Information Organizations, 1945), vol. VI, 507; Leland M. Goodrich and Edvard Hambro, *Charter of the United Nations: Commentary and Documents* (Boston: World Peace Foundation, 1946), 111.

end, an Australian sponsored amendment at the San Francisco conference would ensure that the domestic jurisdiction (non-intervention) principle would not prejudice the application of the UN's enforcement measures.[6]

Asia was hardly engaged in the making of the UN Charter. The only Asian countries (excluding West Asia or Arab Middle East) present at the San Francisco Conference were India, still a British colony, and the Republic of China. Hence Asian countries did not have the opportunity to participate in the debates about the meaning and scope of non-intervention.[7] Moreover, in the immediate post-war period, Asia's leaders had more urgent normative concerns. They were preoccupied with a common enemy—colonialism, and the issue of racial equality. The anti-colonial struggle called for a policy of mutual assistance, rather than a posture of indifference or strict non-intervention. India offered some political as well as material support to Indonesian nationalists after they proclaimed independence from the Dutch in July 1945, including aerial supply missions to break the Dutch air and sea blockade of the republic, and offering to set up its government-in-exile in New Delhi. The idea of non-intervention also clashed with the pan-Asian aspirations of some of Asia's nationalist leaders, which may be regarded as part of a regional cognitive prior. In 1939, for example, India's nationalist leader Jawaharlal Nehru had contemplated an Asian federation: "My . . . picture of the future is a federation which includes China and India, Burma and Ceylon, Afghanistan and possibly other countries."[8] In 1945, Nehru argued that "[i]n the world of tomorrow smaller countries will either have to federate into three or four big confederations or big countries will absorb them as satellites."[9] And in the same year, he spoke of an Asian federation being a "possibility in the near future."[10] Prime Minister S.W.R.D. Bandaranaike of Ceylon (now Sri Lanka) called for a "federation of free and equal Asian countries,"[11] whereas Aung San of Burma envisaged an Asiatic Federation.[12] Overall, however, the force of these pan-Asian

6. *UNCIO Documents*, vol. VI, 334, 435–40.

7. In 1947, only eight of the delegations at the Asian Relations Conference were UN members. Godfrey H. Jansen, *Afro-Asia and Non-Alignment* (London: Faber, 1966), 52. This limits the UN's claim to be a "teacher" of the norms of sovereignty in the early post-war period.

8. Dorothy Norman, *Nehru: The First Sixty Years* (New York: John Day, 1965), 636.

9. "A South Asian Federation," *India Today*, (September 1945), 1–2, cited in Constance Ann Freydig, *India and Indonesia's Independent Foreign Policy*, M.A. thesis, University of California, Berkeley, 1954, 22.

10. Extracts from Nehru's interview with B. Shiva Rao, ICWA ARC Files, Indian Council on World Affairs, New Delhi.

11. Jansen, *Afro-Asia and Non-Alignment*.

12. On 24 July 1946, Aung San said in a speech that Burma would "stand for an Asiatic Federation in a not very, very remote future, we stand for immediate mutual understanding and joint action, wherever and whenever possible, from now for our mutual interests and for

aspirations was not great.[13] There was no ideology of pan-Asianism comparable to pan-Arabism, which regarded the principle of state sovereignty and the division of the Arab nation into separate independent states as an aberration and a temporary phenomenon.[14] Nonetheless, pan-Asian visions did make Asia's leaders less sensitized to the importance of non-intervention as a foreign policy principle, at least in the 1940s.

The fact that non-intervention was not a key demand of Asian leaders in the immediate post-war period was quite evident in the agenda and deliberations of the Asian Relations Conferences (ARCs) convened by India's leader Jawaharlal Nehru in 1947 and 1949. (See table 3.1 for a list of countries in attendance at these and other Asian conferences.) The agenda of the first ARC, held in New Delhi in 1947, listed eight issues: national movements for freedom, racial problems, inter-Asian migration, transition from colonial to national economy, agricultural reconstruction and industrial development, labor problems and social services, cultural problems, and status of women and women's movements.[15] The term "non-intervention" was not mentioned in its agenda, proceedings, or statements. On the contrary, the conference witnessed controversy over demands by some participants over the need for countries like India to provide greater material assistance to the region's national liberation struggles. The Conference called on countries not to support "foreign domination" in any part of Asia, but did not shy away from prescribing rules affecting countries' domestic racial policies.[16] The 1947 ARC urged "people belonging to one country and living in another should identify themselves with the latter," and called upon countries (e.g., Indonesia, Burma, and Ceylon) to refrain from drafting constitutions that would discriminate against the racial minorities (e.g., Chinese and Indian) on their soil. A key agreement to emerge from this conference was that the principle of equality among all citizens, irrespective of race and creed, should be the rule in all countries. The notion of equality was divided into four components: "(i) complete legal equality of all citizens; (ii) com-

---

the freedom of India, Burma and indeed all Asia" ("'Welcome India' Address Delivered at the Reception Given in Honor of Mr. Sarat Bose, a Member of the Working Committee of the Indian National Congress, at the City Hall of Rangoon on July 24, 1946." In *Bogyoke Aung San Maint-Khun-Myar (1945–1947): General Aung San's Speeches* [Rangoon: Sarpay Bait Man Press, 1971], 86).

13. As Jansen put it, "Pan-Asian talk by the Asian nationalist leaders is always vague, with no great force of conviction behind it. It never even amounted to a very palpable political myth" (*Afro-Asia and Non-Alignment*, 38).

14. Michael Barnett, "Sovereignty, Nationalism and Regional Order in the Arab States System," *International Organization* 49, no. 3 (Summer 1995), 479–510.

15. A. Appadorai, "The Asian Relations Conference in Perspective," *International Studies* 18, no.3 (July–September 1979), 275–85.

16. Appadorai, "The Asian Relations Conference," 279.

plete religious freedom; (iii) no public social disqualification of any racial group; and (iv) equality before the law of persons of foreign origin who had settled in the country."[17]

What is especially striking about these principles is that they were essentially concerned with the domestic jurisdiction of states. This may be partly due to the fact that it was technically a non-official gathering, organized as it was by the non-governmental Indian Council on World Affairs and because several of the key participating countries, such as Burma and Indonesia, were not yet independent. But the chairman of the conference was Nehru, already prime minister-designate of India at the time, underscoring the political and at least semi-official nature of the conference. The real reason could be that participants in the 1947 ARC, as well as the strictly "official" Conference on Indonesia also convened by Nehru in New Delhi in 1949 (also known as the Second New Delhi Conference or the Second Asian Relations Conference) to discuss the specific issue of Indonesian independence in the light of the second Dutch "police action," were concerned primarily with self-determination and racial equality. This unity and sense of common purpose would allow them to set common rules for the domestic affairs of states that would become unthinkable in subsequent regional multilateral gatherings and institutions, as they would be seen as a violation of the non-intervention principle.[18]

This shift toward non-intervention was the result of several factors. First, pan-Asian sentiments, weak to begin with, were further discredited because of the unwillingness of Asia's key nationalist leaders to offer more than moral support for the anti-colonial struggles of fellow Asian countries. India's, albeit limited, assistance to the Indonesian freedom fighters facing the Dutch police action was not extended to Ho Chi Minh in his struggle against the French—a stand that attracted criticism at the 1947 ARC.[19] Although Nehru remained a champion of Asian cooperation, often speaking eloquently about Asia's political and spiritual revival after centuries of colonial rule and of the need for coordinated Asian action on regional and international affairs, his interest and those of other Asian leaders in

17. Appadorai, "The Asian Relations Conference," 280.

18. Paradoxically, this also suggests that the Asian debates played an important role in the development of the non-intervention norm.

19. *Asian Relations: Proceedings of the Asian Relations Conference*, (New Delhi: Asian Relations Organization, 1948), 71–90. To such complaints, one Indian delegate replied that "short of a declaration of war, it was difficult to visualize what form such help could take, except moral support. He emphasised that it was necessary that any support should not have the effect of enlarging the area of conflict" (*Asian Relations*, 82). Independent India would put an immediate halt to the British practice of using Indian troops (widely criticized at the ARC) to suppress anti-colonial rebellions. Jansen, *Afro-Asia and Non-Alignment*, 51–73.

pan-Asian unity vanished in the 1950s, leading to the closure of the Asian Relations Organization set up at the 1947 ARC.

Because Asia's leaders only had a weak aspiration for pan-Asian integration, the emerging international norm of non-intervention did not run into any fundamentally incompatible Asian regionalist cognitive prior. More important, although Asia's leaders had initially given non-intervention a lesser priority in their "norm hierarchy,"[20] compared to self-determination and racial equality, they gradually came to recognize the growing congruence between the norm and the desire of Asian leaders to resist pressure and domination by outside powers—a desire closely related to the prevailing sentiments of nationalism and anti-colonialism. This congruence was actively constructed by a group of Asia's leaders, largely in response to a host of new geopolitical developments that made them view non-intervention as an integral element of the overall project of national and regional autonomy. This growing salience of non-intervention in the 1950s attests to the fact that it was not simply a concept inherited from the colonial powers or their practices, but had to be actively constructed in response to changing geopolitical circumstances in Asia, a construction that reflected the worldviews and the political interests and needs of Asian leaders. Far from being an alien and irrelevant Western concept, non-intervention could be usefully applied to the local context to deal with the challenges they faced.

Foremost among these challenges was the escalating superpower rivalry, with the attendant tendency of their competitive interventionism in Asia and the Third World. Another crucial challenge was the 1949 communist takeover in China, which created a new danger to national and regime security of its Asian neighbors. The emergence of the Chinese communist state as a subversive force would make non-intervention an urgent normative concern throughout Asia. In parallel with these developments, non-intervention acquired a new importance with the advent of Asian neutralism (discussed later in this chapter), "a term applicable to those policies and attitudes representing a rejection of extensive commitment to either side now engaged in the cold war," adopted by India, Indonesia, and Burma.[21]

20. Norm hierarchy refers to the relative ordering of norms. Theo Farrell, "Transnational Norms and Military Development: Constructing Ireland's Professional Army," *European Journal of International Relations* 7, no. 1 (2001): 81.

21. Robert A. Scalapino, " 'Neutralism' in Asia," *American Political Science Review* 48, no. 1 (March 1954): 49. But Asian neutralists "resented" the label "neutralism" because "such an appellation is too negative and too passive," and might imply "a lack of responsibility concerning world affairs." Asia neutralism was supposed to be based on "positive action" and "positive beliefs" (Scalapino, " 'Neutralism' in Asia," 49).

The rationale behind Asian neutralism was both domestic and international. Following independence, the new states of Asia faced a growing number of domestic problems; they sought to avoid their escalation, which might be caused by the ever present danger of foreign intervention.[22] Apart from internal consolidation, acquiring prestige before domestic audience through activist neutralism was a key motivating factor behind Asian neutralism.[23] Internationally, neutralism was seen by its Asian proponents as a tool for preserving newfound independence, either through isolation or the activist policy of playing one great power against another, attracting aid from both, preventing dominance by either, and securing opportunities for playing a mediating role among great powers, thereby reducing the danger of war.[24]

The appeal of neutralism and non-intervention was magnified by the growing crisis in Indochina, as the United States stepped up support for the struggling French forces and the related pursuit of a regional collective defense strategy by the United States. Faced with an escalating crisis in Indochina, prime ministers of five Asian countries (India, Pakistan, Burma, Indonesia, and Ceylon) organized a group that became known as the Colombo Powers, because it was an initiative of Ceylon's prime minister John Kotelawala, and held its first meeting in April 1954 in Colombo. This loose and informal grouping would act as the "insider proponent" of the non-intervention principle, making it the basis of its response to the Indochina crisis and for the organization of Asian regional cooperation. Invoking this internationally accepted principle offered the Colombo Powers a convenient basis for assuming a role in a regional conflict to an extent their combined material power could not have.

Thus, at the first summit of the Colombo Powers, U.S. support for the French forces in Vietnam attracted criticism as a form of intervention. In proposing the terms of a settlement in Indochina, a draft resolution of the summit initially suggested "a solemn agreement of non-intervention" by the United States, USSR, UK, and China "to refrain from giving aid to the combatants or intervening in Indo-China with troops or war material."[25] Pakistan, although not being "opposed to the principle of non-intervention,"

22. George Liska, "The 'Third Party': The Rationale of Nonalignment," in *Neutralism and Non-Alignment*, ed. Laurence W. Martin (New York: Frederick Praeger, 1962), 88–89.

23. As Wolfers put it, "a reputation for being important in the world arena may spell victory in the fierce struggle with domestic rivals" (Arnold Wolfers, "Allies, Neutrals, and Neutralists," in *Neutralism and Non-Alignment*, ed. Martin,158–59.

24. Laurence W. Martin, "Introduction: The Emergence of the New States," in *Neutralism and Non-Alignment*, ed. Martin, xii.

25. Colombo Conference Minutes, Unarchived unpublished official documents (henceforth UUOD).

objected to the language's inclusivity (presumably because U.S. assistance to South Vietnam would have been delegitimized at a time when Pakistan had decided to join a collective defense pact with the United States). Ultimately, a softer language was used to urge the external powers (China, the United States, USSR, and UK) to agree on "steps necessary to prevent the recurrence or resumption of hostilities" so that "the success of . . . direct negotiations [as opposed to the prospects for a ceasefire] will be greatly helped."[26]

In the wake of the first Colombo Powers summit, Indonesia proposed an Asia-Africa Conference to be held under the sponsorship of the Colombo Powers. The final preparations for the Conference were made during a second meeting of the Colombo Powers held in December 1954 in Bogor, Indonesia. The objectives of the Asian-African gathering would be to solve "problems affecting national sovereignty and racialism and colonialism"; "to explore and advance" the "mutual and common interests" of Asian and African nations; and "establish and further friendliness and neighborly relations." The principle of non-interference appeared in three key decisions of the Colombo Powers at Bogor. First, they stated that "acceptance of the invitation by any one country would in no way involve or imply any change to the status of that country or its relationship with other countries." Second, they recognized the "principle that the form of government and the way of life of any one country should in no way be subjected to interference by any other."[27] Third, no invitations were to be issued to the representatives of independence movements in dependent countries, as such a gesture would suggest, in Nehru's words, "interference in internal affairs, while the Colombo countries had advocated the principle of non-interference."[28]

The principle of non-intervention found progressive elaboration and extension in Asian regionalist ideas and approaches. It came to replace any lingering pan-Asian sentiments in the cognitive prior of Asian regionalism. But the Asian construction of non-intervention was not simply a restatement of the original European or the subsequent Latin American concept. The norm would take on additional meanings, including the creation of an injunction against participation in collective defense pacts organized under

26. Ibid.
27. Joint Communiqué by the prime ministers of Burma, Celyon, India, Indonesia, and Pakistan, Bogor Conference Minutes, UUOD.
28. First Session, Bogor Conference Minutes, UUOD.

**Table 3.1.**  Representation at Regional Conferences in Asia, 1947–1955

| Asian Relations New Delhi March 1947 | Asian Relations (Conference on Indonesia) New Delhi January 1949 | Asian-African Bandung April 1955 |
|---|---|---|
| Afghanistan | Afghanistan | Afghanistan* |
| Armenia | — | — |
| Azerbaijan | — | — |
| Bhutan | — | — |
| **Burma** | **Burma** | **Burma*** |
| Cambodia, Cochin-China, and Laos | — | Cambodia* |
| **Ceylon** | **Ceylon** | **Ceylon*** |
| China | China (o) | China (Communist) |
| Egypt | Egypt | Egypt |
| — | Ethiopia | Ethiopia |
| Georgia | — | Gold Coast (o) |
| **India** | **India** | **India*** |
| **Indonesia** | **Indonesia** | **Indonesia*** |
| — | Iraq | Iraq |
| — | — | Japan** |
| — | — | Jordan |
| Kazakhstan | — | — |
| Kirghizia | — | — |
| Korea (South) | — | — |
| — | — | Laos |
| — | Lebanon | Lebanon** |
| — | — | Liberia |
| — | — | Libya |
| Malaya | — | — |
| Mongolia | — | — |
| Nepal | Nepal (o) | Nepal |
| — | **Pakistan** | **Pakistan** |
| Palestine (Hebrew University) | — | — |
| Persia | Persia | Persia |
| Philippines | Philippines | Philippines** |
| — | Saudi Arabia | Saudi Arabia |
| — | — | Sudan |
| — | Syria | Syria |
| Tajikistan | — | — |
| Thailand | Thailand (o) | Thailand** |
| Tibet | — | — |
| Turkey | — | Turkey** |
| Turkmenistan | — | — |
| Uzbekistan | — | — |
| Vietnam (Viet Minh) | — | Vietnam (North) |
| — | — | Vietnam (South)** |
| — | Yemen | Yemen |

*(continued)*

**Table 3.1.** *(continued)*

| Asian Relations New Delhi March 1947 | Asian Relations (Conference on Indonesia) New Delhi January 1949 | Asian-African Bandung April 1955 |
|---|---|---|
| Australia (o) | Australia | — |
| — | New Zealand (o) | |
| Arab League (o) | — | Arab League (o) |
| UK (o) | — | — |
| Soviet Union (o) | — | — |
| United States (o) | — | — |
| United Nations (o) | — | — |

*Source*: UK Foreign Office Research Department, "Asian Conferences, 1947–1955," 2 December 1955. DO35/6099; author's own research.

*Notes*: Countries in bold are Colombo Powers (Conference of South-East Asian Prime Ministers) members; (o)=observer; *=neutralist nation at Bandung; **=main pro-Western nation at Bandung; a dash (—) indicates that the country in that row did not participate.

"great power orbit,"[29] an idea that had been evolving since the end of World War II. This further construction of non-intervention is discussed in the next section, which examines the fate of the Southeast Asia Treaty Organization (SEATO), as well as in chapter 4, which elaborates on the overall

29. Liska summarizes the idea of "great power orbits" as follows: "According to the idea, regional groupings of small states ought to cluster around the local Great Power and pool military, economic, and other resources in peace and war. . . . The smaller communities would extend to the local Great Power facilities and amicable cooperation, and receive in return a realistic measure of independence, aid, and protection. They stand to gain by transferring into stronger hands the chief responsibility for organizing regional security, and the Great Powers would also profit from having dependable allies within their strategic area. There would be more security and prosperity both intra- and interregionally" (George H. Liska, "Geographic Scope: Patterns of Integration," in *Regional Politics and World Order*, ed. R.Falk and S. Mendlovitz [San Francisco: W.H. Freeman, 1973], 236). Claude offers the following critique of regionalized security systems within great power orbits: "The status of the great powers offers particular difficulties for the development of regionalism. On the one hand, the segmentation process may take into account the fact that the great powers are *world* powers, or states with a general interest. In that case, the regional body tends to include the multiregional great powers and along with the local small fry, and loses its geographical sense as well as assumed emancipation from involvement in the unwelcome complexities of the wider world. . . . On the other hand, regional organizations are often built around the local great power, taking on the character of a solar system, with subsidiary members revolving about the central sun. One might conceive of a world divided into, say, American, Soviet, and Chinese regional blocs, but this arrangement might not constitute anything more than a formalization of spheres of influence; it might contribute little or nothing to the elimination of conflicts among the great powers, or the alleviation of the anxieties of the small states with regard to their security against domination by the neighborhood giant" (Inis Claude, *Swords into Plowshares* [New York: Random House, 1964], 96–97). For a critical appraisal of ideas about regional collective defense organizations prevalent in the United States at this time, see Hamilton Fish Armstrong, "Regional Pacts: Strong Points or Storm Centers," *Foreign Affairs* 27, no.3 (April 1949): 351–68.

enhancement of the scope of non-intervention at the Asian and international levels, and its contribution to the making of the cognitive prior of Asian regionalism.

## Regional Collective Defense, 1954–1955

In May 1943, during a conversation with Roosevelt administration officials in Washington, DC, British prime minister Winston Churchill proposed that the future world be organized as a "three-legged stool": a Supreme World Council "resting on" three Regional Councils—one for Europe, one for the American Hemisphere, and one for the Pacific.[30] In a book published a year later, American opinion maker Walter Lippmann articulated the vision of a world consisting of regional systems under great power management. There could thus be an Atlantic system managed by the United States and the Soviet Union, a Russian system, a Chinese system, and eventually an Indian system.[31] Although both these ideas were prescriptive in nature, they recognized that regions do matter in world politics. As Churchill later wrote, "I attached great importance to the regional principle. It was only the countries whose interests were directly affected by a dispute who could be expected to apply themselves with sufficient vigour to secure a settlement. If countries remote from a dispute were among those called upon in the first instance to achieve a settlement the result was likely to be merely vapid and academic discussion."[32]

Churchill's advocacy of regional security systems under the influence of a great power did not sway the Roosevelt administration's preference for a universal security organization, although regional groupings were accorded a role under the UN system.[33] But the idea of regional collective defense pacts within "great power orbits" would attract greater support with the outbreak of the Cold War. As post-war efforts by the victorious allies to manage international order through the UN-based collective security system showed its limitations (mainly due to the Soviet veto at the UN), collective defense became a central part of the U.S. strategy to contain the Soviet bloc. Some American legislators, including Senator Arthur Vandenberg, embraced

30. Winston S. Churchill, *The Second World War*, vol. 4 (London: Reprint Society, 1953), 646.

31. Walter Lippmann, *U.S. War Aims* (New York: Da Capo Press, 1976).

32. Churchill, *The Second World War*, 646.

33. Francis Wilcox, "Regionalism and the United Nations," *International Organization* 19, no. 3 (1965): 789–811; Minerva Etzioni, *The Majority of One: Towards a Theory of Regional Compatibility* (Beverley Hills, CA: Sage).

the idea. In 1948, Vandenberg sponsored a resolution by the U.S. Senate Foreign Relations Committee, which called for the United States to pursue the "progressive development of regional and other collective defense arrangements for individual and collective self-defense" in accordance with the UN Charter.[34] The establishment of the North Atlantic Treaty Organization (NATO) in 1949 gave a concrete expression to the idea of collective defense. The United States insisted that NATO, like other proposed collective defense systems, was consistent with the UN Charter, especially with its right to self-defense clause (Article 51).

The U.S. government had resisted ideas and proposals for a regional organization for Asia until the outbreak of the Korean War, partly due to a concern that organizing such a group might be perceived as a prop to the European colonial powers in the region. As noted in a Policy Planning Staff Paper on U.S. policy toward Southeast Asia in March 1949:

> We should avoid at the outset urging an area organization. Our effort should initially be directed toward collaboration on joint or parallel action and then, only as a pragmatic and desirable basis for intimate association appears, should we encourage the areas to move step by step toward formal organization. If Asian leaders prematurely precipitate an area organization, we should not give the impression of attempting to thwart such a move but should go along with them while exerting a cautiously moderating influence. . . . In order to minimize suggestions of American imperialist intervention, we should encourage the Indians, Filipinos and other Asian states to take the public lead in political matters. Our role should be the offering of discreet support and guidance.[35]

Instead, between 1942 and 1943, President Roosevelt had proposed an international trusteeship system for the Southeast Asian colonies to prepare them for independence.[36] In 1949, the Truman administration showed scant interest in pursuing a proposal—mooted by President Elpidio Quirino of the Philippines and supported by President Syngman Rhee of South Korea and General Chiang Kai-shek of the National Government of the Republic

34. Cited in Paul E. Gallis, "NATO: Article V and Collective Defense," CRS Report for Congress, 97–717 F, Congressional Research Service, Library of Congress, Washington, DC (17 July 1997), available at http://www.fas.org/man/crs/97-717f.htm. A "working paper" submitted to the Senate Foreign Relations Committee in May 1948 by Arthur Vandenberg in the form of a Senate resolution called for development of regional arrangements for collective self-defense under Article 51, and the "association" of the United States with such groupings. These regional pacts would be based on "self help and mutual aid" ("Blueprint," *Time*, 24 May 1948, available at http://www.time.com/time/magazine/article/0,9171,794349,00.html.

35. Cited in C. Mahapatra, *American Role in the Origin and Growth of ASEAN* (New Delhi: ABC Publishing House, 1990), 48.

36. David Capie, Power, Identity and Multilateralism: Rethinking Institutional Dynamics in the Pacific, 1945–2000, PhD diss., York University, Toronto, 2003, 36.

of China—for a Pacific equivalent of NATO, with the involvement of South Korea, India, Australia, New Zealand, Thailand, and Indonesia. But the situation changed considerably after the Korean War.

There was no stronger champion of a collective defense framework for Asia than John Foster Dulles, who after the end of World War II negotiated a peace treaty with Japan on behalf of the Truman administration and who later served as Eisenhower's secretary of state.[37] He saw collective defense as a necessary element of U.S. security strategy for the Pacific to counter the communist advance. After the conclusion of the U.S.-Japan alliance and the ANZUS (Australia, New Zealand, and the United States) security treaty, Dulles turned his attention to the creation of a multilateral collective defense system for the Pacific. In a 1952 article in *Foreign Affairs*, he articulated the need for an Asian collective defense organization. In this article, Dulles dismissed objections to the proposed system, including the perceptions among the "Orientals" that treaties with the United States will be a fundamentally unequal enterprise (to him, this was an understandable concern, but not an insurmountable barrier to collective defense). He viewed the necessity of collective defense not just in strategic or utilitarian terms, but also in normative terms. They were "demanded by considerations of justice and morality."[38] He also rejected suggestions that the threat faced by U.S. interests in Asia did not require a collective defense system. Even the US-Japan Treaty and the ANZUS were not sufficient for this task. Asia was more vulnerable to communist expansion than Europe; unlike in Europe, the communists in Asia were prepared to resort to violent action. In his opinion:

> It is in Asia that Russian imperialism finds its most powerful expression. The countermeasures taken in 1951 have been good, but they are not good enough to justify a mood of relaxation. We must go forward to achieve greater unity and greater strength.[39]

37. Before joining the Truman State Department, Dulles had called for an "Association of the Free Nations of Asia and the Pacific." This was "not, at least at the beginning, to be an essentially *military* alliance" John Foster Dulles, *War or Peace* [New York: MacMillan, 1950], 229–30). After joining the Truman administration in March 1950, Dulles would soon reveal that his preference was not for a NATO type organization for Asia, but a Monroe Doctrine kind of declaration. He believed that the Monroe Doctrine formula recognized that the "the only real source of security for the other members lay in U.S. power" (David W. Mabon, "Elusive Agreements: The Pacific Pact Proposals of 1949–1951," *Pacific Historical Review* 57, no. 2 [May 1988]: 160). This shows that Dulles's thinking on pacts was consistent with the great power orbit concept, rather than the concert model, which assumes a certain degree of equality among the allies.

38. John Foster Dulles, "Security in the Pacific," *Foreign Affairs* 30, no. 2 (January 1952): 186.

39. Dulles, "Security in the Pacific," 187.

But the idea of great power-organized collective defense pacts aroused considerable suspicion among the leaders of Asia's newly independent states. First, it conflicted with the prior normative beliefs of a section of Asian nationalists against great power blocs, most prominent among them being Jawaharlal Nehru. In an essay written in prison in 1944, titled *Realism and Geopolitics: World Conquest or World Association?* Nehru explicitly rejected regional security systems under great power "orbits," as proposed by Lippmann, characterizing them as "a continuation of power politics on a vaster scale. . . . [It] is difficult to see . . . world peace or co-operation emerging out of it."[40] His desire and hope for greater international cooperation took the form of a "commonwealth of states" or a "world association" rather than a military alliance that reflected the dynamics of power politics.[41]

Some of Asia's other nationalist leaders also saw regional pacts as a threat to national sovereignty and regional autonomy. They shared Nehru's rejection of collective defense despite their personal differences with Nehru over regional leadership.[42] Burma's Aung San used the experience of Japanese colonialism to argue against regional security arrangements organized by great powers. In January 1946, he contended that "a new Asian order . . . will not and must not be one like the Co-prosperity Sphere of militarist Japan, nor should it be another Asiatic Monroe doctrine, nor imperial preference or currency bloc."[43] In the first major study of comparative regionalism published

40. This essay appears in Jawaharlal Nehru, *The Discovery of India*, 23rd (New Delhi: Oxford University Press, 2003), 539. The framing of regional collective defense systems as a form of power politics was also evident in a speech delivered by Nehru on 7 September 1946: "We propose, as far as possible, to keep away from the power politics of groups, aligned against one another, which have led in the past to world wars and which may again lead to disaster of an even vaster scale. We believe that peace and freedom are indivisible and that denial of freedom anywhere must endanger freedom elsewhere and lead to conflict and war. We are particularly interested in the emancipation of colonial and dependent territories and peoples and in the recognition in theory and practice of equal opportunities for all peoples . . . We seek no domination over others and we claim no privileged position over other peoples . . . The world, in spite of its rivalries and hatreds and inner conflicts, moves inevitably towards closer cooperation and the building up of a world of commonwealth. It is for this one world free India will work, a world in which there is free co-operation of free peoples and no class or group exploits another" (cited in V. S. Mani, "An Indian Perspective on the Evolution of International Law on the Threshold of the Third Millennium," in *Asian Yearbook of International Law, vol. 9 (2000)*, ed. B. S. Chimni, M. Masahiro, and S. P. Subedi [Netherlands: Brill, 2004], 66).

41. Nehru, *The Discovery of India*, 536; Mani, "An Indian Perspective," 66.

42. Nehru did exercise considerable influence over other Asian Nationalists. He had "long . . . been in correspondence with other Asiatic leaders," such as Indonesia's premier Mohamed Hatta, whom he first met at an anti-imperialist rally in Brussels in the 1920s, and was "a close friend and backer of Burma's Premier Thakin Nu" ("Anchor for Asia," *Time*, 17 October 1949. Scalapino observes that Nehru's influence extended far beyond India" (Scalapnio, "'Neutralism' in Asia," 51).

43. Aung San, "Problems for Burma's Freedom," Inaugural Address at the Anti-Fascist People's Freedom League Convention, January 1946, in *The Political Legacy of Aung San*, ed.

in post-war Asia (1948), Indian diplomat and scholar K. M. Panikkar cited Nazi imperial blocs in the 1930s and Japanese Greater East Asian Co-Prosperity Sphere to object to Churchill's and Lippmann's proposals, because such proposals might lead to the "establishment of the paramountcy of a Great Power in a defined geographic region."[44]

The idea of regional collective defense pacts was also at odds with the "neutralist" orientation and foreign policy strategy of Asian nationalists. Nehru, who never liked the term "neutralism,"[45] had developed a doctrine of "area of peace" and "non-involvement" (which later acquired promi-nence as "non-alignment"), even before Dullesian ideas about regional pacts became prominent. Nehru wrote in 1948, "We shall take care not to align ourselves with one group or another . . . remaining neutral on those [ques-tions] not affecting us directly. . . . India obviously cannot join either of the two blocs. . . . What she desires is an understanding between Russia and the U.S."[46] Burmese leader U Nu had argued in September 1950, "If we . . . trust the Union of Burma into the arms of one bloc, the other bloc will not be content to look on with folded arms."[47]

Together with their anti-power politics and foreign policy beliefs, Asian neutralism constituted a prior normative framework in terms of which the legitimacy of great power-led regional pacts came to be judged. Liska sum-marizes the stance of Asian neutrals toward regionalism:

> Asian neutralism typifies the preference of smaller states for regional orga-nization without Great Powers. According to this school of thought . . . [r]egional arrangements around a Great Power are merely disguises for domi-nation over weaker associates; they could not enforce sanctions against an-other Great Power if they conformed literally with the Charter. Instead, re-gional organizations should be set up among states with approximately equal resources and development, certain to respect each other's sovereignty and in-dependence. They should concentrate on socio-economic and cultural tasks and stay aloof from Great-Power conflicts.[48]

Josef Silverstein (Ithaca, NY: Southeast Asia Program, Cornell University, 1992), 101.

44. K.M. Panikkar, "Regionalism and World Security," in *Regionalism and Security*, ed. K.M. Panikkar et al. (Bombay: Oxford University Press, 1948), 1.

45. Apparently because it was a term used in wartime, and indicated "a sort of war mental-ity." In the Indian context, "neutralism" simply meant it had an "independent policy" and "judged questions on their merit" (Peter Lyon, "Neutrality and the Emergence of the Concept of Neutralism," *Review of Politics* 22, no. 2 (April 1960): 255.

46. "Anchor for Asia."

47. Thakin Nu, *From Peace to Stability* (Rangoon: Ministry of Information, 1951), 102.

48. Liska, "Geographic Scope," 233. But the neutralist position on pacts was more complex than the summary rejection of pacts. It contained many different strands. Summarizing the position of new states of Asia and Africa on alliances, and drawing on Liska's analysis, Sing-ham and Hume note that it was not a general opposition to or rejection of all pacts, but these

The rejection of regional pacts was also rooted in anti-colonialism, which had remained robust throughout the region at the time the idea of collective defense pacts was mooted by the United States. Just as norm advocates legitimize a new idea by associating it with (or grafting it onto) a prior local belief or practice, Asian nationalists sought to delegitimize the idea of collective defense pacts by associating it with colonialism. For the neutralist leaders of Asia, the offer of "protection" by superpower-led collective defense pacts was "a condition of colonialism or dependency."[49] This was consistent with the general pattern of nationalist and anti-colonial ideas in Asia and Africa in the post-war period, surveying which Rupert Emerson noted "a widespread sentiment" that associated membership in collective defense pacts with "return . . . to colonial rule."[50]

Another source of neutralist objection to collective defense pacts was its conflict with the prior and evolving norm of non-intervention. Nehru believed that the proliferation of regional pacts would reduce the "area of peace" and encourage great power intervention in the internal affairs of the

---

countries "had a special hostility to the global alliance system that was held over from their historic colonial association with European powers." There was also a "general opposition—especially from the smaller and less powerful states—to an exclusive alliance system which restricts membership" (A.W. Singham and Shirley Hume, *Non-Alignment in an Age of Alignments* [Westport, CT: Lawrence Hill, 1986], 381). George Liska, *Nations in Alliance* (Baltimore: Johns Hopkins University Press, 1962), 206. Also, there was less aversion to bilateral alliances. Incidentally, Nehru was not against any kind of defense cooperation. In 1945, he had envisaged a "close union of the countries bordering on the Indian Ocean for defense and trade purposes." Extracts from Nehru's Interview with B. Shiva Rao, ICWA ARC Files, Indian Council on World Affairs, New Delhi. Later, he had demonstrated that he was not opposed to bilateral defense ties between states, including Third World countries and outside powers, because these were needed for legitimate national defense against overt aggression. But regional pacts conceived in the Cold War context were viewed by Nehru in an entirely different light.

49. Cecil Crabb, *The Elephants and the Grass: A Study of Non-Alignment* (New York: Praeger, 1967), 67.

50. Rupert Emerson, *From Empire to Nation: The Rise of Self Assertion of Asian and African Peoples* (Cambridge, MA: Harvard University Press, 1962), 395; Lynn H. Miller, "The Prospect for Order Through Regional Security," in *Regional Politics and World Order*, ed. Richard A. Falk and Saul H. Mendlovitz (San Francisco: W.H. Freeman), 58; Sisir Gupta, *India and Regional Integration in Asia* (Bombay: Asia Publishing House, 1964), 59. Liska argues that in addition to the traditional motivations such as fear of provoking the other side by aligning with one, or creating more enemies if the number of parties to a conflict increases, the anti-alliance policy of non-aligned countries was due to the fear of weapons of mass destruction and the perceived relationship between Western alliance policy and Western colonialism. The non-aligned opposition to NATO might be partly due to the perception that "it helped the metropolitan members resist the trend toward 'decolonization' by reducing a colonial metropole's defense burden against the Soviet bloc in Europe." On the anti-alliance aspect of neutralism, see Liska, "The 'Third Party,'" 85.

new states. For him, the sanctity of the non-intervention norm was closely linked to the non-involvement of states in superpower rivalry by refraining from membership in regional collective defense pacts. Such pacts did more harm than good to the sovereignty of nations, and as a principle non-intervention would be best pursued through agreements such as the Five Principles of Peaceful Coexistence, which India and China made in 1954. (These principles included mtual respect for each other's territorial integrity and sovereignty, mutual non-aggression, mutual non-interference in each other's internal affairs, equality and mutual benefit, and peaceful co-existence.) In a conversation with the British high commissioner in Delhi on 14 April 1954, Nehru's close adviser V.K. Krishna Menon argued that "collective defense under United States auspices would mean renewed intervention by the West in the East which would in principle be repugnant to all decent Asian opinion."[51]

In December 1954 at the Bogor Conference of the Colombo Powers, Nehru attacked SEATO for introducing "quite a new conception" in international relations, because unlike NATO, "members of this organization are not only responsible for their own defense but also for that of areas they may designate outside of it if they so agree, this would mean creating a new form of spheres of influence." Nehru contrasted it with the Geneva Agreement on Indochina, which he endorsed "because of its clause that no outside interference will be allowed in Indo-China."[52] Responding to the British overtures to take a more sympathetic view of the Southeast Asian pact, Indian officials described SEATO as "a roving commission to protect people who did not want to be protected, affecting the sovereignty of the nations of the area."[53]

Nehru's and India's resistance to collective defense was not entirely devoid of strategic motives. He perceived SEATO and the Central Treaty Organization (CENTO) as threats to India's security, especially because of Pakistan's involvement in both. These alliances brought the Cold War to India's doorstep. Moreover, some Indian scholars have argued that Nehru's rejection of SEATO reflected India's own aspiration for regional dominance.[54] This would constitute an alternative realpolitik explanation of Nehru's position on collective defense. Such self-interested behavior need not be incompatible

51. Inward Telegram, from the UK High Commissioner in Delhi to Commonwealth Relations Office, 14 April 1954, FO 371/112053.
52. Second Session, Bogor Conference Minutes.
53. Cited in Gupta, *India and Regional Integration in Asia*, 59.
54. Bharat Karnad, *Nuclear Weapons and Indian Security: The Realist Foundations of Strategy* (Delhi: Macmillan, 2002), 80.

with normative approaches to international relations.[55] The existence of a Pakistan factor in Nehru's opposition to collective defense pacts obscures the fact that his opposition had been articulated (at least in 1944) *before* the creation of Pakistan and *before* the creation of NATO, and thus could not be simply dismissed as an opportunistic stance against SEATO per se.[56] It even predated the partition of India and the first Kashmir War of 1947.

To attribute Nehru's position on regional defense pacts to his own aspiration for regional dominance would overstate his realpolitik.[57] Nehru's belief that a cooperative international order leading to a "world of commonwealth" was emerging despite ongoing international conflicts clearly went against a realpolitik view of international relations. His rejection of Cold War collective defense pacts was not simply a response to India's changing strategic circumstances; it had a basis in his prior moral beliefs. The Cold War pacts conflicted with Nehru's vision of international relations, which rejected power politics, denounced colonialism, advocated non-exclusionary international and regional cooperation, and demanded equality and justice for the newly independent states. As a biographer of Nehru put it, collective

55. As Finnemore and Sikkink write, some "frequently heard arguments about whether behavior is norm-based or interest-based miss the point that norm conformity can often be self-interested, depending on how one specifies interests and the nature of the norm" (Martha Finnemore and Karyn Sikkink, "Norm Dynamics and Political Change," *International Organization* 52, no. 4 (1998): 913.

56. The evidence presented here that Nehru was already normatively predisposed against great power-led regional pacts before the creation of Pakistan or SEATO is important in a methodological sense—to avoid tautology. Tautology occurs when the norm in question derives mainly from the behavior of the actors espousing the norm in responding to current challenges. In this book, I show two independent sources of the articulation of Asia's anti-collective defense norm before Bandung. The first source was the ideas and beliefs of Asia's nationalist leaders, including but not limited to Nehru, which were articulated prior to the emergence of the Cold War alliances in Asia. The second source was the international norm of nonintervention, which predated the Cold War alliances.

57. Indeed, Nehru was widely criticized as an idealist. Jaswant Singh has criticized Nehru's "idealistic romanticism" in *Defending India* (Basingstoke: Macmillan, 1999), 34. K. Subrahmanyam argues that Nehru was influenced by Gandhian non-violence during the freedom struggle and thus not attuned to defense preparedness. "Evolution of India's Defence Policy 1947–64," in *A History of the Congress Party* (New Delhi, All India Congress Committee and Vikas Publishing House, 1990), cited in Singh, *Defending India*, 41. Karnad draws on Nehru's own words that India would provide " 'leadership [to] a large part of Asia' . . . without joining in 'the old game of power politics on a gigantic scale,' or having anything to do with . . . 'realism and practical politics,' " to conclude that the Nehruvian vision "eschewed all the means of traditional statecraft and international relations, like a strong military, primary and subsidiary alliances, buffer states, security *cordons sanitaire*, secret understandings and defence pacts, and still hoped to lead" (Bharat Karnad, "India's Weak Geopolitics and What to Do About It," in *Future Imperiled: India's Security in the 1990s and Beyond*, ed. Karnad [New Delhi: Viking, 1994], 21).

defense pacts were to him a reminder of India's "long experience with colonial rule"; they represented "an indirect return of Western power to an area from which it had recently retreated."[58]

Nehru was not only the most articulate opponent of military pacts, but also the main figure behind early post-war Asian regionalism. Although far from uncontroversial, his views on pacts influenced nationalist elites of other Asian nations. Not surprisingly, regional defense cooperation was not on the agenda of the first post-war multilateral conference in Asia—the ARC of 1947—organized by Nehru. The ARC's agenda focused on national liberation, excluding defense and security issues because of concern that it could draw in external powers, and turn into the kind of great power orbit that Nehru and Aung San decried.[59] Indeed, none of the major regional conferences held in Asia between 1947 and 1955 would consider initiating any form of multilateral defense cooperation among Asian nations.[60]

The critique of regional collective defense pacts developed by at least some of Asia's nationalist elite would have a major bearing on the fate of SEATO. This was partly because the participation of the Colombo Powers was a key to the legitimation of any U.S.-backed Asian collective defense system—a fact recognized by sections within the Eisenhower administration itself along with the British government.

The British were especially aware of the necessity of the Colombo Powers' participation in SEATO. Following the first Colombo Powers meeting, British Foreign Secretary Anthony Eden told U.S. secretary of state John Foster Dulles that the United States "should avoid taking any action which might lead the Governments represented at Colombo to come out publicly against our security proposals."[61] In May 1954, he wrote to the British ambassador in Washington, "Without Asian countries, the pact would simply be a white man's pact imposed from the outside and robbed of popular support."[62] He asked the Americans to make "strong efforts to secure the participation of the Colombo Powers in the collective security arrangement or at least their

58. Michael Brecher, *Nehru: A Political Biography* (New York: Oxford University Press, 1961), 584, 555.

59. *Asian Relations*, 43, 48, 49.

60. For a list of these conferences, see note 73, chapter 2. Another event, the May 1950 Baguio Conference organized by the Philippines and attended by India, Indonesia, Pakistan, Thailand, Australia, and New Zealand, also did not consider defense cooperation partly due to objections by India and Indonesia.

61. Anthony Eden, *Full Circle: The Memoirs of Sir Anthony Eden* (London: Cassell, 1960), 99.

62. Foreign Office to Washington, 26 May 1954, FO 371/111869.

acquiescence in its formation should be made prior to the negotiation of the treaty."[63] On 10 July 1954, Britain informed the United States that "in the long run," the Colombo Powers' backing for SEATO "was of highest importance," and that even if a pact were to be signed in the near term, it would be an "ad hoc" measure pending the outcome of the "prolonged negotiations with these powers . . . for their later accession or association."[64] Without this larger Asian representation and participation, the British felt "a military alliance inspired and dominated by the United States would be futile . . . agreements with Siam and the Philippines only would merely alienate more important Asian opinion."[65]

U.S. officials were less keen on the participation of the Colombo Powers in the proposed collective defense organization. Yet during a top-secret planning meeting on SEATO on 24 July 1954, Secretary of Defense Charles Wilson "asked about India and added his view that without the Colombo Powers we wouldn't have much in Southeast Asia." At the same meeting, a White House aide urged "giving the whole project an Asian flavor from the start."[66] The State Department's Regional Planning Adviser urged in a 23 July 1954 memo that the administration "should give real consideration to the British position—that is, that we should go slowly in forming such an organization [SEATO] in order to give ourselves time to persuade Burma, Pakistan, Ceylon, Indonesia and India to join in or, at least, to look with favor upon it."[67] Even Dulles, himself no fan of the Colombo Powers, on 1 May 1954 had recognized the importance of "seeking the largest possible gathering of countries in the area, including the so-called Colombo countries."[68] Despite his dislike for Nehru (reciprocated by the latter), Dulles saw India's support for SEATO as vital: "If the British succeed in bringing in India . . . [into SEATO], it would constitute a triumph for Brit-

63. "Report of the Joint U.S.-U.K. Study Group on Southeast Asia," 17 July 1954, *Foreign Relations of the United States (FRUS)*, 1952–54, vol. XVI, p. 1415. Dulles recognized Indian influence on the British approach to SEATO. See Memorandum of Conference with President Eisenhower, Augusta, GA, 19 May 1954, John F. Dulles Papers, Library of Congress.

64. Telegram from British embassy in Washington to the Foreign Office in London, 10 July 1954, FO 371/111868. This also means the United States was informed of and accepted the British move to invite all the Colombo Powers to join SEATO.

65. Eden to Casey via Foreign Office, 22 May 1954, FO 371/111863.

66. "Minutes of a Meeting on Southeast Asia," 24 July 1954, *FRUS*, 1952–54, vol. XII, pt. I, 667.

67. "Memorandum by the Regional Planning Adviser in the Bureau of Far Eastern Affairs (Ogburn) to the Acting Assistant Secretary of States for Far Eastern Affairs (Drumright)," 23 July 1954, *FRUS*, 1952–54, vol. XII, pt. I, 664.

68. This is how the British read Dulles's position. "Parliamentary Question: Controversies Regarding S.E. Asia Security Arrangements," Memo dated 12 May 1954, FO 371/111862.

ish diplomacy. It would also be a triumph for us, even if we couldn't claim it to be."[69]

But a triumph it was not to be. On 30 July 1954, Eden sent letters to the leaders of India, Ceylon, and Pakistan (Indonesia and Burma received similar letters) to inform them about a conference of "governments interested in the collective defence of South-East Asia and South-West Pacific" to be convened in early September, and asking them "whether an invitation to be represented at the proposed meeting would be acceptable" to them. "Your participation," Eden wrote, "would do much to determine the nature and policies of the projected organization. I have always hoped to see the Asian powers play a leading role in the defence of South-East Asia."[70] The presumed initiation was met with resistance. Nehru's reply came two days later, arguing that the proposed alliance would not be a "collective peace system" under the UN Charter, but a "military alliance" that would result in a "counter-military alliance." Referring to Eden's point that SEATO would facilitate the "role of Asian Powers in the defence of South-East Asia," Nehru argued that "the majority of Asian countries and the overwhelming majority of Asian peoples will not be participants in the organization" and that "[s]ome . . . would even be strongly opposed to it, thus rendering South-East Asia a potentially explosive theatre of the Cold War."[71]

Replying to Eden, Indonesia's premier argued that "any one-sided defence arrangement . . . should be avoided, since it would add a new element to the causes of tensions in that area which eventually could lead to war."[72] Indonesia was to refrain from "taking sides"[73] Because participation in the planned conference would be "detrimental to [its] independent foreign policy."[74] According to Indonesia's leaders SEATO's offer of protection even to non-members who were targets of communist aggression "contravened the principle of international law forbidding armed interference by foreign powers in the internal affairs of a nation" and "brought the Cold War to the South East Asian region."[75]

69. "Regional Grouping in Southeast Asia," attached to "Memorandum of Discussion at the 198th Meeting of the National Security Council," 20 May 1954, *FRUS, 1952–54*, vol. XII, pt. I, 497.
70. Outward Telegram from the Commonwealth Relations Office, FO 371/111875.
71. Nehru to Eden, 2 August 1954. Telegram No 739. From Delhi to Commonwealth Relations Office, FO 371/111875.
72. *Milestones on My Journey: The Memoirs of Ali Sastroamijoyo*, ed. C. L. M. Penders (Brisbane: University of Queensland Press, 1979), 271. Ali was prime minister of Indonesia and the originator of the Bandung Conference idea as well as the conference chairman.
73. Jakarta to Foreign Office, FO 371–111875.
74. Foreign Office to Jakarta, FO 371–111875.
75. *Milestones on My Journey*, 271.

<u>SOUTH EAST ASIA DEFENCE</u>

Following for Prime Minister from Foreign Secretary.  <u>Begins</u>.

As I said in my message of July 19th, we have long been in favour of creating a broadly based defensive organisation in South-East Asia and the South-West Pacific.  After careful study of this problem, our ideas have now crystallised sufficiently for me to seek your views on them, and I hope you will give them very serious consideration.

2.  Your participation would do much to determine the nature and policies of the projected organisation.  I have always hoped to see the Asian powers play a leading role in the defence of South-East Asia.  The area is of such importance and its peace is as yet so insecure, that we feel it vital to safeguard its peaceful development and ensure its stability.  Even if you feel that you must stand aside therefore  (following for Nehru only – and I shall understand your reasons if you do – )  (following for all) I am sure you will (following for Nehru only – equally) (following for all) understand why we for our part shall feel it right to go ahead with such countries as are willing to join with us.  Though we should still do our best to take account of your views, our task would be far more difficult without your participation at least in some form.

3.  It is in the light of these arguments that I invite your earnest and early consideration of the following proposal.  A meeting should be convened by the beginning of September, preferably in a country in the area, of representatives of Governments interested in the collective defence of South-East Asia and the South-West Pacific. The Governments we should like to see represented, besides of course those of the five Colombo Powers, are those of Australia, New Zealand, Siam, the Philippines, France, the United Kingdom and the United States.  The purpose of the meeting would be to consider possible measures of collective defence for South-East Asia and the South-West Pacific in the hope of producing agreed recommendations for consideration by the participating Governments and a draft collective
defence/

A

7.  You have referred to the role of the Asian powers in the defence of South East Asia and mentioned its vital importance. Yet the majority of Asian countries overwhelming majority of Asian peoples will not be participants in the organisation.  Some it may be anticipated would even be strongly opposed to it, thus rendering South East Asia a potentially explosive theatre of the cold war.

B

**Figure 3.1.**  Colombo powers' reaction to SEATO. A: Eden's Message to the prime ministers of India, Pakistan and Ceylon, 30 July 1954 (similar messages were sent to Prime Ministers of Burma and Indonesia separately). The last sentence of paragraph 3 ended with the word "agreement." B: Nehru to Eden, 2 August 1954; C: Kotelawala to Eden, 3 August 1954; D: U Nu to Eden, 4 Aug 1954; E: Indonesian response to Eden, 14 August 1954.
Source: The National Archives, United Kingdom, FO 371/111868, FO 371/111875, and FO 371/111876.

2.    I regret that the general opinion is against the collective
defence proposals set out in your messages.  In the circumstances
the Colombo countries would not be able to participate in the
conference anticipated in your message of July 30th.  India and
Indonesia do not favour the proposals and I have little doubt
that Burma is of the same mind although I have had no reply yet.

3.    I appreciate the purpose and objects of the defensive
organisation adumbrated in your last message, but cannot help
feeling that the object of peace in this region might be achieved
in a different way and by other means.  In this connection India
has stated in some detail why she does not favour your proposals
and Mr. Nehru will no doubt state them to you.  He has also
indicated that he will communicate to you his proposals for a
constructive alternative approach to a collective peace system.  I
feel that this alternative or any other that might be put forward
deserves our serious consideration.  I have therefore suggested
to the other four Colombo countries that we might have a conference
regarding these matters, perhaps in Burma, at a very early date

C

    I have received your message of July 30, and carefully con-
sidered the proposal contained therein.  Our view, however, is
that our sending of representative, or even observer, to the
meeting would not be in keeping with the policy of non alignment
which we have adopted.  On the other hand, we are reluctant to
close our consideration of this question of a consolidation of
peace in South East Asia on our giving everybody this reply only.
It would not be fair to you who have so sincerely believed in the
proposal.  We have, therefore, considered that it would be most
advantageous if the Colombo Powers could meet and seek a
solution acceptable to all.  At such a conference, even if

D

    The Indonesian Ambassador today presented his Prime
Minister's message.

    2.    It reiterates that Indonesia cannot participate in any
collective defence arrangement  in South East Asia and the South
West Pacific, since this "would be detrimental to the independent
foreign policy which has been conducted by Indonesia in and
outside the United Nations".

    3.    In the Indonesian Government's view, the creation of
a collective defence organization in South East Asia so shortly
after agreement at Geneva "must necessarily provoke a similar move
from some other countries", and would thus create new tension.

    4.    The message ends: "I therefore regret that my Govern-
ment is unable to send either a representative or an observer
to the proposed meeting".

E

Burma's premier U Nu "made clear" to the British that his country "could not join or publicly approve of any agreement that was 'anti' either side."[76] Accepting Eden's "invitation" "would not be in keeping with the policy of non alignment" adopted by Burma."[77] A year later, U Nu told a U.S. audience that "an alliance with a big power immediately means domination by that power. It means the loss of independence."[78]

Ceylon's premier John Kotelawala replied to Eden that although Ceylon remained "realistic about communist dangers," he "could not ignore the position of India," or his own domestic political difficulties in supporting such a move.[79] He noted, "the object of peace in this region might be achieved in a different way and by different means."[80] Later, Kotelawala would recall that: "what was wrong about S.E.A.T.O. was that the opinion of Free Asia had not been sought with regard to the troubles in Viet Nam and Korea."[81]

To sum up, in rejecting the U.S. collective defense scheme for Southeast Asia, four of the Colombo Powers employed three main arguments. First, it was inconsistent with their policy of non-intervention and non-alignment, which were prior norms of their international conduct. Second, it considerably increased the risk of superpower domination and intervention, and challenged the desire of Asian states not to be drawn into the vortex of the Cold War. Third, it was unrepresentative of Asian opinion at a time when the region was trying to find an independent voice in international affairs.

This provided the backdrop for the Asia-Africa Conference at Bandung, which was dominated by Asian nations and reflected their normative concerns.[82] While earlier Asian conferences focused on self-determination and the West's relations with its colonies and ex-colonies, the 1955 Bandung Conference was primarily concerned with the management of relations among the new states in the context of their twin fears of Chinese-backed subversion and superpower rivalry. Roselan Abdulghani, the Secretary-General of the Bandung Conference, saw the purpose of the Conference as not only "to continue the struggle toward a full materialization of national

76. Rangoon to Foreign Office, 8 July 1954, FO 371–111868, TNA.

77. Rangoon to Foreign Office, FO 371/111868, TNA.

78. U Nu's speech to the National Press Club, Washington, DC, in July 1955, cited in James Barrington (Foreign Secretary of Burma), "The Concept of Neutralism: What Lies Behind Burma's Foreign Policy?" in *Perspective of Burma, An Atlantic Monthly Supplement* (n.d.), 29.

79. Colombo to Commonwealth Relations Office, 3 August 1954, FO 371/111876, TNA.

80. Ibid.

81. John Kotelawala, *An Asian Prime Minister's Story* (London: George Harap, 1956), 119.

82. Some Arab and African representatives were unhappy over Asian dominance at Bandung, and this might have contributed to their lack of enthusiasm for a permanent Asian-African regional organization.

independence," but also "to determine . . . the standards and procedures of present-day international relations."[83] Although participants were already united behind the idea of national independence,[84] they were not in agreement over how to organize their relationships and develop rules of conduct in regional and international relations. Hence, one of the most important objectives of the conference was to discuss "the formulation and establishment of certain norms for the conduct of present-day international relations and the instruments for the practical application of these norms."[85] Bandung's agenda was much broader and much more political in nature than that of the ARCs. In addition to addressing some of the issues addressed at the 1947 ARC—especially self-determination and racism—it focused on human rights and "World Peace and World Cooperation." Participants in the Bandung Conference would later regard the Declaration on World Peace made at the conference as a "most important resolution," because it defined "the principles regulating their relations with each other and the world at large."[86]

Sovereignty, especially the threats to it and how best to protect against them, held the center stage at the Bandung Conference. The key issue was non-intervention—"[T]he word and the idea of intervention was everywhere, especially in Southeast Asia."[87] The main culprits were not just the United States and the USSR; China was also being implicated, not because of its overt military intervention, but because of its sponsorship of subtler forms of interference through its official and non-official relationships with, and support for, communist movements in Southeast and South Asia. A review of the debates at the closed sessions of the Political Committee of the Bandung Conference shows that self-determination issues, such as in Africa, Palestine, and West Irian, attracted less passion and preoccupied the leaders to a much lesser extent than debates about non-intervention and non-involvement (in regional pacts).

The Political Committee deemed three types of acts as "intervention" (used interchangeably with "interference") at Bandung. The first one, described as both "interference" and "intervention," was supply of arms by external powers—including China, the United States, USSR, and Britain—for the two sides in the Indochina conflict. The second, generally referred to as "interference," was Chinese support for communist insurgencies in Asia. This was exemplified in Ceylon's prime minister Kotelawala's attack on communism as

83. Roselan Abdulghani, *The Bandung Spirit* (Jakarta: Prapantja, 1964), 72.
84. Abdulghani, *The Bandung Spirit*, 18.
85. Abdulghani, *The Bandung Spirit*, 103.
86. *The Report of the Arab League on the Bandung Conference* (Cairo: League of Arab States, 1955), 151.
87. Abdulghani, *The Bandung Spirit*, 63.

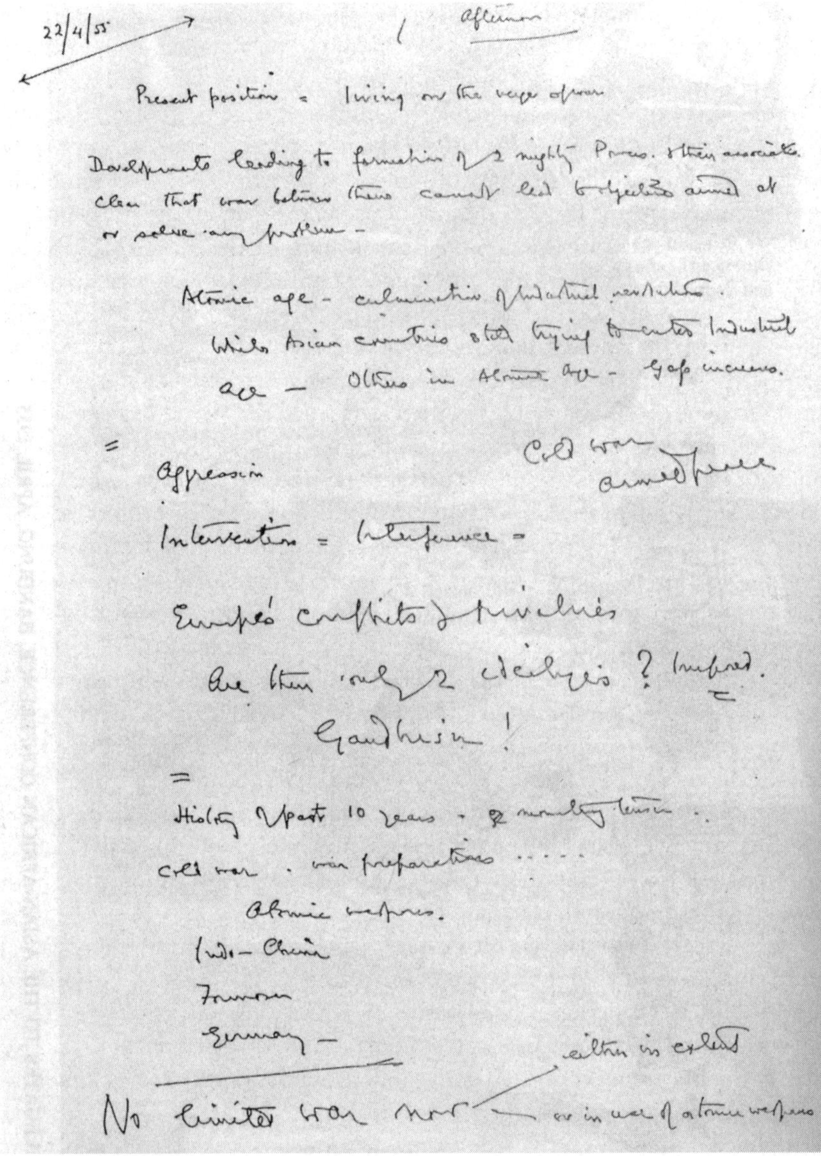

**Figure 3.2.** Nehru's reflections on intervention at Bandung. Although some of it is undecipherable, note the reference to the "danger of war" in the "present" situation, Nehru's equating "intervention" with "interference" and "Europe's conflicts and rivalries." Also note the reference to Cold War as "armed peace" and to "Gandhism."

a second and newer form of colonialism.[88] The third, and most controversial conception of intervention, was membership in military pacts. As the conference progressed, the line between these forms of intervention, especially interference by a regional power in the domestic political affairs of its neighbors, and intervention by extra-regional powers in the security of the region as a whole through the creation of regional defense pacts, became increasingly blurred. The Bandung Conference would thus end up highlighting a link between abstention from *membership in regional collective defense pacts* and non-intervention as a principle of international conduct.

Kotelawala's attack on communism as a new form of colonialism sparked a heated debate at the Conference. Referring to "those satellite states under Communist Domination in Central and Eastern Europe," Kotelawala asked, "If we are in opposition to colonialism, should it not be our duty to openly declare opposition to Soviet colonialism as much as to Western imperialism?"[89] His anger against communist colonialism was supposedly induced by his failure to elicit a pledge from Zhou En-lai to put an end to Cominform propaganda and Chinese assistance to communists in Ceylon. Elsewhere, the view of communism as a new form of colonialism was shared by Iraq, Turkey, and the Philippines—all ruled by pro-Western governments.

Nehru stood on the other side of the argument. He defended the sovereign status of East European communist states, noting that "[t]here is a distinct and great difference in criticizing the very basis of independent nations that are represented in the United Nations and with whom we have diplomatic relations . . . and our talking about Algeria, Morocco or Tunisia," because the latter were "represented in the UN by the colonial powers." The latter lacked independence, whereas the East European countries were "represented directly at the UN by their own representatives and should be regarded as sovereign states."[90] Nehru also argued that non-interference in the domestic affairs of its neighbors could not be pursued in isolation from non-intervention by superpowers in regional conflicts. Unlike Kotelawala, who was concerned as much, if not more, with Chinese interference as with superpower intervention, Nehru was most concerned with superpower intervention through regional pacts.[91]

88. Proceedings of the Bandung Conference Political Committee, 23 April 1955, UUOD.
89. Proceedings of the Bandung Conference Political Committee, 23 April 1955, UUOD.
90. Speech at the Closed Session of the Bandung Conference, Proceedings of the Bandung Conference Political Committee, 22 April 1955, UUOD.
91. Ceylon's anti-communist government had stayed away from SEATO, but attacked Chinese interference, while Nehru dismissed the threat of Chinese subversion as a danger to Asian stability.

On 23 April 1955, speaking before the Political Committee, Nehru argued that membership in such pacts rendered a country a "camp follower" and deprived it of its "freedom and dignity." "It is an intolerable thought to me," declared Nehru, "that the great countries of Asia and Africa should come out of bondage into freedom only to degrade themselves or humiliate themselves in this way."[92] Nehru bitterly condemned NATO as "one of the most powerful protectors of colonialism,"[93] demonstrating his anger over pressures from some European NATO members on India to leave Portugal alone in Goa. Nehru's position, although not his strong language, was shared by the neutral nations of Burma, Indonesia, and Ceylon. U Nu argued at Bandung that "[m]ilitary alliances and pacts do not . . . provide any solution. . . . Indeed, they may often do more harm since they add to existing tension."[94]

These arguments were countered by the proponents of collective defense pacts, which included the Philippines, Pakistan, Turkey, and Lebanon. They held that collective defense was necessary against the threat of communist meddling and defended SEATO as the first pact to cover such threats. SEATO could not violate their sovereignty, because the consent of the party concerned was required before the alliance's mutual assistance provisions could be activated.[95] Responding to Nehru's attacks, Prime Minister Mohamed Ali of Pakistan, a member of both CENTO and SEATO, asserted that as "an independent sovereign nation" Pakistan followed its "national interest," and hence did not feel it "necessary for us to justify our actions to anybody except to ourselves."[96] A more eloquent response to the Indian prime minister came from Carlos Romulo, the lead delegate of the Philippines—a SEATO member. In a barely disguised dig at Nehru, Romulo urged delegates to be "realistic and not be starry-eyed visionaries dreaming utopian dreams." He reminded Nehru that as a smaller nation, the Philippines could not follow India's path in renouncing collective defense to safeguard its new-found independence. Defending SEATO as a necessary guarantee against the growing menace of communist interference in the domestic affairs of Asian states, he issued a warning, "May your India, Sir, never be caught by the encircling gloom."[97]

92. Speech by Nehru, Proceedings of the Bandung Conference Political Committee, 23 April 1995, UUOD.

93. Proceedings of the Bandung Conference Political Committee, 22 April 1955, UUOD.

94. Proceedings of the Bandung Conference Political Committee, 22 April 1955, UUOD.

95. Speech by Mohamed Ali, Proceedings of the Bandung Conference Political Committee, 23 April 1955, UUOD.

96. Ibid.

97. Speech by Mohamed Ali; the text of Romulo's response can be found in Carlos Romulo, *Meaning of Bandung* (Chapel Hill: University of North Carolina Press, 1956), 91.

The conference resolved the two debates on intervention with compromise formulations. On the issue of *communism as a new form of colonialism*, it declared that "colonialism in all its manifestations is an evil which should be brought to an end." The shift from "colonialism in all its forms" to "colonialism in all its manifestations" satisfied China, which interpreted it to mean not the existence of two forms of colonialism (western and communist), but of one "colonialism in its political, military, economic, cultural and social manifestations." On the issue of membership in military pacts the compromise was reflected in the sixth of the ten principles adopted by the Conference's Final Declaration. Point five of the Declaration expressed "respect for the right of each nation to defend itself, singly or collectively," while point six called for the "abstention from the use of arrangements of collective defence to serve any particular interests of the big powers."[98]

The impact of the Bandung Conference on Asian collective defense has been contested. Some Western officials interpreted the Conference as a victory for the pro-pact camp. For example, the U.S. ambassador in Indonesia told his Australian counterpart that "the Conference was . . . more than an 85% victory" for the West.[99] "It is no exaggeration," Romulo would assert to a U.S. audience, "that the anti-communist states put both communism and neutralism on the defensive, scoring a signal diplomatic triumph for the free world."[100]

But an unofficial observer at Bandung, Homer Jack, predicted that "Bandung will mean the eventual neutralization of such committed powers as Thailand and the Philippines."[101] Another observer, Guy Pauker, described the "injunction" against the "use of arrangements of collective defence to serve the particularistic interests of any of the big powers" as the "most significant aspect" of the conference.[102] Declassified Western assessments show the fate of collective defense to be more in keeping with the "Bandung injunction." It certainly made SEATO enlargement impossible. "[A]ny hope that might have existed that additional states could be attracted to SEATO," a secret British Foreign Office assessment of the conference noted, had

98. Final Communiqué of the Asian-African Conference, Proceedings of the Bandung Conference Political Committee, 24 April 1955, UUOD.

99. Personal Impressions by the Australian Ambassador to Indonesia, W.R. Crocker, DO35/6099, TNA.

100. Romulo, *Meaning of Bandung*, 22.

101. Homer A. Jack, *Bandung: An On-the-Spot Description of the Asian-African Conference* (Chicago: Toward Freedom, 1956).

102. Guy J. Pauker, *The Bandung Conference* (Cambridge: Centre for International Studies, MIT, 1955), 18.

"now vanished."[103] What is more, Bandung also led to a rethinking of SEATO on the part of the Philippines and Thailand. A U.S. State Department memo issued after the Conference expressed concern that Thailand could be "reverting to their historic policy of having at least a toe in either camp."[104] After Bandung, Thailand and Philippines expected and demanded aid from the Western members of SEATO "as a compensation for the liability incurred through [their] association with non-Asian, alien forces."[105] In 1959, a British Foreign Office memo assessing the progress of the alliance concluded:

> developments which have taken place in the area as a whole since 1954 . . . has led to a strengthening of the *principles and ideas* which lie behind first the meetings of the so-called *Colombo Powers* . . . and later *the Bandung meeting*. . . . We may indeed have reached a point where the *Asian wish to avoid entangling alliances and outside interference* on the one hand and Asia's collective disapproval of force on the other, can serve the purpose of contributing to the stability of the area *as well as* be a treaty of mutual guarantee among the Great Powers.[106]

## Comparison and Alternative Explanations

Since the constitutive localization perspective takes institutional outcomes as indicators of the diffusion of ideas and norms, how was the contrasting fate of non-intervention and collective defense reflected in Asia's post-war regional institutional architecture? The main indicator of the rejection of the collective defense idea was the crippling of SEATO. The institutional indicators of the diffusion and localization of non-intervention are more complex and multifaceted. It was indicated in the emergence of Asia's soft and open institutionalism, and the policy of all Asian regional groupings to avoid any kind of collective defense arrangement (see chapter 4 for a discussion of soft institutionalism). Why did the idea of non-intervention find acceptance in Asia while that of collective defense failed?

103. "The Afro-Asian Conference," Foreign Office Research Department, 5 May 1955, FO 371/116986, TNA.
104. "Letter from the Acting Officer in Charge of Thai and Malayan Affairs (Foster) to Ambassador in Thailand (Peurifoy)," *FRUS*, vol. XXII, Southeast Asia, 826.
105. George Modelski, "The Asian States' Participation in SEATO," in *SEATO: Six Studies*, ed. Modelski (Vancouver: University of British Columbia Publication Centre, 1962), 155–6.
106. "Review of South-East Asia Treaty Organization During Its First Five Years," Memo from Mr. Selwyn Lloyd to Mr. Peck (Singapore), Secret, 2 September 1959, DEFE 13/542, 4 (emphasis added), TNA.

This outcome can be explained in terms of the constitutive localization model. As table 2.1 indicates, the progress of localization depended on four key conditions: 1) the extent to which the target norm has been internally discredited or seen as being inadequate in addressing new challenges, 2) the discursive reach of insider proponents, 3) the scope for grafting, and 4) the extent to which norm borrowing is seen as offering a scope for the wider diffusion of some elements of a local norm hierarchy.

The principle of non-intervention might have conflicted with the early pan-Asian sentiments of some of Asia's nationalist leaders. But pan-Asianism was weak to begin with and had been discredited at Asian regional conferences because of the inability of countries like India to offer concrete material assistance to national liberation struggles in Indochina. Conversely, non-intervention resonated strongly with the prior norms of anti-colonialism and anti-power politics held by Asian leaders, norms that were enjoying a robust legitimacy. The nature and identity of norm entrepreneur also mattered. In the case of non-intervention, the idea was espoused by the likes of Nehru and the Colombo Powers, whose ability to convene as a group enhanced their discursive reach and the regional appeal of the norm. The norm could be grafted onto the emerging neutralist beliefs of some of Asia's leading nationalists.

By contrast, the idea of collective defense was first proposed to Asia by the United States, an external power. This idea—associated with Dulles, a man who opposed neutralism and called non-alignment "immoral"—clashed with the "neutralist" beliefs already prevailing in Asia. This over-shadowed the efforts of Anthony Eden, who played the role of entrepreneur (on behalf of the United States) on collective defense. The insider proponents of SEATO (Pakistan, the Philippines, and Thailand) enjoyed weaker regional legitimacy compared to its insider critics—India and Indonesia in particular, who were able to frame collective defense as a form of neo-colonial dominance of Asia by the West. This delegitimized the position of the outsider proponents of SEATO, such as the United States and Britain. The latter could not find a prior tradition of collective defense or security multilateralism in the region, because it had been divided into different security zones under the colonial powers—Britain, France, the Netherlands, and the United States, onto which collective defense could be grafted.

Finally, the idea of non-intervention, far from threatening the identity of Asian leaders, was seen as a way of amplifying their profile and role in regional and international affairs. It was an integral part of their belief in active neutralism, the rationale for which included a desire to acquire a recognizable voice in international affairs. Championing this norm gave them a clout that these countries could not have achieved through economic or

**Table 3.2.** Non-Intervention and Collective Defense

| External idea | Cognitive prior | Outcome |
|---|---|---|
| Non-intervention | Anti-colonialism, Pan-Asianism | Enhanced non-intervention, non-alignment |
| Collective defense | Anti-colonialism, "neutralism" | No Asian NATO, defense bilateralism |

military means, whether individually or collectively. By contrast, the advent of a collective defense mechanism backed by external powers threatened to harm rather than help the quest for regional autonomy and identity on the part of some of the most active Asian states. Although collective defense had been accepted by its insider proponents (e.g., Pakistan and Turkey) as a way of bolstering their security, its insider critics (e.g., India and Indonesia) saw in it no way of enhancing the regional identity and authority of Asian nations (in the way the Colombo Powers had seen the role of non-intervention in enhancing their regional moral authority and role). On the contrary, collective defense had been framed in the opposite way, described by Nehru, in a rather extreme fashion, as "degrading."

There are two categories of alternative explanations to the above argument. The first category is generic in the sense that it subsumes the issue of SEATO's failure under a wider explanation of why post-war Asia did not develop a multilateral security institution in general. The second category is specific to the failure of SEATO.

The first category includes both realist and constructivist perspectives. First, from a realist perspective, Donald Crone blames the absence of multilateralism in the immediate post-war period on the huge power differentials between the United States and its Asian allies, a condition he calls "extreme hegemony." Power differentials between the U.S. and its Asian allies then were so immense that there would have been no point in a regional security organization because the Asian states had little material resources to offer either individually or collectively to such a security grouping.[107] U.S. policymakers not only recognized the above reality, they also expected their Asian allies to remain permanently weak, in contrast to their European allies, who were expected to recover from the ravages of World War II. Seeing multilat-

---

107. Donald Crone, "Does Hegemony Matter? The Reorganization of the Pacific Political Economy," *World Politics* 45, no. 4 (July 1993), 501–25. The power disparity argument shaping U.S. strategic choice also forms a major part of Galia Press-Barnathan's explanation of why the United States did not create a NATO-like security organization in Asia. Galia Press-Barnathan, *Organizing the World: The United States and Regional Cooperation in Asia and Europe* (New York: Routledge, 2003).

eralism as a superficial aid and a needless constraint, Washington preferred bilateralism in its approach to Asian security. Its Asian allies also shunned multilateralism, calculating that it would have reduced their opportunities for free-riding.[108]

But the "power gap" explanation suffers from three major limitations. First, as pointed out by Hemmer and Katzenstein, if alliances between great powers and weak Asian post-war states were of little value, then why did the United States not bring Japan (a once and future great power) into SEATO?[109] Second, available evidence does not show the United States (or for that matter, its allies like South Korea and the Philippines) to have been irrevocably predisposed to a primarily bilateral mode of security cooperation in early post-war Asia. Crone does not take into account several U.S. initiatives for Pacific security cooperation, such as President Roosevelt's proposed post-war Pacific collective security system and the Truman and Eisenhower administrations' ideas about Asian collective defense. These early post-war efforts to create a multilateral security organization in Asia were enthusiastically backed by the would-be free-riders like South Korea and the Philippines.

The third problem is the assumption that the fear of being constrained often leads a great power to avoid multilateralism with less powerful states.[110] If so, then the United States should have had a greater fear of being constrained in dealing multilaterally with its European allies whose recovery was expected. It is doubtful that being involved in a regional multilateral institution in Asia would have really constrained independent decision making in Washington any more than it did in Europe.

A constructivist explanation of the puzzle of the absence of a multilateral security organization in post-war Asia is offered by Hemmer and Katzenstein.[111] Multilateralism, they argue, requires a strong sense of collective identity in addition to shared interests. But U.S. policymakers of the early post-war era "saw their potential Asian allies . . . as part of an alien and, in

108. Crone, "Does Hegemony Matter?" 505.

109. Christopher Hemmer and Peter J. Katzenstein, "Why Is There no NATO in Asia: Collective Identity, Regionalism, and the Origins of Multilateralism," *International Organization* 56, no.3 (Summer 2002): 575–607.

110. Steve Weber, "Shaping the Postwar Balance of Power: Multilateralism in NATO," in *Multilateralism Matters*, ed. Ruggie, 233–92.

111. Hemmer and Katzenstein, in "Why Is There no NATO in Asia," reject the power disparity explanation, as well as neoliberal explanations, which would see alliance design as a function of differing calculations about what would be the most efficient institutional response to the threat at hand. Europe and Asia differed in this area; the threat in Europe was a massive cross-border Soviet invasion, whereas the threat in Asia was insurgency and internal conflict. But cross-border threats, argue Hemer and Katzenstein, were also plausible in Korea as well as Taiwan, yet the United States did not address them through a multilateral alliance, an interesting outcome since the Korean War itself was a major catalyst of the creation of NATO.

important ways, inferior community."[112] This was in marked contrast to the perception of "their potential European allies [who were seen] as relatively equal members of a shared community." Hence, Europe rather than Asia was seen as a more desirable arena for multilateral engagement because the United States recognized a greater sense of a transatlantic community than a transpacific one. From this perspective, it was not the preponderance of U.S. power ("extreme hegemony"), but its conception of Europe as part of the "self" and Asia as the "other," which explains why Washington seemed disinclined to develop a "NATO in Asia." Hemmer and Katzenstein conclude that differing conceptions of collective identity were crucial in explaining why Washington favored multilateralism in Europe and bilateralism in Asia.

But this is at best an incomplete explanation. Despite their relative emphasis on perception over power, Hemmer and Katzenstein share with Crone a tendency to explain the absence of regional security organization in post-war Asia from the U.S. vantage point, ignoring the role of Asian normative debates and intra-regional interactions. This neglect is symptomatic of the literature on Asian regionalism, which, as Katzenstein himself once wrote, needs to accord greater recognition to "local, national, or regional political contexts.[113]

This chapter has argued that the reasons for the absence of a multilateral security organization in post-war Asia cannot be explained in terms of U.S. preferences, whether derived from strategic calculations or cultural prejudice. These factors might have played a role, but a key reason had to do with the strong normative opposition to the idea of an Asian regional defense organization from one influential section of Asian leaders for whom military alliances with superpowers meant renewed Western dominance. Their arguments, manifested both before and after the creation of SEATO and especially at the Bandung Conference, limited Asian participation and representation in SEATO, and undercut the feasibility of any form of collective defense system in Asia.

On the specific question of the failure and demise of SEATO, the main alternative explanation blames it on "the half-hearted commitment of the

112. Hemmer and Katzenstein, "Why Is There no Asian NATO," 575.

113. Peter Katzenstein, "Introduction: Asian Regionalism in Comparative Perspective," in *Network Power: Japan and Asia*, ed. Peter Katzenstein and Takashi Shiraishi (Ithaca, NY: Cornell University Press, 1997), 6. Hemmer and Katzenstein acknowledge that they had "not explored all empirical and analytical aspects" of the issue, including "the effects that the policies of the European and Asian states had on U.S. foreign policy." They also acknowledge that "there remains a great deal of potentially valuable historical material that could shed further light on the development of these regions"—precisely the kind of material I have drawn upon. Hemmer and Katzenstein, "Why Is There no Asian NATO," 598–99.

U.S. administration to the alliance."[114] Unlike NATO, SEATO had no permanent military command, no automatic U.S. commitment, which was subject to its "constitutional processes," and no guarantee of action, only of consultations. Unlike the NATO formula of "attack on one, attack on all," the United States applied the Monroe Doctrine formula to SEATO, under which the parties merely recognize that an armed attack in the treaty area "would endanger its own peace and safety."

However, it would be flawed to consider this the main justification for SEATO's failure. There is good reason to believe that SEATO's weakness and failure had more to do with its lack of legitimacy than teeth. SEATO was not the only U.S. alliance in the Pacific to have a Monroe Doctrine-like commitment. Other U.S. alliances in the Pacific (with Japan, South Korea, Thailand, the Philippines, and ANZUS) were based on the Monroe Doctrine formula.[115] Neither was weak institutionalization an exclusive feature of SEATO. ANZUS, a far more successful alliance than SEATO, did not even have SEATO's small secretariat. And like SEATO, it "made no effort to establish integrated forces under central command."[116]

The fact that the United States saw the most likely communist threat in Southeast Asia to be subversion, rather than outright invasion as in Europe, would not by itself explain a "half-hearted" U.S. commitment to SEATO.[117] To see the threat differently than in Europe did not mean it was not perceived

114. Leszek Buszynski, *SEATO: The Failure of an Alliance Strategy* (Singapore: Singapore University Press), 221. See also Liska, *Nations in Alliance*, 121. It is important to note that the realist alternative explanation focuses on the degree of U.S. commitment, rather than lack of a common threat to SEATO members, because communism was viewed as a danger by all the members of SEATO (as well as by the Colombo Powers).

115. Cited in Robert Osgood, *Alliances and American Foreign Policy* (Baltimore: Johns Hopkins University Press, 1968), 81. See pages 77–82 for an elaboration of the similarities in security commitments among the U.S. Pacific alliances with Japan, South Korea, Philippines, Thailand, ANZUS, and SEATO.

116. Osgood, *Alliances and American Foreign Policy*, 81.

117. In 1953, while explaining the Domino Theory, Dulles had used the language, "all for one, one for all" as the formula for a collective defense system in Southeast Asia. "It is because that situation [possibility of a domino effect, 'as each state goes, the position of the others become more vulnerable'] existed in Southeast Asia that we have indicated our readiness, if the states in the region wanted it, to join in a collective security pact which will mean all for one, one for all." "In answer to a question about the 'domino' theory," 12 May 1954, Dulles Papers, Library of Congress, Washington, DC. Dulles's comments show that the United States had not settled the nature of its commitment, and that "if the states in the region wanted it," was an important condition. And as late as 23 July 1954, the administration had been considering three possible types of organizational structure for collective defense, including "an elaborate structure comparable to NATO's," a simple standing council, or a council that could meet periodically when called together. "Memorandum on the Substance of Discussions at a Department of State-Joint Chiefs of Staff Meeting," *FRUS*, 1952–1954, vol. XII, pt. I, 654. Hence, the final U.S. decision on SEATO's nature was influenced by ongoing political developments, especially its assessments of the attitude of India and other Colombo Powers.

to be serious. The Eisenhower administration believed the communist threat in Southeast Asia to be a military, as well as political and ideological, challenge. Before the Battle of Dien Bien Phu, the United States had taken the prospect of Chinese intervention in the conflict very seriously and developed contingency plans for "collective action,"[118] including the possible use of nuclear weapons. Britain too had "contemplated" operations that could be undertaken "in the event of a communist invasion [of Malaya] from Siam."[119]

Moreover, the principal architect of SEATO, Secretary of State Dulles, certainly did not view the U.S. commitment to the alliance to be "halfhearted." At the Manila Conference, which established SEATO in September 1954, he forcefully derided as an "illusion" the perception "that the NATO formula was somewhat stronger" than the Monroe Doctrine formula for SEATO. The Monroe Doctrine formula could be "as effective as that we used in the North Atlantic Treaty Organization." To minimize the contrast, he argued that there was no sense of "automatic action" in NATO because "[w]ould the United States be obligated to react to an attack on Copenhagen in the same way as an attack upon the city of New York? . . . The answer . . . is no." The main rationale for adopting the Monroe Doctrine formula for SEATO was political because Congress had interpreted the NATO formula to mean that any attack outside the United States would require Congressional sanction.[120] This requirement would be too constraining. Dulles assured U.S. Asian allies that the provisions of SEATO regarding each member having to act in accordance with its constitutional processes "gives all the freedom of action and power to act that is contained in NATO."[121]

A second alternative explanation for the failure of SEATO would stress intra-regional rivalries and quarrels among prospective Asian allies of the United States. Instead of focusing on the US-Asia power gap, such an expla-

---

118. Buszynski, *SEATO*, 2–3. According to the *Pentagon Papers*, "In the event of a massive Chinese troop intervention . . . it is quite possible that the U.S. would have retaliated with strategic nuclear weapons against targets in China" (*The Pentagon Papers: The Defense Department History of United States Decision Making on Vietnam*, ed. Mike Gravel (Boston: Beacon Press, 1971). Available at http://www.scribd.com/doc/958746/The-Pentagon-Papers-Volume-1–Gravel-Edition, 107. See also George C. Herring and Richard Immerman, "Eisenhower, Dulles, and Dien Bien Phu: 'The Day We Didn't Go to War' Revisited," *Journal of American History* 71, no. 2 (September 1984), 343–63.

119. "The Prime Minister of the United Kingdom (Churchill) to President Eisenhower," 21 June 1954, *FRUS*, 1952–54, vol. XII, East Asia and Pacific, pt., 570.

120. "Verbatim Proceedings of the Third Plenary Session, Manila Conference," 7 September 1954, *FRUS*, 1952–54, vol. XII, East Asia and Pacific, pt. I, 878–79.

121. Cited in Ralph Braibanti, "The Southeast Asia Collective Defense Treaty," *Pacific Affairs* 30 (December 1957): 329.

nation would be found at the intra-regional level. From this perspective, U.S. Asian allies were too divided among themselves due to bilateral disputes to join a collective defense system under the U.S. umbrella. The main inter-state rivalry among the five Colombo Powers countries who were at one stage seen as possible members of a U.S.-led collective defense organization was between India and Pakistan. There was no conflict among the other Colombo Powers nations; or between any of them and the countries that became members of SEATO (Thailand, the Philippines, and Pakistan). But the Kashmir dispute between India and Pakistan should not have prevented other Colombo Powers—especially Indonesia, Ceylon, and Burma— from joining SEATO had they chosen to do so. This is especially striking because at least two of them, Ceylon and Burma, took the threat of communist subversion extremely seriously, hence the Ceylonese prime minister Kotelawala's speech at Bandung labeling communism as a new form of colonialism, a formulation that was both encouraged and endorsed by Britain and the United States. This suggests that normative factors mattered in addition to inter-state disputes.

Furthermore, multilateral alliances between a hegemonic power and weaker states have been feasible despite quarrels among the latter. A hegemonic power usually possesses the resources to bring such quarrelling partners into a system of collective defense, as the United States was able to do in relation to Greece and Turkey in NATO. Since Crone and others characterize U.S. power position vis-à-vis Asian allies as a condition of "extreme hegemony," if material power was really what mattered, then it should have helped the United States to bring Asian local actors together, despite rivalries among the non-communist Asian states.

Another alternative explanation was that key regional actors could count on UN protection, instead of a regional defense pact. However, the Bandung Conference participants saw the UN as a tool of the great powers, and were skeptical about its role as the protector, especially after the Dutch tried to use it to hold on to their Indonesian colony. The UN's failure to resolve the West Irian issue was resolutely criticized at Bandung. For the neutralists, the UN was too unrepresentative, prompting Ceylon's John Kotelawala to lament,

> It is not the United Nations which has preserved the uneasy peace of the last decade. In all the major issues of world politics, such as the Korean and Indo-Chinese disputes, negotiations for settlement had to be carried on outside the framework of the United Nations . . . what we of Asia and Africa can appropriately demand, is that the United Nations Organization should be so

reconstituted as to become a fully representative organ of the peoples of the world, in which all nations can meet in free and equal terms.[122]

Hence, for countries like Ceylon (not yet a UN member), a regional multilateral defense arrangement should have been desirable to compensate for the UN's deficiencies. That they thought otherwise limits the power of this alternative explanation.

WHY was there no collective defense organization in post-war Asia? Both realist and constructivist explanations take a U.S.-centric view, emphasizing U.S.-Asian power differentials and U.S.-Asian identity dissonance. This chapter has focused on the role of local actors and normative beliefs in delegitimizing collective defense. In post-war Asia, the newfound interdependence of Asian states that had to be safeguarded, and the existing ideas of nationalist leaders such as Nehru or Aung San rejecting great power spheres of influence, provided the basis for their reaction to the ideas of collective defense and non-intervention. This led to the rejection of collective defense and not only the acceptance, but also the reformulation and extension of non-intervention. The scope of non-intervention was broadened to include rejection of multilateral defense pacts within great power orbits. In other words, while localizing non-intervention, Asian states not only enhanced their prior anti-colonial norms and identity as independent actors, they also gave an extended and expanded meaning to the non-intervention norm in the regional context. This and other normative outcomes of the early post-war regional interactions in Asia had important implications for subsequent regional institution-building efforts. Chapter 4 provides a detailed discussion of these outcomes and their legacy.

122. See text of Kotelawala's speech to the opening session of the Bandung Conference in *Asia Africa Speaks from Bandung* (Jakarta: Department of Foreign Affairs, 1955), 40.

# 4 Constructing Asia's Cognitive Prior

This chapter traces the emergence and development of a regionalist cognitive prior in Asia from the 1947 Asian Relations Conference through the 1955 Bandung Conference and beyond. These interactions led to the acceptance of non-intervention and rejection of collective defense. The framework of constitutive localization suggests that the outcome of localizing an external norm could lead to its enhancement in the local context and the amplification of local beliefs and practices at the international level. These outcomes of localization are expressed by the creation of new institutions or modification of existing ones. This is precisely what happened to the non-intervention norm (and the notion of state sovereignty more generally) following the Bandung Conference. Not only was this norm enhanced by its acceptance by Asian states, the injunction against collective defense constructed at Bandung diffused beyond Asia through the Non-Aligned Movement, thereby amplifying the anti-colonial and anti-power politics orientations of Third World states. In particular, the Asian construction of non-intervention would include an injunction against participation in superpower-led collective defense that was absent in the original European formulation and Latin American extension of the norm.

Such consolidation of non-intervention at the regional level also served to strengthen the global sovereignty regime. Although no standing regional institution was created immediately after Bandung, the localization of non-intervention was evident in certain characteristics of Asia's subsequent regional institutions, beginning with ASEAN in 1967. These characteristics include consensus-based decision making, an aversion to legalization, and avoidance of any form of supranational bureaucratic structure. The institutional-design was also notable for its rejection of great power-led regionalism, and of other forms of collective defense function (with or without the participation of Western powers), because of the concern that any form of collective defense would be associated with the discredited SEATO. Instead, defense cooperation would be undertaken on a bilateral basis. ASEAN would develop a framework of regional conflict reduction and extra-regional political and security dialogues as part of a strategy of building security interdependence. Similarly, ASEAN would reject West European style regional economic integration and pursue a developmental regionalism that would limit the scope for more ambitious ideas regarding Pacific economic community. Together these ideas constituted the foundation of a regional cognitive prior, which would shape Asian regional institution-building for decades and condition the reception of new ideas about multilateralism after the Cold War.

## An Asian Construction of Global Sovereignty

The regionalist debates and compromises in Asia played an important role transforming the idea of sovereignty into rules of conduct in post-war international affairs. They enhanced the global sovereignty regime, broadening and strengthening the scope of the doctrine of non-intervention beyond its earlier European and Latin American formulations.

The most notable European writer on non-intervention, Emenic de Vattel, allowed intervention for the sake of maintaining Europe's balance of power. And "intervention in the interests of the balance of power was sometimes included in treatises on international law as an act of deriving its legitimacy from the right of self-defense."[1] But the leaders of many newly independent Asian states would not accept the legitimacy of intervention to maintain the regional or global balance of power. Latin American states invoked the non-intervention norm in the late nineteenth and early twentieth centuries to counter U.S. hegemony,[2] but this did not prevent the Organization of American States (OAS) from entering into a collective defense system with the United States.[3] In contrast, some Asian states led by India's prime minister Nehru believed collective defense pacts to be threats to their

1. Richard J. Vincent, *Nonintervention and International Order* (Princeton, NJ: Princeton University Press, 1974), 290.
2. Ann Van Wynen Thomas and A.J. Thomas, Jr., *Non-Intervention: The Law and Its Import in the Americas* (Dallas: Southern Methodist University Press, 1956).
3. On the Latin American norm of collective defense, see J. Lloyd Mecham, *The United States and Inter-American Security 1889–1960* (Austin: University of Texas Press, 1962); J. Lloyd Mecham, *United States-Latin American Relations* (Boston: Houghton Mifflin, 1965). On collective defense in the Arab League, see Robert W. Macdonald, *The League of Arab States: A Study in the Dynamics of Regional Organization* (Princeton, NJ: Princeton University Press, 1965).

sovereignty. Furthermore, the emphasis on non-intervention led to legalistic regional institutions in Latin America, whereas the same principle of non-intervention produced only informal and consultative regional groups in Asia.[4]

Such regional variations are important to our understanding of the global diffusion of sovereignty norms. Although constructivist literature on sovereignty go beyond the "static" accounts of its evolution and view it as a "social construct,"[5] they need to shed more light on the local/regional processes and mechanisms of this "social construction," including how local actors influenced the reception of European notions of sovereignty and non-intervention, and how these local interpretations reinforced the global sovereignty regime by creating additional support for non-intervention. Post–World War II Asian debates about non-intervention are a good place to search for evidence of non-Western contributions to the global sovereignty regime.[6]

The Bandung Conference, along with its predecessors, provided crucial platforms for playing out differences and reaching compromises over the social construction and diffusion of sovereignty norms. The conference legitimized and expanded the two core norms of sovereignty—non-intervention and sovereign equality—in several ways. First, it highlighted the danger of communist interference, a genuine source of apprehension for leaders concerned with regime security as well as for those concerned with democracy and human rights. Second, although the right of collective defense was upheld as a sovereign right, it was only given a conditional approval. Third, the concept of non-intervention was extended beyond the mere idea of self-determination to include the concept of non-involvement in superpower rivalry and membership in unequal multilateral security pacts. By critiquing

---

4. Other intra-regional variations over the impact of sovereignty norms may be seen in the context of territorial sovereignty, which held firm in Africa in the form of a norm of inviolability of postcolonial boundaries. In Asia, this norm had far less resonance, thereby leading to conflicts between India and Pakistan over Kashmir, between India and China over the British-mandated boundary line, and between Malaysia and Philippines over Sabah.

5. The social construction perspective sees sovereignty as being "negotiated out of interactions within intersubjectively identifiable communities" (Thomas J. Biersteker and Cynthia Weber, "The Social Construction of State Sovereignty," in *State Sovereignty as a Social Construct*, ed. Biersteker and Weber [Cambridge: Cambridge University Press, 1996], 11).

6. The best-known work on this question is rather Africanocentric. Robert Jackson assumes that the spread of the negative sovereignty (i.e., non-intervention) regime began in the mid-1950s and was completed by the late 1960s. But he pays scant attention to the period leading to the Bandung Conference in Asia during which non-interference had made significant inroads into Asian thinking. Robert Jackson, *Quasi-States: Sovereignty, International Relations and the Third World* (Cambridge: Cambridge University Press. 1991); see also Robert Jackson and Carl C. Rosberg, "Why Africa's Weak States Persist: The Empirical and Juridical in Statehood," *World Politics* 35, no. 1 (October 1982): 1–24.

regional pacts, Nehru sought to delegitimize collective defense arrangements because they served "the particularistic interests" of great powers.

In examining the importance of early Asian regionalism in establishing the rules of sovereignty, one must acknowledge that these norms had already been enshrined in the UN Charter. However in the drafting of the charter, non-intervention had received less prominence than other core norms of sovereignty, such as the doctrine of sovereign equality of states. Indeed, the proponents of collective security felt that giving too much emphasis on non-intervention would prejudice the authority of the Security Council to carry out its peace and security functions.[7]

The non-intervention norm was used by the Dutch to defend their colonial possession of Indonesia,[8] an effort which contributed directly to Nehru's determination to convene the second Asian Relations Conference in New Delhi in 1949. As Nehru developed his theory of an "area of peace" and non-alignment, the infusion of these concepts into the traditional meaning of non-intervention broadened the definition and scope of the norm.

The Bandung Conference did not reject the UN's authority and role as the key arbiter of sovereign status. However, as noted in chapter 3, many participants at Bandung also felt that the UN could not defend sovereignty norms sufficiently. This criticism not only came from true advocates of pacts like the lead delegate of the Philippines Carlos Romulo, who felt that the UN did not have enough "teeth," but also from some members of the neutralist camp. The latter group wanted the Conference to pass a resolution to acknowledge that the UN had not done enough on the issue of West Irian. Moreover, many participants at the Asian meetings were not yet UN members, and had no guarantee of future membership. Hence, although non-intervention and sovereign equality were "universal" norms enshrined in the UN Charter, their diffusion and development required the advocacy and support of regional conferences, underscoring the importance of the "social construction" perspective.

Early Asian regional interactions were therefore fundamental in setting the stage for the evolution of Asian regional order, especially in defining the nature and role of a regional organization. These interactions explain why Asia failed to develop a permanent regional organization (an Asian NATO or OAS) in the post-war period. Yet, these interactions succeeded in shaping

---

7. See Documents of the United Nations Conference on International Organization, Commission 1, General Provisions, vol. 6 (New York: United Nations Information Organizations, 1945).

8. J.G. Starke, *Starke's International Law*, 11th ed., ed. I.A. Shearer (London: Butterworths, 1994), 111–13.

an alternative normative framework for Asian regionalism. They supported claims by norm theorists about the importance of norms in shaping the behavior of international actors, even in the absence of formal institutions.

The Asian construction of non-intervention is different from its Latin American trajectory where non-intervention was designed to counter U.S. hegemony. The Latin American construction of the non-intervention norm reflected the political aspirations of settler societies whose intellectual underpinnings had considerable association with Western political traditions and legal ideas. It was part of a regional bargaining exercise in which Latin American countries, through the Inter-American System, negotiated U.S. acceptance of non-intervention in exchange for their acceptance of U.S. security role in the region. The Asian construction of non-intervention was distinctive in the sense of being geared toward a bipolar international structure. It did not allow for collective defense pacts with either superpower. Moreover, the Asian construction of sovereignty preceded and influenced Africa's own contribution. By participating in Asian dialogues and conferences African states were influenced in their own regionalist attitudes toward sovereignty.[9]

Another aspect of the Asian construction of non-intervention deserves notice. At the height of their balance of power diplomacy prior to the two world wars, Europe's great powers sometimes reached agreement on non-intervention to keep the balance of power stable by telling each other to keep their hands off weaker allies or states in their respective spheres of influence. Such non-intervention was a strategic doctrine. In Asia, Nehru's conception of non-intervention was a moral doctrine, aimed not at keeping relations among the strong powers stable, but to protect the weak from the strong.

The Asian construction of non-intervention also had an impact at the larger international level. The Non-Aligned Movement (NAM)—an off shoot of the Bandung gathering—served to diffuse the norm of non-intervention and abstention from superpower-led collective military alliances

---

9. On the normative link between Bandung and African regionalist concepts, see Colin Legum, *Bandung, Cairo and Accra* (London: The Africa Bureau, 1958). The Conference of Independent African States (CIAS), convened by Kwame Nkrumah in 1958, explicitly invoked Bandung principles, including its rejection of Cold War pacts. Kwame Nkrumah, *I Speak of Freedom* (Westport, CT: Greenwood Press, 1961), 151–52, 219. Bala Mohammed, *Africa and Nonalignment* (Kano, Nigeria: Triumph, 1978), 21, 54–55, 184. On Africa's sovereignty regime, see Jackson and Roseberg, "Why Africa's Weak States Persist"; Jeffrey Herbst, "Crafting Regional Co-operation in Africa," in *Crafting Cooperation: Regional International Institutions in Comparative Perspective*, ed. Amitav Acharya and Alastair Iain Johnston (Cambridge: Cambridge University Press, 2007), 129–44.

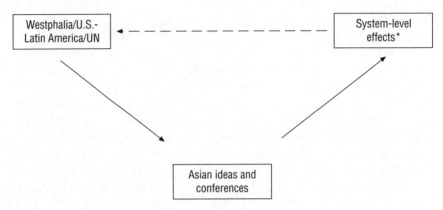

**Figure 4.1.** Asian construction of non-intervention.
 * The reference here is to the Non-Aligned Movement, which diffused the stance against collective defense pacts.

in the global South.[10] Before the first summit of NAM in Belgrade in 1961, the Preparatory Meeting of Foreign Ministers held in Cairo in June 1961 issued criteria that restricted invitations to states that were not members of "a multilateral alliance concluded in the context of Great Power conflicts."[11]

Around the same time that the decolonized states in Asia embraced a particularly restrictive interpretation of sovereignty and non-intervention, their former colonial masters in Western Europe began to move away from Westphalian sovereignty toward a greater degree of solidarism and supranationalism. Hence, a gap opened up in the practices around sovereignty among the former colonial powers (the original site of sovereignty) and the recently decolonized states. This fault line not only shaped the pattern of North-South relations in the post-war period, but it continues to be reflected in recent debates about intervention in world politics, with Asia remaining at the forefront of resistance to post–Westphalianism.[12]

10. Godfrey H. Jansen, *Afro-Asia and Non-Alignment* (London: Faber, 1966); and A.W. Singham and Shirley Hume, *Non-Alignment in an Age of Alignments* (Westport, CT: Lawrence Hill, 1986).

11. Mohammed Ayoob, The Third World Security Predicament: State Making, Regional Conflict and the International System (Boulder, CO: Lynne Reinner, 1995), 104.

12. "Naked pursuit of Westphalian sovereignty epitomize[s] the essence of Asian security today" (Chung-in Moon and Chaesung Chun, "Sovereignty: Dominance of the Westphalian Concept and Implications for Regional Security," in *Asian Security Order*, ed. M. Alagappa [Stanford: Stanford University Press, 2003], 107).

## The Power of Process Politics

Post-war Asian regionalist interactions hold the clue to why the region did not develop a regional institution—not just a security institution, but any kind of standing macro regional body—as could be found in the Middle East, Latin America, or Africa. Moreover, these interactions contributed to the development of a process diplomacy, which would shape the design of subsequent Asian institutions and explain why Asian regionalism would remain underinstitutionalized and non-legalized—the second puzzle discussed in this book.

The genesis of this process diplomacy can be traced to the Asian Relations Conference (ARC) of 1947.[13] Delegates to this and subsequent Asian regional gatherings were divided over the issue of setting up a permanent regional organization; while some backed it, others had only a "minor and desultory interest" in the idea.[14] Debates over procedure at the ARC was resolved in favor of the following principles: regional meetings should be in the nature of "informal talks without commitments"; "there should be no question of majority or minority votes as the consensus of opinion should form the basis of conference decision"; and the "draft communiqués should simply give the consensus of opinion on each subject rather than individual resolutions."[15]

The ARC considered two schemes for a regional organization. One scheme called for "a permanent institution meeting once in three years in an Asian country" whose purpose would be to facilitate the "exchange of ideas and cultivation of personal contacts between Asian thinkers and public workers." The other scheme would be to set up a "new central organization" that would collect and disseminate information, conduct studies and research, hold periodic conferences, and foster cultural and social contacts among Asian countries. It would deal with peace and security issues and be

13. Deliberations at the 1947 ARC, hosted by India and attended by twenty-eight delegations, were marked by "sharp differences" on the issue of establishing a central permanent organization. Those who argued against a permanent official organization, such as nationalist China and the Philippines, insisted that the time was not yet ripe for such a body, because many delegations were from countries that had not yet attained independence or were not fully representative of their countries. Another factor against setting up such a body was the concern that it would be dominated by India or China; thus "it was better to have nothing than to have an organization dominated by one government" (Jansen, *Afro-Asia and Non-Alignment*, 69–70). The conference finally agreed to set up an unofficial body, Asian Relations Organization, to be headquartered in New Delhi. The plan was for members of the ARC to set up national units, but only six would do so.

14. Jansen, *Afro-Asia and Non-Alignment*, 68–73, 221–22.

15. Jansen, *Afro-Asia and Non-Alignment*, 148–49, 193. See also Guy J. Pauker, *The Bandung Conference* (Cambridge, MA: Centre for International Studies, MIT, 1955), 6.

governed by an Asian Council consisting of two representatives from each constituent national unit. The Asian Council would meet twice a year and its resolution would be determined by a majority voting rather than consensus.[16]

Emerging from these discussions was a "new central organization" set up in New Delhi—the Asian Relations Organization (ARO). But this organization was moribund from the outset. A reading of the Indian Council on World Affairs Files (which organized the 1947 ARC) shows that the ARO secretariat in Delhi was unable to elicit response to its information requests from national units despite repeated attempts. The ARO folded its operation quietly in the middle of 1955 when Nehru, in the capacity of ARC President, told Secretary-General A. Appadurai, "I think it is better to wind up the Organization because in the present political climate, nothing much can be done . . . almost from the start of the organization there has been conflicts among member-states and in such a situation I don't think any useful work can be done."[17]

The Second ARC, or the Conference on Indonesia, convened by Nehru in New Delhi in January 1949 to discuss Dutch "police action" against Indonesia, also raised the possibility of a permanent Asian regional organization. Carlos Romulo spoke of "how many members looked beyond [the Conference toward] the formation of a permanent organization, a regional association strictly within the framework of the United Nations."[18] Romulo's desire went unfulfilled. Following the Conference on Indonesia, Nehru, already disillusioned by the ARO experience, expressed India's reservations about a regional association. In a speech to the Indian parliament on 8 March 1949, Nehru said, "We have not yet decided as to what region that cooperation should relate to. India is interested in several regions of Asia and whether all of these should be grouped together or dealt with separately is still to be considered." He also laid down "two conditions for Indian participation in a regional grouping: (1) it must be wholly within the scope and spirit of the Charter of the United Nations; and (2) it must be largely confined to consultation and cooperation with no binding covenant in it."[19]

16. Draft Scheme for a Permanent Conference Organization, ICWA ARC Files, Indian Council on World Affairs, New Delhi.

17. A. Appadurai, "The Asian Relations Conference in Perspective," *International Studies* 18, no. 3 (July–September 1979): 283.

18. *The Conference on Indonesia, 20–23 January 1949* (Delhi: Ministry of Information and Broadcasting), 27, 40.

19. Cited in Norman D. Palmer and Howard. C. Perkins, *International Relations: The World Community in Transition* (London: Stevens & Sons, 1954), 804–5; Mohammed Ahsen Chaudhri, *Pakistan and the Regional Pacts* (Karachi: Royal Books, 1958), 50.

The Colombo Powers met as an ad hoc group, rather than as members of an institutionalized concert of powers. Neither of their two meetings in 1954 mentioned the idea of a permanent regional organization. Some Western and Asian circles had expected the Bandung Conference to lead to the creation such an organization. In a Telegram to the Canadian High Commissioner in Delhi, dated 12 April 1955, the Canadian Secretary of State for External Affairs noted that there was "the possibility that a permanent organization will develop from the Asian-African Conference, and to a certain extent duplicate the work of the United Nations and its specialized agencies."[20]

As recently declassified Chinese documents reveal, the issue of creating a permanent institution out of the Bandung Conference was the subject of debate between China and India. China supported such a move, as early as January 1955. Its Working Plan for the Conference noted that although China did not need to "take the initiative to raise this issue," it could "encourage other countries to propose the establishment of a permanent institution for economic and cultural cooperation or the permanent institution of Asian-African Conference in the meeting."[21] However, when the issue came up during a conversation among Zhou, Nehru, and U Nu in Bandung on 16 April 1955, Nehru—unaware of the Chinese intention—opposed a permanent regional organization. According to a document from the Chinese archives, Nehru argued that setting up a "permanent political institution . . . after the conference" would be unwise because the twenty-nine countries represented at the conference "had much difference in opinion so that it was unimaginable how this institution would effectively perform its function." He also argued that any such "permanent institution must have a headquarters, and if the headquarters was in Jakarta, many of the participating countries had no representatives in Indonesia." Burmese premier U Nu took the position that "the only purpose" of the Bandung Conference "was to provide an opportunity for the delegations of various countries to meet." While the conference "could announce several general principles to the world," setting up "a permanent institution" would take time. Setting up a permanent institution at this point would be premature, as it would not have the resources to implement the resolutions of the Bandung Conference

20. Telegram from Secretary of State for External Affairs to High Commissioner in India, 12 April 1955. Department of External Affairs, Canada, *Documents on Canadian External Relations*, vol. 21, 1995, available at http://dfait-maeci.gc.ca/department/history/dcer/details-en.asp?intRefid=1308.

21. "Draft of the Tentative Working Plan for Participating the Asian-African Conference," signed by Zhou Enlai on 13 January 1955, no. 207–00004–03, Ministry of Foreign Affairs Archive, People's Republic of China.

and as such "could not win respect from the world due to its ineffectiveness." It "would be much better to form a small but effective institution later."

On the contrary, Chinese Premier Zhou held that:

> if the conference could succeed in two matters, it would be of great significance. The first was to use a document, no matter what form it would be, to express our common aspirations, including the Five Principles stressed by Prime Minister Nehru in the Rangoon talks. The second was to set up a permanent institution. We could find a way that would not bind the participating countries too tightly, such as a liaison institution. Such an institution could facilitate the governments of the participating countries to contact each other; especially some of the participating countries of the conference were not the UN members. If the headquarters of the institution was set up in Jakarta, the participating countries with diplomatic envoys there could join the institution, and the countries without diplomatic envoys in Jakarta could dispatch their secretaries to joint it, and the too faraway countries might contact by mail. . . . Such institution not only did not contradict the UN Charter, but was also in conformity with the purpose of this conference, i.e. the friendly and good-neighborly relations among the Asian-African countries.

Despite Zhou's assurance, Nehru still doubted the merit of setting up a permanent institution. He thought such an institution could not be "effective and . . . it was not wise if the conference did anything to enter into rivalry with UN."[22] By the time the Conference ended, the idea of a permanent organization had already dissipated. Only the Economic Committee of the Bandung Conference considered creating a regular body. The Final Report of the Economic Committee discussed the organizational aspects of such a body. The proposals varied from having a permanent organization with a permanent secretariat, to having only informal discussions without any secretariat, with majority of Conference members against a permanent economic organization with a permanent secretariat.[23] While still at Bandung, Zhou En-lai asked Nehru about maintaining a "liaison office" for the next meeting of the Asia-Africa Conference due to be held in Egypt two years later. In a note to his principal aide Krishna Menon, Nehru revealed that the Joint Secretariat for the Bandung meeting could play such a role. However, Burma's U Nu reacted strongly against this idea, preferring that "there

22. Summary of the talks among Zhou, Nehru, and U Nu, Bandung, 16 April 1955, no. 207–00015–01, Ministry of Foreign Affairs Archive, People's Republic of China.

23. Proceedings of the Political Committee of the Asian-African Conference, Bandung, 20–24 April 1955, UUOD.

should be no kind of organization or liaison office." Nehru later concurred with this view.[24]

Although the Bandung Conference and previous regional gatherings did not produce any permanent organization, they did shape a process (including many procedural norms) that would leave a long legacy for Asian regional institution-building efforts, including the so-called ASEAN Way. The ASEAN Way came to be known for its informality, preference for consensus over majority voting, avoidance of legalistic procedures, preference for non-binding resolutions and tendency to avoid contentious bilateral issues in multilateral discussions. Contentious issues such as those related to the Cold War were avoided at the 1947 ARC as they were likely to "divide the conference."[25] Among Asia's leaders, Nehru, in particular, was insistent on soft rules for the conduct of deliberations at Asian summits, not unlike those of the Commonwealth Heads of Government meetings. Nehru was most impressed by the "friendly spirit" of the Commonwealth meetings' proceedings as "there would be no attempt by states to impose their will on one another." Instead, they were conducted in an atmosphere of "mutual equality and respect amongst its members," in which, "when differences arise, they are accepted with tolerance and mutual respect."[26]

At the first Colombo Powers meeting, Nehru asked that the member states "follow the precedent set by the Conferences of Commonwealth Prime Ministers," where disputes between members . . . were never discussed.[27] In deciding the procedure for Bandung, the Bogor summit declared that "any view expressed at the conference by one or more participating country would not be binding on or be regarded as accepted by any other, unless the latter so desired."[28] Bogor confirmed that "acceptance of [an] invitation by any one country would in no way involve or imply any change in the status of that country or its relationship with other countries."[29] This position was shaped by participants' respect for non-interference, and "the principle that the form of government and the way of life of any country should in no way be subject to interference by another."[30]

24. "Note to VK Krishna Menon," Bandung, 23 April 1955, in *Selected Writings of Jawaharlal Nehru*, second series, vol. 28, (New Delhi: Jawaharlal Nehru Memorial Fund, 2001), 124.
25. Appadurai, "The Asian Relations Conference in Perspective," 279.
26. Indian ambassador to the United States, G.L. Mehta, cited in Francis Low, *Struggle for Asia* (London: Frederick Muller, 1955), 203.
27. Colombo Conference Minutes, UUOD.
28. Bogor Conference Minutes, UUOD.
29. Bogor Conference Minutes, UUOD.
30. Bogor Conference Minutes, UUOD.

Despite being an official gathering, Bandung maintained a close resemblance to the ARC. Three features of the decision-making process adopted at Bandung are noteworthy. First, controversial issues were to be avoided partly due to earlier Nehru's insistence that:

> The first thing to be decided is what subjects should not be discussed. The internal controversial subjects of these countries should not be discussed. Thus we should not discuss the Palestine problem. We must not discuss the Indo-China problems. That would be undesirable in any event and it would be particularly embarrassing for India, which is acting as Chairman. So also other problems as between Indian and Pakistan or Ceylon and India, should not be discussed. We should confine ourselves to broad issues affecting Asia as a whole or Southeast-Asia.[31]

Second, and this was also based on Nehru's earlier insistence at the Bogor conference, that the rules of procedure at Bandung should be "as flexible as possible."[32] The similarity with the ARC, which was based on procedures of the Commonwealth leaders' meetings, is worth noting. The Bandung Conference at the outset agreed that "the conference agenda should be kept as simple as possible in line with what had been decided by the five prime ministers in Bogor."[33] To some extent, the simplicity principle meant not having any rigid formula and allowing the chairman of the conference, Prime Minister Ali Sastraomidjo of Indonesia, to conduct the meetings "in accordance with the generally accepted conventions of Conferences."[34]

Third, "it was not necessary to take decision by majority vote, but rather that the system of consultation and consensus (*musyawarah* and *mufakat*), would be adopted, as proposed by the Indonesian delegation."[35] Roeslan Abdulghani, the secretary-general of the Bandung conference, would describe the consensus principle as a "deep-rooted and unquestioned practice," not only for Indonesians or Asians, but also for African societies.[36] Abdulghani even offered a sociological explanation of the consensus principle, stating that "[t]he object is to reach an acceptable consensus of

31. Indonesian proposal for an Afro-Asian Conference, In *Selected Works of Jawaharlal Nehru*, second series, vol. 26 (New Delhi: Jawaharlal Nehru Memorial Fund, 2001), 432.

32. Bogor Conference Minutes, UUOD.

33. *Milestones on My Journey: The Memoirs of Ali Sastroamijoyo*, ed. C.L.M. Penders (Brisbane: University of Queensland Press, 1979) 288–89.

34. "Proceedings of the Plenary Session," 18 April 1955, Proceedings of the Political Committee of the Asian-African Conference, Bandung, 20–24 April 1955, UUOD.

35. *Milestones on My Journey*, 288–89.

36. Roselan Abdulghani, *The Bandung Spirit* (Jakarta: Prapantja, 1964), 29.

opinion, and one which not only [does not hurt] the feeling or the position of [any member, but reinforces] the community feeling."[37]

Western officials observing Bandung would disparage such rules of procedure. It was noted that "at Bandung, there was a preference for avoiding a number of obvious thorny points; and it may be wondered whether a system of conference which led to no more than the enunciation of high-sounding principles is likely to endure indefinitely, however congenial the emission of such platitudinous pronouncements may be to many Asian minds."[38] In Abdulghani's view, the rules of procedure at Bandung, despite being informal in nature, had a key role in the running of the Conference. The principle of deliberation and consensus were the keys to success of the Conference.[39] The consensus principle was not simply a matter of procedure. Basic but important lines of policy emerged from these principles, including the importance of state sovereignty and the non-interference doctrine.

There is a striking resemblance between the rules of procedure of the various Asian conferences and those of ASEAN. Although the ASEAN Way developed in Southeast Asia, the roots of this "process-driven" approach to regionalism cannot be understood in isolation from the wider Asian conferences held between 1947 and 1955.[40]

## The Strong in the World of the Weak

The early Asian interactions not only delegitimized collective defense within great power orbits, they also contributed to a normative bias against regionalism led by great powers, including Asian great powers. Conversely, regionalism among weaker states acquired greater appeal. SEATO's decline was representative of this trend. But often missed by observers of Asian regionalism is that the Asian Relations Conference and the Bandung conference confirmed, at least in the eyes of the Southeast Asian states, that neither China nor India could be the legitimate leader of an Asian regional organization. In the post-Bandung era, the failure of great power-led regional organizations could be seen by the contrasting experience of two regional institutions created within a year of each other—the Asia and Pacific

37. Abdulghani, *The Bandung Spirit*, 29.
38. British Foreign Office Research Dept Assessment: Far Eastern Dept, DO35/6099, The National Archive, United Kingdom (henceforth TNA).
39. Roselan Abdulghani, *The Bandung Connection: The Asia-Africa Conference in Bandung in 1955* (Jakarta: Gunung Agung, 1981), 76–77.
40. For a critical discussion of the ASEAN Way see Amitav Acharya, *Constructing a Security Community in Southeast Asia* (London: Routledge, 2001).

Council (ASPAC) founded in Seoul in 1966 and the Association of Southeast Asian Nations (ASEAN), established in Bangkok in 1967.

ASPAC was comprised of Australia, Japan, Malaysia, Republic of China (Taiwan), New Zealand, the Philippines, South Korea, South Vietnam, and Thailand. It was described as "the major example to date of a multi-regional organization designed to bring together most of the leading non-Communist nations of Western Pacific to deal with external threats [from Indochina] . . . and to provide a framework for more widespread cooperation."[41] Its proponents sought to present ASPAC as an indigenous (Asian) effort. From South Korea's perspective, ASPAC not only represented "Asia's first regional organization which was launched entirely by Asians themselves," it also had the potential to "serve as a major forum in Asia in which all Asian nations, large and small, democratic as well as Communist, will discuss their common problems and diffuse their differences."[42] According to a memorandum of a conversation between Thai foreign minister Thanat Khoman and U.S. secretary of state Dean Rusk—held at the SEATO Council meeting in Canberra in June 1966—Thanat had "hoped that ASPAC could be maintained as a loosely organized grouping with the primary design of providing an increasingly intimate forum for the candid exchange of views." Such an arrangement Thanat believed, "would permit, taking into account the absence of Western Powers [*sic*], the easier concerting of the views of the Asian nations concerned," and "would perhaps in the future give a greater weight to the expression of Asian opinion."[43]

ASPAC was also notable as a potential instrument for Japanese leadership in regional institution-building in Asia. Tokyo had identified ASPAC and the Ministerial Conference on Economic Development of South East Asia (MCEDSEA) "as the two major vehicles for Japanese participation in regional affairs and tried to promote regional cooperation based on those organizations."[44] As such, ASPAC was to complement, if not substitute, SEATO, providing an Asian voice to regionalism in Asia.

ASPAC's members also declared themselves against a military role, at least initially. At the fourth ASPAC Ministerial Conference, held on 9–11

41. Norman D. Palmer, "SEATO, ASA, MAPHILINDO and ASPAC," in *The ASEAN Reader*, ed. K.S. Sandhu et al. (Singapore: Institute of Southeast Asian Studies, 1992), 28.
42. Byung Kyu Kang, "The Asian and Pacific Peace System in the 1970s," paper presented at the International Institute for Strategic Studies, Fourteenth Annual Conference on East Asia and the World System: China and Japan in the 1970s, 3 October 1972.
43. "Memorandum of Conversation, Canberra, June 28, 1966," US/MC/5, *FRUS*, 1964–1968, vol. 27, Mainland Southeast Asia: 190–91.
44. Susumu Yamakage, "Japan's National Security and Asia-Pacific's Regional Institutions in the Post-Cold War Era," in *Network Power: Japan and Asia*, ed. Peter J. Katzenstein and Takashi Shiraishi (Ithaca: Cornell University Press, 1997), 283.

June 1969, the Australian minister for external affairs Gordon Freeth stated that ASPAC "should not be concerned to become or to set up such [security] organisations." In his view, ASPAC "should be concerned rather with building up the relations of mutual trust and confidence which are essential if such [security] organisations are to succeed."[45] Later, according to a British memo, Thailand was "very much opposed to turning either ASEAN or ASPAC into a military alliance, though [it] agrees that ASEAN might have a politico-security role to play in addition to its economic one."[46]

ASEAN was established in 1967 with the explicit goal of promoting economic, cultural, and political cooperation. Its initial membership included Indonesia, Malaysia, Thailand, Singapore, and the Philippines. Like ASPAC, ASEAN's founders also presented it as an indigenous Asian initiative. Echoing similar claims about ASPAC, Thanat Khoman described ASEAN as the "first . . . indigenous Asian organization" to be "initiated within the community of nations of the area to help themselves."[47] Indeed, ASEAN's founders would strenuously try "not to lend credence to charges that [ASEAN] was a substitute for the ill-fated SEATO." Instead, ASEAN would concentrate on "economic, social, cultural, technical, scientific and administrative fields."[48]

In important ways, ASEAN helped to institutionalize the core principles of Bandung. Its Zone of Peace, Freedom and Neutrality (ZOPFAN) Declaration of 27 November 1971, strongly pushed by Indonesia, affirmed "the continuing validity of the 'Declaration on the Promotion of World Peace and Cooperation' of the Bandung Conference of 1955, which among others, enunciates the principles by which states may co-exist peacefully." The

45. "ASPAC Conference," *Asian Almanac*, vol. 7 (18 October 1969): 3603.
46. From Bangkok to Foreign and Commonwealth Office, 28 February 1969, FCO 24/341, TNA.
47. Cited in Karl D. Jackson et al., eds., *ASEAN in Regional and Global Context* (Berkeley: University of California, Institute of East Asian Studies, 1986), 10. ASEAN was an outgrowth of two earlier experiments in regionalism—the Association of Southeast Asia (ASA) and MAPHILINDO (Malaysia, the Philippines, Indonesia). ASA, formed in 1961 by Malaysia, Thailand, and the Philippines (the latter two were SEATO members), was intended to be an alternative rather than a complement to SEATO. It was noted in ASA's founding declaration that it was "in no way connected with any outside power bloc and was directed against no other country," a clear reference to the demonstrated illegitimacy of SEATO. ASA soon foundered over the non-participation of Indonesia. MAPHILINDO also suffered an early demise, in this case over an intra-regional dispute: the territorial dispute between Malaysia and the Philippines over Sabah. The fate of ASA offered the lesson that for Southeast Asian regionalism to be viable, it must be inclusive of Indonesia, while that of MAPHILINDO showed the importance of intra-regional conflict reduction. Indeed, the longevity and relative success of ASEAN could be attributed to its acceptance of these two lessons.
48. Michael Leifer, *ASEAN and the Security of South-East Asia* (New York: Routledge, 1989), 28.

Treaty of Amity and Cooperation in Southeast Asia, adopted at the first summit of ASEAN members held in Bali in 1976, acknowledged that ASEAN's goals would be "consistent with" the "Ten Principles adopted by the Asian-African Conference in Bandung."

At first, ASEAN and ASPAC were seen as complementary forms of indigenous regionalism. U.S. president Richard Nixon saw the two organizations as signs of an "active regionalism" that was "one of the new realities of Asia." The "vigor" of this active regionalism was "one of the guarantees of the influence of Asia's smaller states in the future political structure of the region."[49] Yet, although both ASEAN and ASPAC professed to give an Asian voice to regionalism and both rejected a military role, and although ASEAN's early years of existence were marked by a number of setbacks from disputes among its members (e.g., tensions among Singapore, Malaysia, and Indonesia, and more important, the Malaysia-Philippine dispute over Sabah), ASEAN would far outlive ASPAC. A comparison of ASPAC's fate with ASEAN illustrates the normative conditions that played a crucial role in legitimizing different types of regionalism in Asia.

It has been argued that the Sino-US rapprochement following Nixon's visit to China and the U.S. recognition of the People's Republic of China were the main reason for the eclipse of ASPAC. But this obscures the issue of ASPAC's weak legitimacy, which explains why it failed and why ASEAN succeeded. Despite its pretense to be a voice for Asian opinion, ASPAC continued to be seen as a front for Western powers against China. In Norman Palmer's view, ASPAC was "even more ill-fated and even more irrelevant" than SEATO.[50] As he noted, ASPAC's founding communique announced the signatory states' "determination to preserve their integrity and sovereignty in the face of external threats," while agreeing that it would remain a "nonmilitary, nonideological, and not anti-Communist" grouping. As such, "[e]ven the most closely knit organization would face difficulties in working toward these conflicting objectives, and ASPAC was anything but closely knit."[51]

A British assessment of ASPAC accurately predicted its early demise. Describing ASPAC as a "grandiose scheme . . . attempting to achieve both political and economic cooperation," the assessment concluded that "[i]t is unlikely that ASPAC will achieve much in its present form because the

49. Richard Nixon, "United States Foreign Policy for the 1970's—East Asia and the Pacific: The contribution of Asian Nations working," (n.d.), available at http://www.let.rug.nl/usa/P/rn37/writings/ch7_p7.htm.
50. Palmer, "SEATO, ASA, MAPHILINDO and ASPAC," 28.
51. Ibid.

association is clearly between Western nations, and if Formosa and South Vietnam remain members it will almost certainly not attract the support of any non-aligned South-east Asian countries. . . . The chance that ASPAC will develop into an organisation with a powerful influence over Asian affairs seem poor." The report also assessed correctly that the most viable and likely regional organization for Southeast Asia would be "a union of the present ASA [Association of Southeast Asia—set up in 1961 and comprising Malaysia, Thailand, and the Philippines] countries together with Indonesia and Singapore."[52] A few days after the founding of ASEAN, another British memo offered an interesting contrast between ASPAC and ASEAN. It found ASEAN's origin to have "revealed unsuspected depths of common interest in the participating countries, and a realistic estimate of the difficulties still to be overcome." It cited the speech by Singapore's foreign minister Rajaratnam to the founding meeting of ASEAN in Bangkok, in which he had called for ASEAN members "to marry national thinking with regional thinking," and to develop a sense of "regional existence" even if it meant "painful adjustments" to their interests and policies. This "apparently genuine wish for closer cooperation" was one reason why the British memo believed ASEAN had a "better chance of survival" than "some of its predecessors."[53]

By contrast, ASPAC was given an unfavorable assessment. The same memo identified "excessive Australian zeal" and Japan's disproportionate economic power within ASPAC as among the reasons that might produce the "collapse" of the grouping. It characterized the atmosphere surrounding ASPAC as "unreal" due to "the presence of these two countries (Australia and New Zealand) which, though professing Asian sympathies and loyalties, are in fact much closer to the United States or to Western Europe in their way of looking at the area's problems." ASPAC also had little chance of attracting Indonesian membership because of its "dislike of being drawn into any kind of regional defensive grouping,"[54] which Jakarta still suspected to be a possible goal of ASPAC. Indeed, Indonesian foreign minister Adam Malik was cited in a British diplomatic dispatch to have ruled out not only Indonesian membership of ASPAC, but also any prospect for a merger

52. "Prospects for MAPHLINDO and Other South East Asian Regional Cooperation," South and South-East Asia Section, Joint Foreign Office and Commonwealth Relations Office Research Department, January 1967, FO 370/2878, TNA.
53. "Association of South-East Asian Nations," Mr. Bullard to Mr. Brown, received 11 August 1967, South-East Asia General, FCO 15/23, TNA.
54. Ibid.

between ASPAC and ASEAN. Malik excluded Australia and New Zealand as well as Japan as "possible members" of ASEAN.[55]

New Zealand's High Commissioner in Malaysia also highlighted the weakness of ASPAC vis-à-vis ASEAN. ASPAC was "either unready or unwilling to deal with basic regional economic problems," whereas ASEAN was "at least attempting to grapple with these matters, which are of major importance to its members." New Zealand should oppose any moves that would see ASEAN as "the smaller organisation [to] be absorbed within the larger [ASPAC] because that would lead to ASEAN's goals being "submerged or side-tracked," an outcome that would be contrary to "New Zealand's own interests, let alone those of ASEAN's members."[56]

In contrast to ASPAC, ASEAN was seen as an organization by and for Southeast Asia. At the height of the Sabah dispute between Malaysia and the Philippines, Malaysia refused to attend ASEAN meetings if the Philippines were present but ruled out withdrawing from ASEAN altogether. Zainal Sulong of the Malaysian Foreign Ministry explained the difference between ASPAC and ASEAN: the main difference was that ASEAN "had an identity of Asian-ness which the other grouping had not," an identity that owed to "close links of race, history, aspirations."[57]

The death of ASPAC was symptomatic of the normative resistance in Asia to great power-led regionalism. Whereas SEATO underscored U.S.-led efforts at security multilateralism, the fate of ASPAC symbolized the limits of Japan-led attempts at regional institution-building. Scholarly literature on Japan's role in Asian regionalism has stressed the importance Tokyo placed on soft regionalism, on market driven regionalism, the role of business networks, and on pan-pacific epistemic communities (discussed later in this chapter).[58] However, Japan's network-style regionalism might have been the result of its realization that an inter-governmental regional organization led by Japan would not be acceptable to Asians. It should be noted that Japan was not uninterested in Asian regional organization in which it could play a major role, although it was more keen on an economic and political organization than a military one. Indeed, one Japanese writer has observed that in the 1960s the Japanese government was so "preoccupied" with ASPAC and

55. British Embassy in Jakarta to Foreign and Commonwealth Office, London, "A.S.E.A.N. Membership and A.S.E.A.N. A.S.P.A.C. Relations," 26 August 1968, FCO 15/23, TNA.

56. "ASPAC/ASEAN," from the High Commissioner in Kuala Lumpur to Secretary of External Affairs, 27 August 1968, FCO 15/23, TNA.

57. "Malaysia/Philippines/ASEAN," undated memorandum, FCO 24/341, TNA.

58. Lawrence T. Woods, *Asia-Pacific Diplomacy: Nongovernmental Organizations and International Relations* (Vancouver: UBC Press, 1993); Katzenstein, "Introduction: Asian Regionalism in Comparative Perspective."

the Ministerial Conference for the Economic Development of Southeast Asia (MCEDSEA) that it "did not take ASEAN seriously."[59]

But Japan's leadership of ASPAC lacked regional legitimacy. As a 1972 British memo noted, "ASPAC's effective development as an instrument of regional collaboration has suffered from the hostility of some of its South East Asian members to anything implying Japanese leadership."[60] The following year, another British memo blamed Japan's "half-baked statements about new groupings" on the awareness of the Japanese government "of the continuing resentment in South East Asia against them arising from the War, and also from current Japanese economic domination."[61] Despite Japan's "natural inclination" to join an Asian regional grouping because that would "make her feel secure and less isolated," there were "not many groups to which Japan could naturally belong" in Asia. ASPAC, "despite its imperfections and genesis as an anti-communist alliance, did provide a forum in which Japan could sit down as an equal with other Asian countries." Tokyo did make "some effort to show the importance they attach to the South East Asian Ministerial Conference for Development by always sending a high-ranking Minister to their meetings." But at the end of the day, Japan hoped "that other countries will take initiatives but she will be hesitant to take the initiative herself."[62]

When in July 1973 it was reported that the Japanese appeared to be looking at the MCEDSEA as a "possible successor" to ASPAC, Tokyo was believed to have been lukewarm toward requests by Australia and New Zealand to join the grouping. But there was "no prospect of any early initiative on the Japanese side towards constructing some new regional grouping," because "such a move would arouse suspicion in many quarters."[63] Economic cooperation in formal networks offered a more practical avenue for Japanese regionalism. The fact that the first Pacific regional networks and proposals for free trade in the Pacific emerged as the weakness of AS-PAC became apparent might not entirely be coincidental. After Japanese prime minister Takeo Miki's proposed Pacific Free Trade Area (PAFTA) failed to take off, Australian and Japanese private sectors formed Pacific Basin Economic Council (PBEC) in 1967. PBEC was a nongovernmental

59. Yamakage, "Japan's National Security and Asia-Pacific's Regional Institutions in the Post-Cold War Era," 290.
60. "Asian and Pacific Council," March 1972, FCO 24/1269, TNA.
61. "Japan and Asian Regional Cooperation," British Embassy in Tokyo to Foreign and Commonwealth Office, London, 26 April 1973, FCO 15/1727, TNA.
62. Ibid.
63. "Japan and South East Asia," from British Embassy in Tokyo to South East Asia Department of the Foreign and Commonwealth Office, London, 5 July 1973, FCO 15/1727, TNA.

**Table 4.1.** Selected Asian Regional Forums in the 1960s

| Name | Year established | Membership | Impact/Outcome |
|---|---|---|---|
| Association of Southeast Asia (ASA) | 1961 | Thailand, Malaysia, Philippines | Dissolved in August 1967 after ASEAN's formation but some of its programs "transferred" to ASEAN |
| MAPHILINDO | 1963 | Malaysia, Philippines, Indonesia | A racial concept proposed by the Philippines to unite Malaya peoples, which failed because of Indonesia's "Confrontation" against Malaysia in 1963, although its members joined ASEAN |
| Ministerial Conference on Economic Development in Southeast Asia (MCEDSEA) | 1966 | Japan, South Vietnam, Laos, Cambodia, Thailand, Philippines, Malaysia, Singapore, and Indonesia | Ceased meeting by 1975 |
| Asian and Pacific Council (ASPAC) | 1966 | South Korea, Australia, New Zealand, Japan, Thailand, Republic of China (Taiwan), Malaysia, South Vietnam, Philippines | Defunct in the early 1970s |
| Association of Southeast Asian Nations (ASEAN) | 1967 | Malaysia, Indonesia, Thailand, Philippines, and Singapore (Brunei joined in 1984) | Survived the Malaysia-Philippines dispute over Sabah and the Singapore-Indonesia antagonisms |

organization of businessmen from five Pacific Rim nations later opened to businessmen from other Asian states. In 1968, the Pacific Trade and Development Conference (PAFTAD) was set up, which would later bring together Japan, Canada, Australia, New Zealand, the United States, and the ASEAN states. These initiatives had the implicit backing of the Japanese government. The Fukuda Doctrine, announced by Prime Minister Takeo Fukuda in 1977 at Manila during his much publicized tour of Southeast Asia, was aimed at easing Southeast Asian fears of Japanese hegemony and gave official Japanese backing to ASEAN as a regional institution. Thus, Japan's efforts at regionalism focused on non-governmental organizations, while the initiative for inter-governmental regionalism passed into the hands of ASEAN.


## The Path to Security Cooperation

The norm against regional collective defense also contributed to shaping Asian regionalism in the post-Bandung period. Indeed, what was originally an injunction against "the use of arrangements of collective defense to serve the particular interests of any of the big powers," expanded into a more general norm against regional collective defense, whether sponsored by great powers or not, because of the fear that such defense arrangements, especially if involving pro-Western nations, might be seen as a "SEATO through the backdoor."

ASEAN's approach to security cooperation contained a clear rejection of collective defense. During the negotiations leading to the formation of ASEAN, Indonesia sought the commitment of its members against pacts that served "the particular interests" of great powers.[64] Although this language was eventually dropped, ASEAN never endorsed nor developed collective defense. Philippine foreign minister Narciso Ramos forcefully stated in August 1967 that "There is no obligation on the part of any Asian [sic] member State to go to the aid of another member State in cases of outside intervention; neither is there any intention or commitment for the Asian States to 'share' in the responsibility of resisting foreign intervention. Each state must look after its own security."[65]

Through its early years, reports about ASEAN assuming a military role proved unfounded. One example was remarks attributed to Indonesian acting president Suharto in 1968 about an ASEAN defense pact. The Indonesian government position was summarized in a memo by the British embassy in Jakarta. According to the memo, while "ASEAN could be a vehicle for co-operation in the military field . . . Indonesia would not join any military pact, but (presumably as examples of the kind of cooperation which the Acting President had in mind) the Government was willing to enter into arrangements for the exchange of information and into 'loose military co-operation' such as the existing joint patrols with Malaysia on the Kalimantan

64. Arnfinn Jorgensen-Dahl, *Regional Organization and Order in Southeast Asia* (Basingstoke: Macmillan, 1982).

65. From the British Embassy in Manila to the Foreign and Commonwealth Office, "Philippines Foreign Secretary's Comments on Formation of ASEAN," 14 August 1967, FCO 15/23, TNA.

border."[66] The memo concluded that although the Indonesian Government did not "exclude the possibility of bilateral arrangements with neighbouring countries for military cooperation against subversion and threats arising within the area, or multilateral arrangements for the exchange of information," it remained "genuinely opposed to joining any military grouping."[67]

In 1974, then foreign minister Malik rejected intra-ASEAN defence cooperation on the ground that military "[p]acts are of no value and don't really add strength to a region."[68] Carlos Romulo agreed with this view when he noted that "[w]e did not phase out SEATO in order to set up another one."[69] In a similar vein, the Thai foreign minister declared in 1977 that military alliances were "obsolete" and stressed that ASEAN had "nothing to do with military cooperation."[70] Ali Moertopo, a key adviser to President Suharto of Indonesia who had played an important role in the formation of ASEAN, also rejected military pacts, using reasons that echoed Nehru's concerns, such as the danger they posed to the "sovereignty" of Asian nations and the risk that they would provoke "intervention by outside forces." "Excessive dependence of a country on the might of a foreign power, resulting in the existence of foreign military bases on its soil or its membership in a military pact," Moertopo argued, "may precisely pose a threat to its sovereignty, its national integrity, its peace and security." Moreover, in the event of "an internal upheaval in the host country or in a member country of a military pact," its security dependence would "constitute a sound reason for intervention by outside forces."[71]

At the 1976 Bali Summit, in its Declaration of ASEAN Concord, the Association would only approve of "continuation of cooperation on a non-ASEAN basis between the member states,"[72] which in essence meant an agreement to keep defense cooperation among ASEAN members at the bilateral level. Malaysian prime minister Hussein Onn found it "obvious that the ASEAN members do not wish to change the character of ASEAN from a socio-economic organization into a security alliance as this would only

66. Phillips in Jakarta to Foreign and Commonwealth Office, London, "General Soeharto's Statement on ASEAN and Military Security," 7 March 1968, FCO 15/23, TNA.

67. Ibid.

68. The *Straits Times*, 22 August 1974.

69. The *Straits Times*, 22 December 1975.

70. The *Straits Times*, 6 July 1977.

71. Lt. General Ali Moertopo, "Superpower Interests in Southeast Asia," in *Self-Reliance and National Resilience*, ed. K. Subrahmanyam (New Delhi: Abhinav, 1975), 50.

72. The text of the Treaty of Amity and Cooperation in Southeast Asia and the Declaration of ASEAN Concord can be found at the website of the ASEAN Secretariat in Jakarta, www.aseansec.org.

create misunderstanding in the region and undermine the positive achieve-ments of ASEAN in promoting peace and stability through co-operation in the socio-economic and related fields."[73] The refusal to organize itself into a military pact or develop any form of military cooperation on a multilateral basis would persist through subsequent decades. Noordin Sopiee lists "re-jection of internal and external collective military pacts" and "rejection of emphasis on peace through military deterrence" as fundamental ASEAN norms.[74] Instead, ASEAN members would develop an overlapping system of bilateral military relationships. This included intelligence exchanges, joint operations against communist insurgents on common borders, exchange of senior level officers for training, provision of field training facilities, joint maritime surveillance and patrols, and above all, a range of military exercises to develop common operating procedures and simulate joint action against common threats.[75] These bilateral ties developed as a result of ASEAN's earlier rejection of multilateral defence, and attested to the resilience of the norm against superpower-led collective defense.

ASEAN's stance would survive not only the persistence of concerns about communist subversion, but also the Vietnamese invasion of Cambodia in December 1978. The latter crisis prompted Singapore's prime minister Lee Kuan Yew to propose that ASEAN conduct multilateral military exercises to guard against a possible Vietnamese incursion into Thailand. But the proposal was turned down by Indonesia and by Thailand itself, both of whom did not want to change the non-military character of ASEAN. Indo-nesia rejected the Singapore proposal on the ground that ASEAN exercises would provoke Vietnam and be "similar to ASEAN opening a new front."[76] ASEAN continued to reject multilateral defense cooperation even after the Vietnamese withdrawal of Cambodia in 1989 and the end of the ASEAN-Vietnam divide. ASEAN then faced the prospect of a precipitate reduction in the US military presence in Asia. This was seen by some ASEAN elites as necessitating the creation of an ASEAN "defence community."[77] But the norm against collective defense would hold. The then President of the Phil-ippines, General Fidel Ramos, would still warn that any move to create an ASEAN defence pact "could provoke an arms race, intensify ideology-based

73. *New Straits Times*, 1 April 1976.

74. Noordin Sopiee, "ASEAN Towards 2020: Strategic Goals and Critical Pathways," paper presented at the Second ASEAN Congress, Kuala Lumpur, 20–23 July 1997, 9.

75. For details, see, Amitav Acharya, "A Survey of Military Cooperation Among the ASEAN States: Bilateralism or Alliance," Centre for International and Strategic Studies Occa-sional Paper no. 14, York University, April 1990, 40.

76. *New Straits Times*, 17 September 1982.

77. Amitav Acharya, "Association of Southeast Asian Nations: Security Community or Defence Community?" *Pacific Affairs* 64, no. 2 (Summer 1991): 159–78.

polarisation and conflicts within South-east Asia, encourage the big powers to initiate pre-emptive counteraction and prevent ASEAN from pursuing with undiluted vigour and freedom of action its vision of full regional stability and economic self-sufficiency."[78] More recently, in 2003-04, an Indonesian proposal for closer defense cooperation under an "ASEAN Security Community" was considerably diluted by its ASEAN partners.[79]

ASEAN continued to reject collective defense involving non-Southeast Asian actors. The only exception to this might be the Five Power Defence Arrangements (FDPA)—created in the wake of the British withdrawal from the region—which comprised Singapore, Malaysia, UK, Australia, and New Zealand. But as the author of the most important work on the FPDA writes, it has remained "an essentially loose political consultative framework that is far from being a collective defense system."[80] Despite conducting military exercises, FPDA's contribution to the defense needs of its ASEAN members, Singapore and Malaysia, are rudimentary. The ASEAN Regional Forum (ARF), created in 1994 as Asia's only multilateral security organization, has never seriously considered the NATO model of collective defense. In the words of a senior U.S. official, the ARF is "not a bloc forming against the common threat" but rather a case of "potential antagonists talking to each other trying to clear up any misperceptions, give greater transparency . . . [and] some sense of predictability."[81]

The norm against regional defense cooperation was also evident in the failure of a recent U.S. initiative for a Pacific "Security Community"[82]—which, despite its nomenclature, was aimed at legitimizing an expansive multilateral defense relationship in the region—as well as a 2004 proposal for a "Regional Maritime Security Initiative." Even terrorism, a threat affecting many Asian countries, has been addressed mainly through bilateral security cooperation. Multilateral cooperation has been limited to intelligence-sharing and capacity-building activities. Similarly, despite the fact that several countries in the region see the rise of China as a potential

---

78. The *Sunday Times* (Singapore), 26 November 1989.

79. Adrian Kuah, "ASEAN Security Community: Struggling with Details," *IDSS Commentaries*, 15 June 2004.

80. Chin Kin Wah, "Singapore's Perspective on Asia-Pacific Security," in *Asia-Pacific Security Cooperation: National Interests and Regional Order*, ed. See Seng Tan and Amitav Acharya (Armonk, NY: ME Sharpe, 2004), 175.

81. Interview, the *Straits Times*, 30 July 1993, 34.

82. Dennis C. Blair, "Collective Responsibilities for Security in the Asia-Pacific Region," text of a lecture organized by the Institute of Defence and Strategic Studies, Singapore, 22 May 1999; Dennis C. Blair, "Security Communities Are the Way Ahead for Asia," *International Herald Tribune*, 21 April 2000; Dennis C. Blair, "Security Communities: The Way Ahead for Asia," *Asia-Pacific Defense Forum* (Special Supplement) 2, no. 1 (2000).

common threat, there is no serious advocacy of an Asian NATO. Rather, the United States is falling back on its existing bilateral alliances to deal with this challenge. Despite suggestions by some writers that altered strategic condition—such as reduced US-Asian and intra-Asian power disparities and the rise of China—might create the possibility of a "Nato-like Asian security framework," it can be safely predicted that no such NATO in Asia is forthcoming.[83]

Aside from the rejection of collective defense, ASEAN organized its approach to security cooperation around three elements. The first was its wholehearted embrace of the extended non-intervention principle. The doctrine could be found in all the major political statements of ASEAN, including the founding Bangkok Declaration of 1967, which called on Southeast Asian states to "ensure their stability and security from external interference in any form or manifestation"; the 1971 Kuala Lumpur Declaration, which recognized the "right of every state, large or small, to lead its existence free from outside interference in its internal affairs as this interference will adversely affect its freedom, independence, and integrity"; the 1976 Treaty of Amity and Cooperation adopted by ASEAN, which included the principle of "non-interference in the internal affairs of one another"; and the Declaration of ASEAN Concord, also adopted in 1976, which stipulated that "member states shall vigorously develop . . . a strong ASEAN community . . . in accordance with the principles of self-determination, sovereign equality, and non-interference in the internal affairs of nations."[84]

A second element of ASEAN's approach to security cooperation was subregional conflict reduction and war avoidance. Despite initial aspirations and the provision of a dispute-settlement mechanism under the terms of its 1976 Treaty of Amity and Cooperation, ASEAN did not engage in formal conflict resolution among its members, an act that would have been considered intrusive. Instead, the real objective was to prevent armed conflict among the members through persuasion and peer pressure. A Thai foreign minister would describe "the immediate task of ASEAN" as an

83. Press-Barnathan's rationalist argument, echoing that of Crone, suggests that the reduction of power disparities could lead to greater prospects for the creation of an Asian security arrangement by making it more useful to the United States. See Galia Press-Barnathan, *Organizing the World: The United States and Regional Cooperation in Asia and Europe* (New York: Routledge, 2003), 208. See also Galia Press-Barnathan, "The Lure of Regional Security Arrangements: The United States and Regional Security Cooperation in Asia and Europe," *Security Studies* 10 (Winter 2000–2001): 49–97; Derek Chollet, "Time for an Asian NATO?" *Foreign Policy*, no. 123 (March/April 2001); Sunanda K. Dutta-Ray, "Signs Look Promising for Nato-Like Asian Security Framework," the *Straits Times*, 22 April 2004.

84. All the declarations may be accessed on the ASEAN Secretariat website at www.aseansec.org.

"attempt to create a favourable condition in the region whereby political differences and security problems among Southeast Asian nations can be resolved peacefully."[85] This could be seen in the original circumstances surrounding ASEAN's emergence; negotiations to establish ASEAN had closely paralleled efforts undertaken by Thailand to bring an end to the Indonesia-Malaysia confrontation of 1966–67. ASEAN's role was tested during the Sabah dispute between Malaysia and the Philippines in 1968–69, when the two parties broke off diplomatic relations and brought the ASEAN diplomatic process to a standstill. But their common ASEAN membership did prove to put a brake on the further deterioration of ties, including the possibility of armed conflict. To quote a 1968 memo from the UK embassy in Jakarta to the Foreign and Commonwealth Office in London, "although the practical achievements of ASEAN's first year have been very limited, the idea is sound and . . . it is incontestable that the idea is a political force of some importance; indeed a major influence restraining both Malaysia and the Philippines from open rupture after the Bangkok talks on Sabah seem to have been their reluctance to imperil their standing as ASEAN members."[86]

Third, as already noted, it was in ASEAN that the process diplomacy that emerged through the Asian conferences found its institutional expression. This included a preference for consultations and consensus over formalistic and legalistic mechanisms.[87] This approach was described by Malaysian analyst Noordin Sopiee as ASEAN's "non addiction to Cartesianism and to legalism."[88] Speaking at the height of the 1997 Asian financial crisis, Singapore's foreign minister would list the principles that were considered integral to ASEAN's decision-making process—"informality, organization minimalism, inclusiveness, intensive consultations leading to consensus and peaceful resolution of disputes."[89]

Apart from developing its own security approach, ASEAN organized and represented a microcosm of what may be called Asia's proto-multilateralism in regional security affairs. This was a regionalism bereft of the formal com-

85. Cited in Acharya, Constructing a Security Community in Southeast Asia.

86. Mr. H. C. Hainworth in Jakarta to the Foreign and Commonwealth Office, London, 30 August 1968, FCO 15/23, TNA.

87. Jorgensen-Dahl, *Regional Organization and Order in Southeast Asia*; Askandar Kamarulzaman, "ASEAN and Conflict Management: The Formative Years of 1967–1976," *The Pacific Review* 6, no. 2 (1994): 57–69; Tuan Hoang Anh, "ASEAN Dispute Management: Implications for Vietnam and an Expanded ASEAN," *Contemporary Southeast Asia* 18, no. 1 (June 1996): 61–81; Acharya, *Constructing a Security Community in Southeast Asia*.

88. Sopiee, "ASEAN Towards 2020," 9.

89. Lee Kim Chew, "ASEAN Unity Showing Signs of Fraying," the *Straits Times*, 23 July 1998, 30.

mitments or mechanisms of collective security or collective defense organizations, and marked by features that suggested basic continuities with the normative ideas and outcomes of Asia's earlier regionalist interactions.

One feature was represented by ASEAN's Zone of Peace, Freedom and Neutrality (ZOPFAN) initiative. The latter combined the non-allowance of pacts with emphasis on intra-regional conflict resolution through the application of the non-intervention norm. The 1971 ZOPFAN Declaration committed ASEAN members to 1) resist alliances with foreign powers, 2) abstain from inviting or consenting to intervention by external powers in the domestic affairs of the regional states, 3) resist involvement in any conflict of powers outside the zone, and 4) ensure the removal of foreign military bases in the territory of ZOPFAN's states.[90] ZOPFAN's goal was to reduce the role of external powers in the affairs of the region, with an even more important aim to provide a framework for intra-regional conflict management, based on the fear that regional conflicts that were mismanaged at the regional level would invite intervention by outside powers.

Thus, ZOPFAN and Bandung reached a similar compromise between pro-alliance and non-aligned states. Like Bandung, ZOPFAN did not allow multilateral pacts that served the interests of the Cold War, but allowed separate defense arrangements between ASEAN members and outside powers. It reflected Philippines' and Thailand's disenchantment with external security guarantees and addressed Malaysia's and Indonesia's concerns over the dangers of being engulfed by the ambitions of great powers. At the same time, it contained enough ambiguity to allow for the continuation of the existing security relationships between ASEAN members and external powers.

Through ZOPFAN, ASEAN sought to limit the strategic role of external powers in regional security so that the region did not become a cockpit of the Cold War superpower rivalry; however, this did not preclude it from engaging with selected external powers in consultations and dialogues. Beginning in the 1970s, ASEAN developed a number of "dialogue partnerships" (table 4.2) with external powers, including the United States, Canada, the European Union, Japan, Australia, and New Zealand.

The aim of these dialogues was to engage the outside powers, and to turn ASEAN into the hub of Asian regional interactions, a pattern that would influence and be evident in regional institution-building efforts in the 1990s. The dialogue relationships initially focused on economic and

90. Heiner Hanggi, *ASEAN and the ZOPFAN Concept* (Singapore: Institute of Southeast Asian Studies, 1991), 25.

**Table 4.2.** The Evolution of ASEAN's Dialogue Partnerships

| Country | Year joined | Comments |
|---|---|---|
| Australia | 1974 | In 1974, Australia became ASEAN's first full dialogue partner. First Australia-ASEAN Summit was held in 1977. |
| Japan | 1977 | Informal dialogues had begun in 1973. |
| United States | 1977 | The United States was represented at this meeting by its Under Secretary of State for Economic Affairs. |
| United Nations Development Programme (UNDP) | 1977 | UNDP is the only multilateral body with which ASEAN held a formal dialogue. |
| New Zealand | 1977 | Informal cooperation since 1975. |
| Canada | 1977 | |
| EEC | 1978 | This was the first ministerial level meeting. An informal meeting had been held in 1974. |
| South Korea | 1991 | |
| India | 1996 | India had been a sectoral dialogue partner since 1993. |
| Russia | 1996 | In July 1991, the then deputy prime minister of the Soviet Union attended the opening session of the Twenty-Fourth ASEAN Ministerial Meeting held in Kuala Lumpur as a guest of the Malaysian Government. |
| China | 1996 | ASEAN and China had held consultative relations since 1992. |

*Source*: ASEAN Secretariat.

technical issues, as was decided at the Second ASEAN Summit in Kuala Lumpur in 1977, which agreed that "the association's economic relations with other countries or groups of countries needed to be expanded and intensified." It was here that ASEAN leaders had their first meeting with prime ministers of Australia, Japan, and New Zealand, for whom it was also "the first time that they had held consultations as a group with the leaders of non-ASEAN countries."[91] The next year, the first Post-Ministerial Conference took place immediately after the ASEAN Ministerial Meeting, and included Australia, Canada, the European Community, Japan, New Zealand, and the United States. The agenda of these Post-Ministerial Conferences was broad, covering regional security issues, especially the conflict created by the Vietnamese invasion and occupation of Cambodia in December 1978.[92] Although initially featuring friendly nations from outside the region, these post-ministerial conferences would form the basis of an "inclusiveness," which would expand into a cooperative security institu-

91. See http://www.aseansec.org/92.htm. The PMCs have since expanded. See Table 4.2.
92. http://www.aseansec.org/92.htm.

tion involving former adversaries, such as the U.S, Russia, and China in the post–Cold War period.

## The Path to Economic Cooperation: Developmental Regionalism and the Pacific Community Idea

Following World War II, ideas about regional economic cooperation in Asia were also influenced by the conceptions of sovereignty held by Asia's newly independent states. The Bandung Conference offered important clues to the nature and limits of post-war Asian economic regionalism. First, as noted earlier in this chapter, Bandung showed that Asia would forsake any form of standing regional economic organization in the foreseeable future (see section on the power of process politics). At the same time, Japanese participation at the conference and the approach it took there indicated that Japan would make economic cooperation the vehicle for its reengagement with Asia and that Tokyo's approach to regional cooperation would be mainly in the economic arena.

Bandung revealed that economic nationalism, import-substitution strategies, and collective bargaining, rather than a move toward a regional trade bloc, would shape Asian countries' approach to regional economic cooperation. This was indicated in a secret assessment of the economic outcomes of the Bandung Conference by the British Commissioner-General's Office in Singapore, dated 7 June 1955. It listed some "bad" outcomes of the conference (meaning "contrary to the interests" of UK), such as calls for a study on freight rates intended to increase pressure on Western shipping companies, demands for the processing of more raw materials before export, setting up of national and regional banks and insurance companies to increase financial self-reliance of Asian countries, exchange of information on oil prices—which some saw as a precursor to the Organization of the Petroleum Exporting Countries (OPEC), and a call for countries present at Bandung to consult before international meetings—which might "reinforce existing tendency" for Afro-Asia to "form a bloc" at the UN. Most serious were "harmful ideas about the desirability of economic autarchy and about the right of the underdeveloped countries to blame any shortcomings in their economic situation on the failure of the richer nations to ladle out large and uncontrolled grants for economic development." The assessment also noted several "good" outcomes of the Conference—also from the British point of view—including an agreement on the need for cooperation with countries outside the region, recognition of the value of aid, and acceptance of the principle of multilateral trade. The call for collective action to stabilize the prices of, and demand for primary commodities was seen as innocuous and ineffectual and contrary to the communiqué statement that was "not intended to form a regional bloc."[93]

This proved to be an accurate assessment not just of Bandung, but also of subsequent efforts at regional economic cooperation, including those undertaken by ASEAN. Although ASEAN's founders publicly stressed economic cooperation as a key purpose, they did so mainly to avoid the perception of ASEAN as a political and security grouping. There was no intention of turning ASEAN into a regional economic grouping in the manner of the European Economic Community (EEC). As Lee Kuan Yew noted in 1972, "For the present, ASEAN does not aim at integrating a regional economy."[94] Malaysian prime minister Mahathir Mohamad recalled in 1980, "Grand economic designs were discarded at the formation of ASEAN because the differing and conflicting needs of the nations concerned would have made a formula for economic cooperation most difficult to agree upon. . . . An economic community approach a la EEC would have made ASEAN a nonstarter."[95]

ASEAN's approach to economic cooperation in the formative years fits the framework of "developmental regionalism":[96] regional schemes for economic development to achieve "collective self-reliance,"[97] rather than comprehensive market integration.[98] Other elements of developmental regionalism

93. A.G. Gilchrist, Office of the Commissioner-General for the UK, Singapore, to F. S. Tomlinson, Foreign Office, London, "The Economic Recommendations of the Bandung Conference," 7 June 1955, FO 371/116986, TNA.

94. *Eighth Year Cycle of ASEAN* (Jakarta: ASEAN National Mass Media, Department of Information and ASEAN National Secretariat, 1976), cited in Marjorie L. Suriyamongkol, *The Politics of Economic Cooperation in the Association of Southeast Asian Nations*, PhD diss., University of Illinois at Urbana-Champaign, 1982 (Ann Arbor, University Microfilms International, 1984), 121.

95. Mahathir bin Mohamad, "Tak Kenal Maka Tak Cinta," in *Pacific Economic Cooperation: Suggestions for Action*, ed. John Crawford with Greg Seow (Petaling Jaya, Malaysia: Heinemann Asia, 1981), 44.

96. W. Andrew Axline, "Underdevelopment, Dependence, and Integration: The Politics of Regionalism in the Third World," *International Organization* 31, no. 1 (Winter 1977)" 83–105; Maurice W. Schiff and L. Alan Winters, *Regional Integration and Development* (New York: Oxford University Press for the World Bank, 2003).

97. B.W. Mutharika, "A Case Study of Regionalism in Africa," in *Regionalism and the New International Economic Order*, ed. Davidson Nicol, Luis Echeverria, and Aurelio Peccei (New York: Pergamon, 1981), 92.

98. See the editor's introduction and conclusion in Domenico Mazzeo, ed., *African Regional Organizations* (Cambridge: Cambridge University Press, 1984), 9, 238–39. Philip C. Schmitter, *Autonomy or Dependence as Regional Integration Outcomes: Central America*, Research Series no.17 (Berkeley: Institute of International Studies, University of California, 1972).

include collective bargaining and regional conflict resolution.[99] ASEAN's early years were aimed at creating "an environment conducive to economic development" through "the reinforcement of social and political stability" and intra-mural conflict avoidance.[100] And ASEAN economic regionalism was "stronger in its external relations than in intra-ASEAN cooperation . . . [taking] the form of a joint effort in securing a larger external market and better terms for exports rather than in establishing a customs union or a free trade area vis-à-vis the non-ASEAN countries."[101] As an example, in 1973, ASEAN would raise concerns with Japan over the "indiscriminate expansion" of its synthetic rubber industry, which was harming ASEAN's exporters of natural rubber, and send Indonesia's Adam Malik to Japan to successfully persuade Tokyo to reduce its synthetic rubber production.[102] Another example was attempts to secure greater market access for ASEAN products by lobbying for an expansion of the coverage of its exports in the EEC's generalized system of preferences. ASEAN organized a meeting with the EEC in June 1972 to coordinate its economic relations with the group in response to EEC's extension of preferential treatment to forty-two African countries through the Lome Convention. ASEAN also offered a coordinated position at the Tokyo round of the General Agreement of Tariffs and Trade (GATT) talks. This was followed by similar coordination at the Uruguay Round, which assumed increased urgency as the result of the crisis over the agricultural subsidies.[103]

The other key element of ASEAN's economic cooperation was based on a UN report, which called for selective trade liberalization and industrial cooperation within an import substitution framework.[104] ASEAN trade cooperation centered on the scheme called ASEAN Preferential Trading Arrangements (PTA), whose basic agreement was signed in 1977. The PTA provided for a number of measures to liberalize and increase intra-ASEAN trade

99. Björn Hettne, "Developmental Regionalism," in *New Directions in Development Economics: Growth, Environmental Concerns and Government in the 1990s*, ed. Mats Lundahl and Benno J. Ndulu (London: Routledge, 1996), 165.

100. Stuart Drummond, "ASEAN: National Policies Versus Economic Cooperation," *The Round Table* no. 295 (1985): 263.

101. Narongchai Akrasanee, "Issues in ASEAN Economic Regionalism," in *ASEAN Security and Economic Development*, ed. Karl D. Jackson and M. Hadi Soesastro, (Berkeley: University of California, Institute of East Asian Studies, 1984), 72.

102. Dewi Fortuna Anwar, *Indonesia in ASEAN* (Singapore: Institute of Southeast Asian Studies, 1994), 64.

103. For an Overview of ASEAN's role in GATT, see M. Hadi Soesastro, "ASEAN's Participation in GATT," *Indonesian Quarterly* 15, no.1 (January 1987): 107–27.

104. Hadi Soesastro, "ASEAN Economic Cooperation in a Changed Regional and International Political Economy," in *ASEAN in a Changed Regional and International Political Economy*, ed. Hadi Soesastro (Jakarta: Centre for Strategic and International Studies, 1995), 20.

including long-term quantity contracts, liberalization of non-tariff measures on a preferential basis, exchange of tariff preferences, preferential terms for financing of imports, and preference for ASEAN products in procurement by government bodies. Yet the impact of the PTA was limited, despite the rise of intra-ASEAN trade as a proportion of total ASEAN trade from 13.5 percent in 1973 to 20 percent in 1983 (it fell to 16% in 1985). Much of the total intra-ASEAN trade volume was due to bilateral trade between Singapore and Malaysia and between Malaysia and Indonesia. In addition, about 65 percent of intra-ASEAN trade was fuel-related (mineral fuels, lubricants, and related materials).[105]

ASEAN's industrial cooperation schemes fared somewhat better. Of the five projects under the first batch of 1976 ASEAN Industrial Projects scheme (large government-sponsored projects geared to the regional market: urea plants in Malaysia and Indonesia, super-phosphate in the Philippines, soda ash in Thailand, and diesel engine in Singapore), only two could be implemented. Governments were unwilling to surrender their freedom to choose industrial locations and invest under a supranational scheme. Launched in 1981, the ASEAN Industrial Complementation Scheme, which would distribute the production stages of an industry among different ASEAN members, fared worse; only two of its thirty proposals received approval, its effect of intra-regional trade being a miniscule US$1 million. Such schemes, it was realized, could be better pursued through market mechanisms, rather than government intervention, and the existence of such schemes was seen as an excuse for not eliminating trade barriers. A third scheme, ASEAN Industrial Joint Ventures, launched in 1983 and aimed at promoting industrial joint ventures among member countries, also showed poor results, not the least because investors from ASEAN seemed to "prefer joint ventures with partners from outside the region" than from inside.[106]

Indonesian analyst Hadi Soesastro blames the limited achievements of ASEAN's economic schemes on "too much emphasis on regional import substitution instead of export-orientation."[107] Economic nationalism and import substitution remained for some time at the heart of ASEAN's economic cognitive prior of developmental regionalism. They would gradually give way to export promotion in the 1980s spurred by a sharp global decline in commodity prices. But the cognitive prior of developmental regionalism

105. Hadi Soesastro, "Prospects for Pacific-Asian Regional Trade Structures," in *Regional Dynamics: Security, Political and Economic Issues in the Asia-Pacific Region*, ed. Robert Scalapino et al. (Jakarta: Centre for Strategic and International Studies, 1990), 391.

106. Soesastro, "ASEAN Economic Cooperation," 29

107. Ibid., 30.

would still underlie ASEAN's misgivings regarding the Pacific Community concept that emerged in the 1970s and 1980s.

Although its initial articulation can be traced to the Institute of Pacific Relations (1925–61) in the United States,[108] the idea of a Pacific Community (also known as Pacific Economic Cooperation, and Pacific Basin Cooperation) in the post-war era evolved through a series of Japanese and Australian proposals in the 1960s and 1970s (see table 4.3). Two main stages of its evolution can be discerned. The initial articulation of the concept by Japanese scholar Kiyoshi Kojima proposed a Pacific Area Free Trade Association (PAFTA) involving five advanced economies of the Pacific (the United States, Japan, Canada, Australia, and New Zealand) and sought to emulate European integration. However, this approach was discarded with the establishment and gradual consolidation of ASEAN. In the 1970s the emphasis shifted from integration of regional economies toward a more "consultative, informal, and communicative" organization modeled after the Organization for Economic Co-operation and Development (OECD).[109] A key turning point was the proposal for an Organization for Pacific Trade and Development (OPTAD) that would "attempt to improve intergovernmental economic relations and intentionally not attempt to replace them or in any sense become a supranational Government. Nor would such an organization . . . try to evolve into a common market."[110]

The key idea behind the growing interest and interactions around the Pacific Community concept was the emerging concept of "open regionalism," understood mainly as non-exclusionary regionalism. Garnut rightly asserts that the emergence of the open regionalism concept was a matter of "reality shaping an idea," that is, discussions about Pacific cooperation from the late 1970s on "recognized" the "reality of Asia-Pacific trade expansion as it emerged in the post-war decades."[111] The first specific usage of the term is credited to John Crawford, the Australian chair of a tripartite meeting of policy–oriented academics, the private sector, and

108. Woods, *Asia-Pacific Diplomacy*.

109. Peter Drysdale and Hugh Patrick, "Evaluation of a Proposed Asian-Pacific Regional Economic Organization," Research Paper no. 61, Australia-Japan Economic Research Project, Australian National University, Canberra, July 1979, 35. The Paris-based OECD does bring together top policymakers and allows governments to discuss problems and compare views but ultimately its role is that of a high-powered think tank. Although it has a capacity for political persuasion, in the final analysis it lacks institutional bite.

110. Lawrence B. Krause, *Pacific Economic Cooperation: Suggestions for Action* (Petaling Jaya: Heinemann Educational Books, 1981), 136.

111. Ross Garnaut, *Open Regionalism and Trade Liberalization* (Singapore and Sydney: Institute of Southeast Asian Studies and Allen and Unwin, 1996), 6.

**Table 4.3.** The Pacific Community Idea, 1960–1980

| Idea | Year | Source of idea | Goals | Membership | Impact/Outcome |
|---|---|---|---|---|---|
| Asian Marshall Plan to be promoted by Japan | 1960–64 | Morinosuke Kajima, Japanese business-man and MP | "regional solidarity through mutual cooperation" (Soesastro 1983, 16) | "Union of Asian Countries": Pan-Asian rather than Pan-Pacific | Influenced by growing pan-European cooperation idea, undermined by perceived Japanese hegemonism |
| Economic Cooperation in the Pacific Area | 1963 | Japan Economic Research Centre (founded 1963) | To discuss economic relations, transport, communications and cultural exchanges | | JERC emerges as key Japanese institution for research and dissemination on Pacific cooperation concept |
| Economic Cooperation for Development and Trade in the Pacific | February 1964 | East-West Center, Honolulu | The Pacific Community concept was "first discussed and thought through" here (Kojiama 1980, 1) | | Stirred Kojiama's interest in Pacific Community concept |
| Pacific Economic Community | November 1965 | Kiyoshi Kojiama's paper to a JERC Conference | Proposal for a Pacific Free Trade Area similar to EEC | Japan, United States, Canada, Australia and New Zealand | Attracts the interest of Japanese FM Takeo Miki, who sends Kojiama to travel through the Pacific in early 1967 to ascertain interest in the PEC idea |
| Pacific Basin Economic Council | April 1967 | Australia-Japan Business Coopera-tion Committee | "Getting to know you" inaugural meeting of business leaders, which grew into annual meetings to study global trade and investment and coopera-tion between public and private sector in the Pacific | Japan, United States, Canada, Australia and New Zealand. Later developing countries represented | Supportive of Pacific Community concept; joined the coordinat-ing group of Pacific Economic Cooperation Council (PECC) that grew out of the Canberra Seminar |
| Asian Pacific Policy | May 1967 | Japanese FM Takeo Miki | Promote "awareness of common principles,' regional cooperation in Asia, cooperation among advanced nations in the Pacific area" (Drysdale and Patrick, 26) | | First Japanese proposal for a "formal Pacific association . . . at the *official level.*" (Soesas-tro). No policy initiative follows but seen as the precursor to PAFTAD. |

| Organization | Date | Convened by / Report | Objective | Members | Notes |
|---|---|---|---|---|---|
| Pacific Trade and Development Conference (PAFTAD) | January 1968 (Tokyo) | Convened by Kojima with support from FM Miki under the auspices of JERC | "To establish and strengthen contacts among policy-oriented academic economists, governments officials, and business leaders" (PAFTAD 1980, 26) To discuss foreign economic policies of Pacific countries | Initially Japan, United States, Canada, Australia, New Zealand, later expanded to include Pacific developing countries | Became a major platform for promoting the Pacific Community concept and precursor to the OPTAD idea |
| Pan-Pacific Association | 1978 | Masayoshi Ohira (PM of Japan) | | Advanced Pacific countries and ASEAN members (left open association of other countries) | Establishment of Pacific Basic Cooperation Study Group under Japanese Prime Minister's office |
| Pacific Basin Cooperation Study Group | March 1979 | Ohira (Japan), Saburo Okita (Chair) Interim and Final reports on the Pacific Basin Cooperation Concept | "Creation of free and open interdependence," cultural exchanges with "maximum respect for diversity", "free transaction of goods and capital . . . with utmost respect for the developing countries' situations and interests" (Pacific Basin Study Group 1980, 7) | Advanced Pacific countries and ASEAN members (left open association of other countries) | First mention of "open regional cooperation" (Interim Report, 4), which became "open regionalism": the *mantra* of Pacific economic cooperation |
| Organization for Pacific Trade and Development (OPTAD) | July 1979 | CRS Study for U.S. Senate Foreign Relations Committee by Peter Drysdale and Hugh Patrick | To articulate the need for a "wider, flexible, and non-bureaucratized institutional association for Asian-Pacific economies committed to outward-looking trade and development objectives" (Drysdale and Patrick, 24) | Leadership of the United States and Japan, and the full involvement of Australia, South Korea, the non-communist Southeast Asian countries, and other Pacific basin countries" (Drysdale and Patrick, 35) | Abandonment of idea of a free trade area among advanced Pacific Nations in favor of an OECD-type association with "consultative, informal, and communicative" style of operations" (Drysdale and Patrick, 35) |

*(continued)*

103

**Table 4.3.** *(continued)*

| Idea | Year | Source of idea | Goals | Membership | Impact/Outcome |
|---|---|---|---|---|---|
| Pacific Community Seminar, Canberra | 15–17 September 1980 | Mooted by Ohira and Aust PM Malcolm Fraser, Government-sponsored, tripartite (official, business, and academic) representation | Open regionalism | Attended by representatives from Japan, Australia, United States, New Zealand, Canada, Indonesia, Malaysia, Philippines, Singapore, Thailand, South Korea, Papua New Guinea, Fiji, Tonga | Established a standing committee, which would later come to be known as the Pacific Economic Cooperation Council (PECC) to undertake information exchanges and research on regional economic cooperation; stimulated national committees of Pacific Economic Cooperation in Japan, United States, South Korea, Thailand, and Canada, as well as ASEAN Pacific Cooperation Committee |

*Sources:* John Crawford with Grew Seow, ed., *Pacific Economic Co-Operation: Suggestions for Action* (Petaling Jaya, Malaysia: Heinemann Asia for the Pacific Community Seminar, 1981); Peter Drysdale and Hugh Patrick, "Evaluation of a Proposed Asian-Pacific Regional Economic Organization," Australia-Japan Economic Research Project Research Paper no. 61, Australian National University, Canberra, July 1979. This is the report commissioned in April 1978 by the U.S. Congressional Research Service, which grew out of a request by Senator John Glenn, Chairman of the Sub-Committee on East Asian and Pacific Affairs of the Senate Committee on Foreign Relations and submitted in May 1979; Kiyoshi Kojima, "Economic Cooperation in a Pacific Community," Pacific Community Lecture Series, East-West Center, 22 May 1980; Pacific Basin Cooperation Study Group (Prime Minister's Office), *Report on The Pacific Basin Cooperation Concept* (Translation of the Summary Draft), Tokyo: Foreign Press Centre, 19 May 1980; Pacific Basin Cooperation Study Group (Prime Minister's Office), *Interim Report on The Pacific Basin Cooperation Concept* (Translation), Tokyo: Foreign Press Centre, 14 November 1979; Pacific Trade and Development Conference, "The Pacific Trade and Development Conference Series," in Crawford with Seow, *Pacific Economic Co-Operation*, 26; Hadi Soesastro, "Institutional Aspects of Pacific Economic Cooperation," in *Pacific Economic Cooperation: The Next Phase*, ed. Hadi Soesastro and Han Sung-Joo (Jakarta: Centre for Strategic and International Studies, 1983), 3–52; Sir James Vernon, "The Pacific Basin Economic Council," in Crawford with Seow, *Pacific Economic Co-Operation*, 25; Lawrence T. Woods, *Asia-Pacific Diplomacy* (Vancouver: University of British Columbia Press, 1993).

government officials called the Pacific Community Seminar held in Canberra in September 1980, which laid the foundation for the Pacific Economic Cooperation Council (PECC).[112] But Crawford attributed it to Japanese proponents.[113] Indeed, the term "open" to qualify regionalism appeared five times (in seven pages) in a Japanese government-appointed task force report released almost a year before the Canberra seminar.[114] The final report of the same group in May 1980 had also advocated "free and open interdependence" and disavowed "exclusive and closed regionalism."[115]

One of the most serious obstacles to the notion of open regionalism and Pacific Community concept was misgivings expressed by ASEAN. Southeast Asian policymakers and academics also used the concept of open regionalism, but in a somewhat different manner. Malaysia's Cabinet Minister Mohammed Ghazali bin Shafie agreed that "the Pacific basin concept has to aim and be seen to aim at an open as opposed to a closed arrangement."[116] But he argued that open regionalism implied inclusiveness, more in the political and geographic sense than in the economic sense. Hence, the concept must encompass "all the littoral states of the Western and Eastern Pacific seaboard as well as the island states in between, plus hinterland states that may experience a dominant Pacific pull."[117]

Several reasons explained ASEAN's suspicions regarding the Australian-Japanese promoted notion of a Pacific Community. One was the fear of being drawn into great power rivalry. Referring to the fact that the idea originated among the pro-Western Pacific nations, Thailand's deputy prime minister (and former foreign minister) Thanat Khoman, although

112. Garnaut, *Open Regionalism*, 6–7.

113. "Some Japanese views suggests what a Pacific community should not be: it should be non-military, non-political and non-exclusive—that is, it should embrace 'open regionalism'" (John Crawford, "Introduction," in Crawford with Seow, *Pacific Economic Co-Operation*, 2–3).

114. These usages include "open cooperation" (p. 3), "open regional cooperation" (p. 4), "a regional community based upon free and open interdependent relations" (p. 5), "open policies" (p. 5), and "internationally open countries" (p. 6). The Pacific Basin Cooperation Study Group, *Interim Report on the Pacific Basin Cooperation Concept* (Tokyo: Foreign Press Centre), 1979.

115. The Pacific Basin Cooperation Study Group, *Report on the Pacific Basin Cooperation Concept*, Translation of the Summary Part (Tokyo: Foreign Press Centre, 1980), 7.

116. M. Ghazali bin Shafie, "Towards a Pacific Basin Community: A Malaysian Perception," in *Pacific Economic Co-Operation*, eds. Crawford with Seow, 97.

117. Shafie, "Towards a Pacific Basin Community," 97. A Southeast Asian scholar Chong Li Choy in a 1981 paper based on a previously written dissertation, called for "open self-reliant regionalism," implying both collective self-reliance of ASEAN members through intramural cooperation and international cooperation "to maximize their benefits from cooperative relations with outside nations" by presenting "a consistent, united front as a regional coalition." Chong Li Choy, *Open Self Reliant Regionalism: Power for ASEAN's Development* (Singapore: Institute of Southeast Asian Studies, 1981), 68.

generally sympathetic to the idea of a Pacific Community, acknowledged the "apprehension that participation in the Pacific Community with the contemplated membership may draw the accusation of aligning oneself with one group of countries in opposition to another group."[118] Malaysia's prime minister Mahathir Mohamad was concerned with the issue of regional identity: "even as we talk of Pacific regionalism, countries like New Zealand, Australia, the United States and Russia consider themselves more European than anything else."[119] Crawford recognized unease about Japan's leading role in a Pacific Community as an obstacle. Neither Japan nor the United States might be acceptable as a leader of such a group. Although such sensitivity in Crawford's view was "unnecessary," it meant the leadership mantle might fall on ASEAN, "perhaps in the form of quietly arranged semi-summit of ASEAN members and the five developed countries."[120]

ASEAN members were alarmed by what they perceived as the Western dominance of the proposed organization. A key report on the OPTAD (the 1979 Drysdale/Patrick report) was clearly aimed at the U.S. domestic audience, trying to convince Congress that any U.S. participation in the proposed Pacific Community concept would not be at the expense of U.S. commitment to the global multilateral trade regime. Hence, the report's list of five principles for an organizational structure for OPTAD recognized "that leadership of the United States and Japan, and the full involvement of Australia, South Korea, the non-communist Southeast Asian countries and other Pacific Basin countries can best build the cooperation structure."[121] This concession to U.S. and Japanese leadership in an Australian-U.S. report was one source of the misgivings on the part of ASEAN about the nature and purpose of the Pacific Community initiative. ASEAN was also concerned that a multilateral Pacific framework will undermine its own institutional machinery, including its own dialogues with major Pacific nations.[122]

ASEAN would accept the Pacific Community idea under certain conditions. Philippine Minister of Economic Planning Gerardo Sicat put forth three conditions: any new Pacific organization must not "submerge ASEAN's

118. Thanat Khoman, "The Pacific Basin Co-Operation Concept," in *Pacific Economic Co-Operation*, ed. Crawford with Seow, 24.

119. Mohamad, "Tak Kenal Maka Tak Cinta," 43.

120. John Crawford, "The Pacific Basin Co-Operative Concept," in *Pacific Economic Co-Operation*, ed. Crawford with Seow, 40.

121. Drysdale and Patrick, Evaluation of a Proposed Asian-Pacific Regional Economic Organization, 35.

122. Gerardo P. Sicat, "ASEAN and the Pacific Region," in *Pacific Economic Co-Operation*, ed. Crawford with Seow, 221.

cohesion and identity," it should not undercut ASEAN's own dialogues with Pacific nations, and it should deal with common problems that cannot be dealt with through ASEAN's own dialogues and bilateral channels.[123] Noordin Sopiee of Malaysia bluntly argued, "It is imperative that the concept is not perceived as a Western, neo-colonial proposal devised for Western neo-colonial purpose."[124] ASEAN worried that it would be forced to accept a formalistic and legalistic organization, or regional economic cooperation that went beyond consultations to negotiations over trade liberalization. For Mahathir, "the first move towards a Pacific Community should not be a comprehensive economic plan of some such clear-cut formula for co-operation but the tedious one of getting to know each other." Echoing the principles of the ASEAN Way, he argued that any such forum "should be created for the discussion firstly of non-controversial issues of interest to everyone, for example meteorology, rescue operations, charting the seas and the oceans." Later, "more and more subjects will be discussed and new areas of co-operation worked out. All the time the numerous contacts, formally or informally, multilaterally or bilaterally will stimulate a greater knowledge and appreciation of each other."[125] Finally, ASEAN members wanted the Pacific organization to adopt its own model of regionalism. As Ghazali Shafie put it, "Essentially, any Pacific basin concept, to be acceptable to ASEAN, must represent a natural extension of ASEAN's activities in the wider regional and global circles."[126]

To sum up, despite being a latecomer to the game, ASEAN played a critical role in shaping the fate of the Pacific Community concept. As Woods writes, "participation from ASEAN has been of central importance, and attempts by the Pacific Economic Cooperation Council (PECC) enthusiasts to placate the fears of this subregional grouping acknowledge that the pace of pan-Pacific cooperation is largely dependent upon the association's attitude towards the concept."[127] But ASEAN resistance to the Pacific Community concept would soften, thanks especially to the role played by Track II meetings and dialogues. Through PECC and PAFTAD meetings, it was not just academics and think tankers, but also government officials who were being socialized into the idea of Pacific economic cooperation. At the very least,

123. Sicat, "ASEAN and the Pacific Region," 223.
124. Cited in Hadi Soesastro, "Institutional Aspects of Pacific Economic Cooperation," in *Pacific Economic Cooperation: The Next Phase*, ed. Hadi Soesastro and Han Sung-Joo (Jakarta: Centre for Strategic and International Studies, 1983), 49.
125. Mohamad, "Tak Kenal Maka Tak Cinta," 45.
126. Shafie, "Towards a Pacific Basic Community," 99.
127. Woods, *Asia-Pacific Diplomacy*, 124.

these meetings provided participants with some confidence that they were not alone in their efforts. The 1980s commodity price crisis was also crucial in encouraging economic nationalists in ASEAN (Singapore had already done so) to switch to export promotion. Most ASEAN countries would sign onto the Washington Consensus, especially unilateral liberalization even before Asia Pacific Economic Cooperation (APEC) was established. Yet, despite these new imperatives for liberalization and influence of norm entrepreneurs, there would be striking parallels between ASEAN's misgivings about the Pacific Community concept and its initial objections to APEC, as discussed in chapter 6.

### Path Breaking to Path Dependence

As ASEAN evolved, the proto-multilateralism it developed and represented acquired significant legitimacy and appeal within the larger region. Asian policymakers came to consider ASEAN as a suitable basis for constructing a larger Asia-Pacific institutionalist framework based on the notion of cooperative security and "open regionalism." ASEAN was initially hesitant in getting involved in these larger Asia-Pacific frameworks as it feared domination by the greater powers and seeing its regional identity diluted. This would change when it realized that involvement in wider regional institutions would give the Association an opportunity to project and validate its sub-regional model onto a larger scale, thereby securing a greater influence.

In South Asia, ASEAN's progress inspired the establishment of the South Asian Association for Regional Cooperation (SAARC) in 1986. President Ziaur Rahman of Bangladesh, the main inspiration behind SAARC, had been working since 1977 on "the idea of an ASEAN-like organization in South Asia,"[128] resulting in an organizational structure that is "largely based on the ASEAN model."[129] The basic norms of The South Asian Association for Regional Cooperation (SAARC) were the same as those of ASEAN, although the degree of adherence to these norms has differed. SAARC's

128. Kishore C. Dash, "The Political Economy of Regional Cooperation in South Asia," *Pacific Affairs* 69, no. 2, (Summer 1996): 186.

129. Nira Wickramasinghe, "Globalization and Regional Insecurities in South Asia," paper presented at the Conference on Globalization and Regional Security: Asian Perspectives, organized by the Asia-Pacific Center for Security Studies, Honolulu, 23–25 February 1999, 23. This influence of ASEAN on SAARC is further underscored by the fact that there had been a growing number of seminars in the SAARC countries focusing on the ASEAN experience and seeking to draw relevant lessons for SAARC itself.

**Table 4.4.** Path Dependency in Asian Security Multilateralism

|                     | ARC and Bandung | SEATO | ASEAN | Asia Pacific (ARF) |
|---------------------|-----------------|-------|-------|--------------------|
| Collective security | No              | Yes   | No    | No                 |
| Collective defense  | No              | Yes   | No    | No                 |
| Cooperative security| Yes             | No    | Yes   | Yes                |

exclusion of contentious bilateral issues from the multilateral agenda was similar to ASEAN's approach, which left bilateral disputes to be handled bilaterally, rather than be brought to the agenda of ASEAN.

Northeast Asia would later develop proto-institutional frameworks, such as the Four-Party Talks (later the Six-Party Talks), and the security dialogues conducted under the auspices of the Council for Security Cooperation in the Asia Pacific (CSCAP) North Pacific Group and Northeast Asian Cooperation Dialogue, which have been influenced by the idea of cooperative security championed by ASEAN and the ARF.[130] The ARF would adopt ASEAN's Treaty of Amity and Cooperation as its basic normative framework, and the ASEAN Way of flexible consensus and organizational minimalism, and would be the most important expression of ASEAN's proto-multilateralism. Moreover, ASEAN was given the "driver's seat" of the ARF, and ASEAN members clearly expected outside powers to accept ASEAN's leadership of the forum and the norms and principles specified by the Association.[131]

THE early regional institution-building experience of Asia contains several important lessons. First, the absence of institutions did not mean the absence of shared norms. These norms continued to be influential in the absence of formal institutions. Proposals for a regional security organization led by superpowers or great powers that conflicted with the norms articulated at the early Asian and Asian-African gatherings, all failed. The fates of SEATO and ASPAC attest to this. Instead of institutionalizing power asymmetries through collective defense or collective security institutions, the evolution of Asian regionalism post-Bandung was shaped by a normative approach to regional order, which was embodied in and developed by ASEAN. The norms of enhanced non-intervention, aversion to great power-led regionalism, avoidance

130. Amitav Acharya, "A Concert of Asia?" *Survival* 41, no. 3 (Autumn 1999): 84–101.

131. Peter Ho, "The ASEAN Regional Forum: The Way Forward," paper presented at the Third Workshop on ASEAN-UN Cooperation in Peace and Preventive Diplomacy, Bangkok, 17–18 February 1994; Michael Leifer, *The ASEAN Regional Forum*, Adelphi Paper no. 302 (London: International Institute for Strategic Studies, 1996); Yang Razali Kassim, "Minister: ASEAN Will Always Have Driver's Seat in Forum," *Business Times*, 25 July 1994, 3.

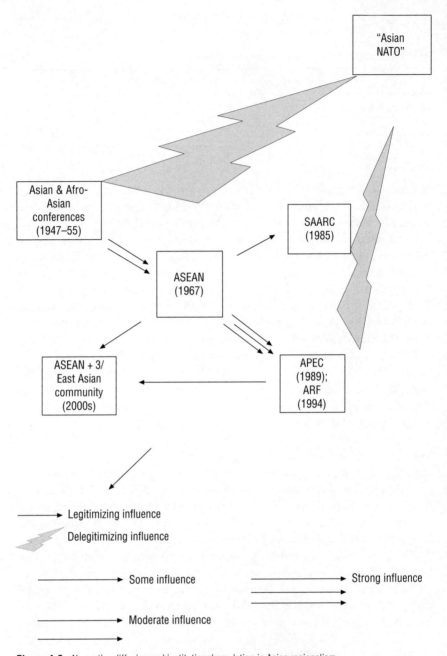

**Figure 4.2.** Normative diffusion and institutional emulation in Asian regionalism.
Apart from the rejection of collective defense, institutional emulation in Asian regionalism includes diffusion of process norms, such as organizational minimalism, exclusion of bilateral disputes from the multilateral agenda, preference for consensus over majority voting, and avoidance of legalistic mechanisms. The ASEAN process norms are remarkably similar to Bandung's, which were shaped by Indonesia; in turn, ASEAN has influenced the process norms of SAARC, ARF, and the ASEAN+3 framework. The "+3" framework represents a diffusion of the ASEAN model to Northeast Asia.

of collective defense, and acceptance of soft institutionalism in both economic and security arenas, provided the foundation for the Asia-Pacific regionalism that emerged in the 1990s. These will play an important role in ASEAN's response to proposals for multilateral security and economic cooperation after the end of the Cold War.

# 5 Resistance and Change
## COMMON SECURITY AND COLLECTIVE INTERVENTION

In the 1990s, Asia faced two sets of ideas about regional cooperation, which challenged its existing institutional architecture that had come into place during the Cold War. The first was the idea of "common security." Originating in Cold War Europe, this norm was framed (prelocalized) in Asia-Pacific discourses as "cooperative security." The second idea concerned the role of regional cooperation, especially that of ASEAN, in addressing transnational problems that would require it to go beyond its traditional adherence to the norm of non-intervention.[1] This effort had its normative roots in the post–Cold War notion of collective (including humanitarian) intervention, although it was framed (prelocalized) in the regional context as "constructive intervention" and "flexible engagement." After a period of contestation, the first proposal led ASEAN to formalize intra-mural security dialogues, adopt a more inclusive posture toward external powers' role in regional order, and anchor a new security institution for the wider Asia-Pacific region. In contrast, the attempt to dilute the non-intervention norm based on the flexible engagement idea failed, producing only weak policy instruments.

## Common Security, 1990–1994

The doctrine of common security emerged in Europe during the Cold War. Its most authoritative statement was the 1982 report of the Independent Commission on Disarmament and Security Issues, chaired by the Swedish

---

1. I have used "non-intervention" and "non-interference" interchangeably, being conscious of the fact that ASEAN policymakers tended to use the latter more frequently during the period under investigation, although they implied no real distinction between the two terms.

prime minister Olof Palme.[2] The report argued, "states cannot achieve security at each other's expense" and security must be achieved "not against the adversary but with him."[3] Warning that unilateral security measures could aggravate the security dilemma, in which one state's defensive preparations may be construed as being offensive by its rivals,[4] it concluded that common security "must replace the present expedient of deterrence."[5]

The Conference on Security and Cooperation in Europe (CSCE), although not directly an offshoot of the common security idea, nonetheless represented the closest institutionalization of it.[6] As an institution, the CSCE—which later emerged into an organization—was noted for its rejection of adversarial or balance of power approaches to security and preference for an "inclusive" approach through reassurance strategies pursued through confidence-building measures.[7] But in a departure from one of the original principles of common security, the CSCE created a "linkage between arms negotiations and political events," which would have a significant bearing on its effectiveness.[8]

The CSCE and its instrumentalities, especially its Confidence-building measures (CBMs), acquired considerable global prominence as a major factor in bringing the Cold War to an end. As such they attracted the attention of policy communities in the Asia Pacific where Cold War tensions had persisted even as the War was nearing an end in Europe. The Soviet leader Mikhael Gorbadev, in 1986, as well as Joe Clark, Canada's secretary of state for external affairs, and Australian foreign minister Gareth Evans, both in 1990, advanced proposals for a multilateral security organization in the

2. Palme Commission, Common Security: The Report of the Independent Commission on Disarmament and Security Issues Under the Chairmanship of Olof Palme (New York: Simon & Schuster, 1982).

3. Palme Commission, *Common Security*, xiii.

4. The Commission established six principles of common security: (1) All nations have a legitimate right to security; (2) Military force is not a legitimate instrument for resolving disputes between nations; (3) Restraint is necessary in expression of national policy; (4) Security cannot be attained through military superiority; (5) Reduction and qualitative limitations of armaments are necessary for common security; and (6) "Linkages" between arms negotiations and political events should be avoided (Palme Commission, *Common Security*, 8–11).

5. Palme Commission, *Common Security*, xiii.

6. Common security was not formally a CSCE norm, although that is how it is widely perceived in Asian debates.

7. The CBM regime of the CSCE included the presence of observers at large military exercises, increased transparency, and information sharing. On the CSCE's CBM agenda, see Joachim Krause, *The OSCE and Cooperative Security in Europe: Lessons for Asia*, IDSS Monograph No. 6 (Singapore: Institute of Defence and Strategic Studies, 2003).

8. The CSCE successfully incorporated human rights issues into the regional confidence-building agenda, thereby setting norms that would regulate the internal as well as external political behavior of states. Philip Zelikow, "The New Concert of Europe," *Survival* 34, no. 2 (1992): 26.

Asia Pacific.[9] These proposals were not only influenced by the concept of common security, they also called for an institution closely modeled after the CSCE.[10]

In 1986 the Soviet leader Mikhail Gorbachev proposed a "Pacific Ocean conference along the Helsinki [CSCE] conference," to be attended by all countries "gravitating" toward the Pacific Ocean to discuss peace and security in the region.[11] The next such proposal came from the Canadian external affairs minister Joe Clark in 1990, envisaging a "Pacific adaptation" of the CSCE.[12] Australia's foreign minister Gareth Evans added to the momentum around the same time by finding it "not unreasonable to expect that new Europe-style patterns of cooperation between old adversaries will find their echo in this part of the world."[13] Asserting that "what Asia needs is a Europe-style CSCA [Conference on Security and Cooperation in Asia]," Evans envisaged "a future Asian security architecture involving a wholly new institutional process that might be capable of evolving, in Asia just as in Europe, as a framework for addressing and resolving security problems."[14]

9. Amitav Acharya, "The Asia-Pacific Region: Cockpit for Superpower Rivalry?" *The World Today* 43, nos. 8–9 (August-September 1997), 155–58; Joe Clark, "Canada and the Asia Pacific in the 1990s," speech delivered at the Victoria Chamber of Commerce, Canada, 17 July 1990; Joe Clark, speech delivered at the Foreign Correspondents' Club of Japan, Tokyo, 24 July 1990; Joe Clark, speech delivered at the Indonesia-Canada Business Council and the Canada Business Association, Jakarta, Indonesia, 26 July 1990; Stewart Henderson, "Canada and Asia Pacific Security: The North Pacific Cooperative Security Dialogue: Recent Trends," NPCSD Working Paper No. 1, York Center for International and Security Studies, York University, Canada, 1992; Gareth Evans, "ASEAN's Past Success a Prelude to the Future," reproduced in Australian Department of Foreign Affairs and Trade's *The Monthly Record*, July 1990, 429–32; and Gareth Evans and Bruce Grant, *Australia's Foreign Relations: In the World of the 1990s*, 2nd ed. (Carlton, Australia: Melbourne University Press, 1995). For a useful summary of some of the early proposals, see Trevor Findlay, *Asia-Pacific CSBMs: A Prospectus* (Canberra: Peace Research Centre, Australian National University, 1990).

10. There is considerable literature attesting to how the European common security norm affected security debates in Asia. See David B. Dewitt, "Common, Comprehensive and Cooperative Security," *Pacific Review* 7, no. 1: 1–15; Geoffrey Wiseman, *Common Security and Non-Provocative Defence: Alternative Approaches to the Security Dilemma* (Canberra: Peace Research Centre, Australian National University, 1989); Kevin Clements, "Common Security in the Asia-Pacific: Problems and Prospects," *Alternatives* 14, no. 1 (1989): 49–76; and Geoffrey Wiseman, "Common Security in the Asia-Pacific Region," *The Pacific Review* 5, no. 1 (1992): 42–59.

11. Ramesh Thakur and Carlyle Thayer, *The Soviet Union as an Asian Pacific Power: Implications of Gorbachev's 1986 Vladivostok Initiative* (Boulder: Westview Press, 1987).

12. Joe Clark, speech delivered at the Foreign Correspondents' Club of Japan, 1990; and speech delivered at the Indonesia-Canada Business Council and the Canada Business Association, 1990.

13. *International Herald Tribune*, 27 July 1990.

14. Cited in ibid. Evans was clearly inspired by the Palme Commission Report and by the Common Security idea. Author's interview with Geoffrey Wiseman, Evans's Private Secretary, New Orleans, 24 March 2002.

Although these proposals called for an Asia-Pacific institution and were not specifically directed at ASEAN, the Association, as the most successful Asian grouping, became an important site for debating them. In its initial reaction, ASEAN feared that these proposals could undermine its existing norms and practices. At stake were three key practices. First was its avoidance of military-security cooperation. This was due to fear of provoking its Cold War adversaries—Vietnam and China—who had in the past denounced ASEAN as a new front for the now-defunct U.S.-backed Southeast Asian Treaty Organization. ASEAN felt that attention to military confidence-building issues, which was a key part of the CSCE process, would be divisive and undermine economic and political cooperation.

Second came ASEAN's regionalist framework ZOPFAN. As discussed in chapter 4, ZOPFAN had called on major powers to refrain from interfering in the internal affairs of ASEAN members and in regional affairs. ZOPFAN was thus to some extent an "exclusionary" framework. A common security institution, in contrast, would bring together ASEAN and the so-called outside powers within a single security framework, allowing them a legitimate role in regional security. ZOPFAN had remained an official goal of ASEAN, although it divided the Association's members. For example, Singapore and Thailand favored closer defense links with the United States whereas Malaysia and Indonesia preferred a more non-aligned posture.[15]

Third at stake was ASEAN's process diplomacy, including organizational minimalism and a preference for informal non-legalistic approaches to cooperation.[16] Challenging this tradition were common security mechanisms, especially the CBM and arms control regime in the Helsinki and Vienna Documents of the CSCE, which imposed formal, reciprocal, and binding obligations, and allowed intrusive verification.[17]

ASEAN's discomfort with the Soviet, Canadian, and Australian proposals was aggravated by the fact that they came from 'outsider proponents.' Accepting them could lead ASEAN to "lose its identity."[18] Senior ASEAN

15. For details, see Amitav Acharya, Constructing a Security Community in Southeast Asia: ASEAN and the Problem of Regional Order (London: Routledge, 2001).

16. Amitav Acharya, "Ideas, Identity, and Institution-Building: From the 'ASEAN Way' to the 'Asia Pacific Way'," *Pacific Review* 10, no. 3 (1997): 319–49.

17. See David Dewitt, "Confidence- and Security- Building Measures in the Third World: Is There a Role?" *International Journal* 52 (Summer 1987): 509–35; Masahiko Asada, "Confidence-Building Measures in East Asia: A Japanese Perspective," *Asian Survey* 28, no.5 (May 1988): 489–508; Trevor Findlay, "Confidence-Building Measures for the Asia-Pacific: The Relevance of the European Experience," in *Building Confidence, Resolving Conflicts*, ed. Muthiah Alagappa (Kuala Lumpur: Institute of Strategic and International Studies, 1988), 55–74.

18. Excerpts from Lee Kuan Yew's interview with *The Australian*, published in the *Straits Times*, 16 September 1988. See also Michael Vatikiotis, "Yankee Please Stay," *Far Eastern Economic Review*, 13 December 1990, 32.

figures also argued that the common security norm and the CSCE model were uniquely suited to "European" conditions. Capturing this sentiment, Ali Alatas, Indonesia'a foreign minister, argued, "You cannot just take European institutions and plant them in Asia because the two situations are totally different."[19] Alatas held that "[u]nlike in the European situation, there has been no commonly perceived, single security threat in the Asia-Pacific region, but rather a multiplicity of security concerns." To this, he added the "wide diversity of cultures, socio-political systems and levels of economic development" among regional countries and their consequent lack of "a distinct sense of a community" as obstacles to a CSCE-type structure in the Asia Pacific.[20]

It was "sensitivity" to such ASEAN's reaction that led Evans to modify his proposal.[21] He dropped the CSCE analogy and the wholesale importation of its model.[22] Evans would now recognize ASEAN's "past success as a prelude to the future," thereby acknowledging the relevance of existing norms and institutions in Asia.[23] In fact ASEAN's position and pressure was

19. Author's interview with Ali Alatas, Kuala Lumpur, Malaysia, 4 June 2002.

20. Ali Alatas, "The Emerging Security Architecture in East Asia and the Pacific—An ASEAN Perspective," lecture delivered at the National University of Singapore Society, 28 October 1992. It should be noted that ASEAN members were not alone in holding such views. Yukio Satoh, a senior Japanese foreign ministry official, closely involved in the formative stages of regional security dialogues, provided one of the most forceful arguments as to why European concepts and processes would not fit the conditions of the Asia Pacific region by offering four reasons. (1) Asia lacked the strict bipolarity of Europe because of the presence and role of China and because many Asian states adopted non-aligned foreign policy postures; (2) military conditions in both regions are different: Asian threat perceptions were more diverse and the structure of Asia's alliances were mostly bilateral. U.S. and Soviet force postures in the region were more asymmetric, with the forward deployment strategy of the U.S. reliance on naval forces whereas the Soviet defense strategy was more land-based; (3) Asia had a larger number of unresolved conflicts and disputes; and (4) during the Cold War, Europe was preoccupied with nuclear war while Asia's main concern was economic development. Thus regional cooperation in Asia was focused on economic rather than political or security concerns. Yukio Satoh, "The Japanese Role," in *Asian-Pacific Security After the Cold War*, ed. T.B. Millar and James Walter (Canberra, Australia: Allen & Unwin, 1993), 5. Author's interview with Yukio Satoh, Singapore, 1 June 2002.

21. Author's interview with Geoffrey Wiseman, Evans's Private Secretary, 24 March 2002.

22. The CSCE framework did, however, contribute several ideas, which have since served to define the terms of the security debate in the Asia Pacific region. These include (a) the idea of a macro-regional framework covering the Asia Pacific as a whole, as opposed to the narrower sub-regionalism represented by ASEAN; (b) the need for a comprehensive notion of regional security as opposed to focusing on military threats and issues alone; (c) the principle of "inclusiveness" in regional security consultations, as opposed to like-mindedness, deterrence, and balance of power; (d) the idea that Asia-Pacific security cooperation should be organized on a multilateral basis; (e) the idea that security cooperation should evolve through institutionalized bargaining as opposed to ad hoc dialogue within existing consultative channels.

23. The *Monthly Record*, Canberra, Department of Foreign Affairs and Trade, Australia, July 1990, 430, cited in David Capie and Paul Evans, *The Asia Pacific Security Lexicon* (Singapore: ISEAS, 2002).

partly responsible for the revision of the concept and its institutional blue-print by Australia and Canada. In the early 1990s, the CSCA morphed into the idea of regional security dialogues and the softer institutional design that ASEAN demanded was reflected in the growing salience of the term "cooperative security," which despite being coined and developed by Canada and Australia, conformed to ASEAN's expectations and demands.

This reframing of common security into cooperative security occurred through exchanges and dialogues hosted by a regional think-tank network—the ASEAN Institutes of Strategic and International Studies (ASEAN-ISIS).[24] Cooperative security retained two key elements of the original common security idea: the principle of "inclusiveness" and the rejection of deterrence-based security systems, but rejected the legalistic measures of security cooperation found in the CSCE process.

Although formally established in 1988, ASEAN-ISIS had been in existence as an informal network for over a decade, organizing "second track" meetings that brought together Asian and Western scholars and policymakers interested in multilateral security.[25] A 1991 ASEAN-ISIS document, "A Time for Initiative," urged dialogues and measures that would result in a multilateral security institution.[26] ASEAN-ISIS thus made proposals from external proponents appear as a local initiative.

Its push for cooperative security was due to a realization that the end of the Cold War and the settlement of the Cambodia conflict, which had hitherto preoccupied ASEAN and contributed to its success, required ASEAN

24. See Dewitt, "Common, Comprehensive and Cooperative Security" for a good account of this reframing.

25. The ASEAN-ISIS brought together think tanks from Indonesia, Malaysia, Singapore, the Philippines, and Thailand with the goal to "encourage cooperation and coordination of activities among policy-oriented ASEAN scholars and analysts, and to promote policy-oriented studies of, and exchanges of information and viewpoints on, various strategic and international issues affecting Southeast Asia and ASEAN's peace, security and well-being" (ASEAN-ISIS, "A Time for Initiative," *ASEAN-ISIS Monitor* 1 (1991): 1.

26. The landmark report issued in June 1991 articulated ideas already mooted and discussed in ASEAN-ISIS circles for some months. The report proposed that the annual meetings of ASEAN foreign ministers with their dialogue partners should be followed by a Conference on Stability and Peace in the Asia Pacific. The meeting, to be held at "a suitable retreat . . . for the constructive discussion of Asia Pacific stability and peace" would comprise such states as China, Russia, North Korea, and Vietnam on a regular basis, and other governments could be invited from time to time depending on the nature of the issues on the conference agenda. See "A Time for Initiative," *ASEAN-ISIS Monitor*, 2–3. See also Lau Teik Soon, "Towards a Regional Security Conference: Role of the Non-Government Organizations," National University of Singapore Department of Political Science Working Paper 1, 1991; ASEAN-ISIS, "Confidence Building Measures in Southeast Asia," *Memorandum*, no. 5, December 1993; and, Malaysian minister of defense Datuk Seri Mohammed Najib Tun Razak, "Regional Security: Towards Cooperative Security and Regional Stability," speech delivered at the Chief of the General Staff Conference, Darwin, Australia, 9 April 1992.

to rethink its focus.[27] Helping to create a cooperative security institution promised a new and enhanced role for ASEAN in the Asia-Pacific region.[28] Underlying this aspiration was a measure of self-confidence that ASEAN represented a proven model of regional security cooperation. Alatas would later argue: "There was a feeling . . . that we had something to offer, not in terms of European-style structures, but in terms of a forum . . . proposals for security cooperation in Asia by Russia, Canada, and Australia were seen by us as outsiders, with good intentions, telling us what to do. So we told them: Why don't you learn from what we have achieved, how we did it."[29]

An equally important factor behind ASEAN's more receptive attitude toward cooperative security was its recognition of some important common ground between this norm and the existing ASEAN principles and processes. The rejection of deterrence fitted well into ASEAN's existing policy of not organizing itself into a regional collective defense system. Moreover, the idea that security should be pursued multilaterally resonated well with Indonesia's prior effort to develop a shared understanding of security in ASEAN through a doctrine of regional resilience.[30] Above all, it was consistent with ASEAN's efforts to develop a proto-multilateralism, featuring dialogue partnerships with several external powers.

Malaysia's defense minister Najib Tun Razak signaled ASEAN's more receptive attitude toward the common security norm. Speaking on the subject of Asia-Pacific security at a conference in Darwin, Australia in April 1992, he invoked the principles of common security enunciated by the Palme Commission. Common security, according to Razak, involved the legitimate rights of all nations to security, the inadmissibility of military force as a problem-solving instrument, the need for restraint in the pursuit of national interests, and recognition of the futility of trying to achieve security through military superiority. Razak argued, "Although the Palme Commission's major preoccupation was with nuclear confrontation, I am of the

27. Author's interview with Jusuf Wanandi, New Orleans, 4 June 2002. Wanandi, chairman of the Supervisory Board of the Centre for Strategic and International Studies, was a founding leader of ASEAN-ISIS.

28. Yang Razali Kassim, "Minister: ASEAN will always have driver's seat in forum," *Business Times*, 25 July 1994.

29. Author's interview with Ali Alatas, Kuala Lumpur, 4 June 2002.

30. Dewitt, "Common, Comprehensive and Cooperative Security." In the 1970s, Indonesia organized a series of seminars to disseminate the concept of national and regional "resilience," which created the basis for a multilateral security approach. Author's interview with Kwa Chong Guan, Singapore, 21 May 2003. Kwa is Council Member of the Singapore Institute of International Affairs.

opinion that these principles are equally valid in the non-nuclear context."[31] In defining the elements of a new approach to security in Asia Pacific, he interestingly used the notion of cooperative security: "The end of the Cold War has certainly provided us with a golden opportunity to find new approach to security. . . . This golden opportunity must be seized by all of us. We must be guided by the notion of cooperative security. 'One man's security should lead to another's assurance,' should be our motto."[32]

With the help of ASEAN-ISIS, ASEAN began to reconstruct the norm of common security so that its institutional expression conformed to the ASEAN Way and acknowledged ASEAN as the main platform for developing a wider Asia-Pacific regional security institution.[33] At its Singapore summit in January 1992, ASEAN agreed to "use established fora to promote external security dialogues on enhancing security as well as intra-ASEAN dialogues on ASEAN security cooperation."[34] As a follow-up, ASEAN-ISIS meetings contributed to an official Japanese initiative for a new regional security institution based on the ASEAN model. In 1993, Japanese foreign minister Taro Nakayama proposed that an existing ASEAN mechanism— the ASEAN Post-Ministerial Conferences (PMC)—be turned into the foundation of a new security organization for the Asia Pacific.[35] The resulting institution, the ASEAN Regional Forum (a proposal to call it Asian Regional Forum was rejected by ASEAN), came into life composed of the

31. Razak, "Regional Security."

32. Razak, "Regional Security."

33. Michael Leifer, "New Framework for Security," the *Straits Times*, 26 July 1994; Michael Leifer, *The ASEAN Regional Forum*, Adelphi Paper no. 302 (London: International Institute for strategic Studies, 1996), 55; Michele Cooper, "ASEAN Seizes Role in Post-Cold War Diplomacy," *Agence France Presse*, 28 July 1994; Acharya, *Constructing a Security Community in Southeast Asia*, 171–72; Kassim, "Minister: ASEAN Will Always Have Driver's Seat in Forum"; Desmond Ball, "A Critical Review of Multilateral Security Cooperation in the Asia-Pacific Region," paper presented at the inaugural conference of the Asia-Pacific Security Forum on The Impetus of Change in the Asia-Pacific Security Environment, 1–3 September 1997, Taipei, Taiwan, 16–17.

34. Association of Southeast Asian Nations, Singapore Declaration, ASEAN Heads of Government Meeting, 27–28 January, 1992, available at http://www.aseansec.org/1396.htm, 2.

35. The Japanese foreign minister's proposal was derived from regional security dialogues already organized by ASEAN-ISIS. Yukio Satoh, head of the policy planning bureau of the Japanese Foreign Ministry, attended a security seminar organized by the ASEAN-ISIS in Manila in 1992, and upon returning to Tokyo, "rewrote" the draft of Foreign Minister Taro Nakayama's speech to incorporate the idea of using the PMC, which was ASEAN's existing framework of dialogue with non-member countries, into a regional security forum for the Asia Pacific. Satoh acknowledges that the Japanese minister's proposal incorporated many ideas borrowed from Track-II debates in ASEAN. Author's interview with Yukio Satoh, Singapore, 1 June 2002.

ASEAN members as well as China, Japan, Russia, the United States, Australia, Canada, and South Korea, with India and others joining later.[36]

As the first Asia-Pacific institution dedicated to security issues, the ARF represents a significant expansion of ASEAN's security agenda. It is the most inclusive regional institution, whose members include all the major powers (including the European Union) of the contemporary international system. Its creation marked a shift from ASEAN's ZOPFAN framework.[37] At the same time, it maintained continuity with two other principles of ASEAN: its rejection of defense multilateralism and the doctrine of non-intervention. In July 1993 Winston Lord, the U.S. Assistant Secretary of State for East Asian and Pacific Affairs, had presaged the ARF's mission by claiming that the aim of multilateral regional security consultations would be:

> to try to get all the significant countries together to talk to each other directly, especially those who may harbor worries or apprehensions about their neighbors or the other countries in the region. . . . So it is not a bloc forming against the common threat. Its potential antagonists talking to each other trying to clear up any misperceptions, give greater transparency . . . so that you have a more stable region . . . one where people have some sense of predictability.[38]

The point was reinforced by Malaysia's then foreign minister Abdullah Badawi:

> the concept of the ARF requires the development of friendship rather than the identification of enemies. The nature of security problems in the Asia Pacific is such that they do not lend themselves amenable for management through the old method of deterrence by countervailing force.[39]

At its first meeting in Bangkok in 1994, the ARF endorsed ASEAN's Treaty of Amity and Cooperation, stressing non-interference, "as a code of conduct governing relations between states and a unique diplomatic instrument for regional confidence-building, preventive diplomacy and political and security cooperation."[40] As such, ASEAN's basic norm matrix (with

---

36. Acharya, *Constructing a Security Community in Southeast Asia.*
37. Leifer, *The ASEAN Regional Forum.*
38. Interview in the *Straits Times*, 30 July 1993.
39. The *Straits Times*, 23 July 1994.
40. Chairman's statement at the First Meeting of the ASEAN Regional Forum (ARF), Bangkok, 25 July 1994.

non-intervention at the top) remained unchanged, whereas a cooperative security approach displaced the ZOPFAN idea.

ASEAN was to occupy "the driver's seat" and "dominate and set the pace" of the ARF.[41] Its central role in the ARF is evident in the fact that the ARF's annual Foreign Ministers' meetings are held in ASEAN member countries only. The ARF's policy instruments have been characterized as "evolutionary developments from extant regional structures rather than the importation of Western modalities or the creation of new structures."[42] Its institutional structure consists primarily of its annual Foreign Ministers' conclave, preceded by a Senior Officials Meeting (ARF-SOM). In between these meetings, the only other inter-governmental meetings are those of the inter-sessional groups, which were instituted following a decision at the 1995 ARF meeting. There is no ARF secretariat or secretary-general. Matters pertaining to the ARF are handled by the annually rotating chair of the ASEAN Standing Committee, although the ASEAN secretariat in Jakarta developed a small bureaucratic apparatus for dealing with ARF-related security issues. The ARF is likened to a dialogue *forum*, rather than a multilateral *institution*. As Singapore's defense minister stated: "The ARF is not a multilateral security mechanism but a forum where Asia-Pacific countries can talk with one another so as to better understand each other's security concerns."[43]

A Concept Paper for the ARF drafted in 1995 envisaged three stages of security cooperation: confidence-building, preventive diplomacy, and "elaboration of approaches to conflicts"—modified from the notion of "conflict-resolution" that was deemed to be too "Western" and intrusive by China.[44] Unlike the OSCE's intrusive and constraining CBMs backed by an inspection regime, the ARF's CBM agenda remains "ASEAN-like" in being non-intrusive and non-legalistic, providing only for voluntary compliance. Hence, the ARF has not yet made the transition to a preventive diplomacy role, mainly because concerns among leading members, especially China, that such a role would violate the principle of non-intervention.

The creation of the ARF *narrowed* the scope of the norm of common security, dropping its more intrusive elements, as well as the CSCE's human security agenda, at the same time *universalizing* the ASEAN process as it included all the major powers of the world. The resulting institutional

41. Kassim, "Minister."

42. Ball, "A Critical Review of Multilateral Security Cooperation in the Asia-Pacific Region," 16–17.

43. Cited in *Jane's Defense Weekly*, 19 February 1994, 52.

44. ASEAN, *The ASEAN Regional Forum: A Concept Paper*, Annex A and B (Jakarta: ASEAN Secretariat, 1995), 8–11.

outcome was twofold: new tasks, such as security cooperation, for an existing regional institution (ASEAN) that displaced a long-standing norm (ZOPFAN), and the creation of a new institution (the ARF), closely modeled after ASEAN. For the first time in its history, the Asia-Pacific region acquired a permanent regional security institution. China's and U.S. participation in the ARF also indicated the diffusion of the cooperative security norm. Initially, neither power was supportive of multilateral security. China saw in it the danger that its neighbors could "gang up" against its territorial claims in the region. But its attitude changed in the mid-1990s. To quote a Chinese analyst, China was "learning a new form of cooperation, not across a line [in an] adversarial style, but [in a] cooperative style." This, he added, would change Chinese strategic behavior in the long term. Chinese policymakers consistently stressed cooperative security as a more preferable approach to regional order than balance of power approaches.[45]

During initial debates about cooperative security, Richard Solomon, Assistant Secretary of State for East Asian and Pacific Affairs in the Bush Sr. administration, argued that the region's problems could not be solved "by working through a large, unwieldy, and ill-defined region-wide collective security forum."[46] The Bush administration feared that an Asian multilateral institution would undermine America's bilateral security alliances in the region.[47] However, the U.S. position changed as ASEAN begun to localize the common security idea. Secretary of State James Baker conceded that

45. This greater acceptance by Chinese officials and analysts of the ARF was indicated to me during a series of field trips and personal interviews conducted during the 1997–2000 period. The interviews were with staff of the Ministry of Foreign Affairs, Beijing; China Institute of International Studies; China Institute of Contemporary International Relations; China Centre for International Studies; Institute of Asia Pacific Studies; Chinese Academy of Social Sciences; Institute for Strategic Studies; National Defense University; and the People's Liberation Army. Johnston suggests that the ARF and multilateral dialogues have reduced the probability of Chinese use of force in the South China Sea (Alastair I. Johnston, "Is China a Status Quo Power?" *International Security* 27, no. 4 [2003]: 5–56).

46. Richard Solomon, "US Relations with East Asia and the Pacific: A New Era," statement given by the Assistant Secretary of State for East Asian and Pacific Affairs, 17 May 1991, reproduced in *US Department of State Dispatch*, vol. 2, no. 21, 27 May 1991, available at http://findarticles.com/p/articles/mi_m1584/is_n21_v2/ai_11409804/pg_2.

47. Richard Solomon, "Asian Security in the 1990s: Integration in Economics, Diversity in Defense," address at the University of California San Diego, 30 October 1990, reproduced in *US Department of State Dispatch*, vol. 1, no. 10, 5 November 1990, available at http://findarticles.com/p/articles/mi_m1584/is_n10_v1/ai_9290222; James Lilley, assistant secretary of defense in the Bush administration in "No need for East Asian Security Grouping: Lilley," *Central News Agency*, 1 March 1993; and Robert Zoellick, U.S. Under Secretary of State for Economic and Agricultural Affairs, "US Engagement with Asia," Statement at the Opening of the ASEAN 6+7 Post-Ministerial Conference, Kuala Lumpur, 22 July 1991, reprinted in *United States Foreign Policy: Current Documents 1991* (Washington, DC: Department of State, 1994), 670.

while America's bilateral ties would remain the most important element of its security strategy in the region, "multilateral actions may . . . supplement these bilateral ties."[48] Bill Clinton, who made Japan and Korea his first overseas destination as president, stated in Korea in July 1993 that "new regional dialogues on the full range of our *common security* challenges" would be one of the priorities for his administration's security strategy for the Asia-Pacific region.[49] Six years later, Ralph Boyce, deputy assistant secretary of state for East Asian and Pacific affairs, defended the cooperative security institution, observing that "nay-sayers expected ASEAN Regional Forum to be short-lived, but it has confounded these pessimists by not only surviving, but also thriving."[50] While the ARF's subsequent record has been somewhat disappointing, it did represent the institutionalization of the cooperative security norm to a degree not anticipated by the early Chinese and U.S. critics of the norm.

## Collective Intervention, 1997–1999

While the notion of common security was a key multilateral concept for ASEAN in the early 1990s, the later part of the decade was dominated by the notion of collective intervention. The establishment of the ARF in 1994 boosted ASEAN's international prestige. But the glory was short-lived. ASEAN suffered a major setback in the wake of the 1997 Asian economic crisis, which revealed the vulnerability of ASEAN to global economic trends. Its failure to respond to the crisis with a united front drew considerable criticism. A key fallout was proposals for reforming ASEAN to make it more responsive to transnational challenges. The emerging post-Westphalian concepts of collective intervention, including the norm of humanitarian intervention, underpinned the most prominent of these proposals, including the proposal for "flexible engagement."[51]

48. U.S. secretary of state James A. Baker, "The US and Japan: Global Partners in a Pacific Community," speech delivered in Tokyo, 11 November 1991.

49. Bill Clinton, "Fundamentals of Security for a New Pacific Community," speech delivered to the National Assembly of the Republic of Korea, reproduced in the U.S. Department of State *Dispatch* 4, no. 29 (10 July 1993): 1–2 (emphasis added).

50. Ralph Boyce, "Moving from Confidence-Building to Preventive Diplomacy: The Possibilities," paper presented at the Thirteenth Asia-Pacific Roundtable, Kuala Lumpur, Malaysia, 30 May–2 June 1999, 1.

51. ASEAN members understood collective intervention broadly to include both humanitarian intervention and collective action against a variety of transnational challenges such as the transboundary effects of state failure, and economic crisis. Author's interview with Surin Pitsuwan, former Thai foreign minister, Singapore, 2 and 7 September 2001. Author's interview with Pitsuwan, Bangkok, 10 May 2002.

Two developments influenced collective intervention as a global normative idea. The first was the proliferation of "failed states," exemplified by
the collapse of political authority in Somalia, Ethiopia, Rwanda, Burundi,
Liberia, and Zaire. The large-scale humanitarian disasters suffered by
these states led to interventions by the UN and other international bodies,
often to the dislike of some political factions within these states. However,
as these interventions were undertaken in countries left with little or no
functional central authority, the question of sovereignty was not seriously
contested. A more controversial challenge to sovereignty and non-intervention
was the increased focus on human rights and democracy in the foreign policy
agenda of the Western nations. Gross violations of human rights, previously
ignored under the pretext of state sovereignty, were now regarded as a
legitimate reason for foreign concern and intervention. As the UN Secretary-
General Javier Perez de Cuellar stated in 1991, "we are clearly witnessing
what is probably an irresistible shift in public attitudes towards the belief
that the defence of the oppressed in the name of morality should prevail
over frontiers and legal documents."[52] He also argued that the Universal
Declaration of Human Rights implicitly called into question the inviolable
notion of sovereignty. Therefore a balance had to be established between
the rights of states and the rights of the individual as confirmed by the
Declaration.

The U.S.-led intervention to provide safe havens to Kurds in Northern
Iraq was the first human rights-related armed intervention in the post–Cold
War era. In the wake of this intervention, French foreign minister Roland
Dumas argued that the international community had a right to intervene
in humanitarian cases, and that national borders may be violated to allevi-
ate human suffering caused by repression, civil disorder, interstate conflict,
or natural disasters.[53] A *New York Times* editorial expressed this view
even more succinctly: "In just a few years the idea has been established
that countries which fail to care decently for their citizens dilute their
claim to sovereignty and forfeit invulnerability to outside political-military
intervention."[54]

52. Cited in Richard N. Gardner, "International Law and the Use of Force," in *Post-Gulf
War Challenges to the UN Collective Security System: Three Views on the Issue of Humanitar-
ian Intervention*, ed. David J. Scheffer, R.N. Gardner, and G.B. Helman (Washington, DC:
United States Institute of Peace, 1992), 21.

53. Thomas G. Weiss and Kurt M. Campbell, "Military Humanitarianism," *Survival* 33,
no. 5 (1991): 452.

54. Reproduced as "Humane Intervention," *International Herald Tribune*, 27 November
1992.

Despite its global prominence, collective intervention was very contro-versial in Asian—including ASEAN—think tanks and policymaking circles. For ASEAN governments, any policy framework that smacked of interven-tion in the internal affairs of states had attracted no insider advocacy, only suspicion and rejection. For example, Malaysia's foreign minister Syed Hamid Albar found the notion of humanitarian intervention "disquieting."[55] He urged the region "to be wary all the time of new concepts and new phi-losophies that will compromise sovereignty in the name of humanitarian intervention."[56] Collective (including humanitarian) intervention's clash with existing ASEAN's policy frameworks was most evident in the case of the Burmese military regime. Western governments—the United States, Canada, Australia, and the European Union—pushed for sanctions against Burma, with the EU threatening to block economic cooperation with ASEAN if it offered membership to Burma. Southeast Asian NGOs such as Forum Asia and Alternative ASEAN, backed by Western donor agencies, demanded a more interventionist posture toward Burma. In contrast, ASEAN pursued a policy of "constructive engagement" toward the regime, display-ing greater deference to its non-intervention norm than to the promotion of human rights and democracy.[57] In 1997, ASEAN granted Burma full membership.

Furthermore, the collective intervention norm did not receive backing from the local epistemic community. Here, criticisms of the doctrine were based on four key uncertainties:

1. whether intervention should be multilateral or unilateral (a question relevant to assessing the 1978 Vietnamese invasion of Cambodia);
2. whether intervention should be carried out strictly with the consent of the government of the country facing a crisis (what if there is no func-tioning government capable of controlling the target country, as in the case of Somalia or Ethiopia?);
3. whether intervention should be strictly limited to alleviating human misery or go further in seeking to reestablish the political system of a failed state (as the United States found out in Somalia, the two were

55. Datuk Seri Syed Hamid Bin Syed Jaafar Albar, "The Malaysian Human Rights Commission—Aims and Objectives," speech delivered at the Bar Council Auditorium, Kuala Lumpur, Malaysia, 28 October 1999.

56. "Malaysia Opposes UN Probe of East Timor Atrocities," *Agence France Presse*, 7 October 1999.

57. The policy of constructive engagement called for avoiding public criticism or shaming of the Burmese regime, rejection of economic or military sanctions, and quiet dialogue with the regime to induce gradual political change in Burma. In reality, ASEAN never held any talks with the Burmese regime on political change.

quite different propositions and confusing or combining them could
have disastrous consequences);
4. whether intervention should be undertaken only if a domestic humanitarian crisis affects international peace and security. Prevailing norms
would not justify intervention unless human sufferings were deemed
to be a major threat to international peace and security.

The only initial support for a diluted form of regional intervention came
from Anwar Ibrahim, then deputy prime minister of Malaysia. In July 1997,
after the collapse of Cambodia's elected coalition government (co-Prime
Minister Hun Sen seized power at the expense of fellow co-Prime Minister
Norodom Ranarridh), Anwar published a commentary in *Newsweek*,
blaming the ineffectiveness of the Cambodian peace-building process on
ASEAN's "non-involvement," which in turn owed to its non-intervention
doctrine.[58] Indeed, ASEAN, after having played an instrumental role in
bringing peace to Cambodia, had done little to consolidate it.

Anwar therefore proposed various political and economic measures, including direct assistance to firm up electoral processes, an increased commitment to legal and administrative reforms, the development of human
capital, and the general strengthening of civil society and the rule of law.[59]
The idea of constructive intervention shared similarities with concepts of
peace-building, humanitarian assistance, and preventive humanitarian action, which topped the collective intervention agenda of the UN and other
regional organizations after the Cold War. However, this was the first time
that a senior ASEAN leader had publicly advocated such a role for the Association. Anwar's proposal raised a major debate within ASEAN over the
possibility of reconciling "constructive intervention" with its doctrine of
non-intervention. The constructive intervention idea was the first major
departure from ASEAN's solidly pro-sovereignty approach toward regional
issues.

Anwar was thus a regional norm entrepreneur who sought out ideas he
thought were relevant to the contemporary challenges facing his region and
modified them to suit local conditions and context. Unsurprisingly, his idea
provoked opposition from other ASEAN members. Condemning the idea,
Indonesian foreign minister Ali Alatas stated that constructive intervention

58. Anwar Ibrahim, "Crisis Prevention," *Newsweek International* 21 (July 1997), 13.
59. Author's interview with Adnan Abdul Rahman, policy adviser to Anwar Ibrahim,
Bangkok, 23 August 1997.

was "not an ASEAN policy. ASEAN continues to pursue the same policy—constructive engagement."[60]

Anwar's ouster from political office in September 1998 put paid to any hopes for ASEAN adopting his approach to state sovereignty.[61] But his cause was taken up by another reform-minded ASEAN leader, Thailand's foreign minister Surin Pitsuwan, who shared Anwar's motivations and articulated the same ideas with even more vigor. Surin was a key member of the new Thai government that took office in November 1997 in the wake of the catastrophic devaluation of the Thai currency four months earlier, causing an immediate contagion effect throughout the region. ASEAN's non-intervention doctrine was blamed for its incapacity to respond effectively to the crisis, especially the failure to alert Thailand to its economic woes. Surin emerged as the strongest critic of the doctrine. "It is time," he said, "that ASEAN's cherished principle of non-intervention be modified to allow it to play a constructive role in preventing or resolving domestic issues with regional implications." He added that "when a matter of domestic concern poses a threat to regional stability, a dose of peer pressure or friendly advice at the right time can be helpful."[62] Instead of a strict adherence to non-intervention as an ASEAN norm, Surin proposed the idea of "flexible engagement," which implied a more flexible interpretation of the certain fundamental approaches undertaken by the Association. Surin argued that ASEAN members needed more "openness" in dealing with one another,[63] meaning that ASEAN members should not refrain from commenting on each other's domestic policies when such policies have regional implications. "Problems in the ASEAN family have become quite complicated that one member of the family can implicate others with its internal problems."[64] According to an official Thai document:

> All the ASEAN members have the responsibility of upholding the principle of non-interference in the domestic affairs of one another. But this commitment cannot and should not be absolute. It must be subjected to reality tests and accordingly it must be flexible. The reality is that, as the region becomes more

60. "Indonesia Says No to 'Constructive Intervention'," *Kyodo News International*, 4 August 1997.

61. Roger Mitton, "ASEAN Loses Critic Anwar," *Asiaweek*, 18 September 1998, available at http://www.asiaweek.com/asiaweek/98/0918/nat6.html.

62. "Surin Pushes 'Peer Pressure'," the *Bangkok Post*, 13 June 1998.

63. The Department of Foreign Affairs in the Philippines defined flexible engagement in suitably vague terms as having "greater flexibility in expressing views and if possible, giving advice to each other on policies pursued by each country that could affect ASEAN as a whole." "Thailand Urges Philippines Support on Flexible Engagement," *Deutsche Presse-Agentur*, 18 July 1998.

64. Author's interview with Surin Pitsuwan, Bangkok, 30 January 2001.

inter-dependent, the dividing line between domestic affairs on the one hand and external or trans-national issues on the other is less clear. Many "domestic" affairs have obvious external or trans-national dimensions, adversely affecting neighbors, the region and the region's relations with others. In such cases, the affected countries should be able to express their opinions and concerns in an open, frank and constructive manner, which is not, and should not be, considered "interference" in fellow-members' domestic affairs.[65]

Although ostensibly geared toward an economic crisis, Surin's real aim was to promote greater political openness and transparency in ASEAN, both at domestic and regional levels. Among the ideational underpinnings of flexible engagement were emerging post-Westphalian concepts of collective action, including the norm of collective intervention and the advocacy of human rights, human security and democratization by the West.[66] Thanks to opposition from fellow ASEAN members, Anwar's proposal had never been officially tabled. Against this backdrop, Surin, who was clearly influenced by Anwar's idea,[67] felt the need to reframe and "prune" the idea further to make it more palatable to his ASEAN colleagues. His flexible engagement idea made no mention of coercive interference or sanction-based regional interactions. Rather, it was needed to fix the deficiencies and problems exposed by the financial crisis and create the basis for more effective regional action.[68] Surin stressed the potential utility of flexible engagement in making ASEAN more transparent and interdependent, which might make it more effective in addressing a range of current transnational issues, including financial crises as well as challenges related to "drugs, environment, migrants."[69]

65. Ministry of Foreign Affairs, Thailand. "Thailand's Non-Paper on the Flexible Engagement Approach," Press Release no. 743/254127, 27 July 1998, available at http://www.thaiembdc.org/pressctr/pr/pr743.htm.

66. Several discussions by the author with Surin Pitsuwan attest to this influence. Surin became a member of the Commission on Human Security and an adviser to the International Commission on State Sovereignty and Humanitarian Intervention, which was tasked to improve the legitimacy and effectiveness of humanitarian intervention. Author's interview with Surin Pitsuwan, Singapore, 27 September 2001. Author's interview with Surin Pitsuwan, Bangkok, 10 May 2002.

67. When Surin first presented his ideas, he used the term constructive intervention. But Thai Foreign Ministry officials felt this sounded "too radical" and coined the less intrusive term "flexible engagement." Capie and Evans, *The Asia-Pacific Security Lexicon.*

68. Domingo Siazon Jr., "Winning the Challenges of the 21st Century," speech delivered to the Thirty-First ASEAN Ministerial Meeting, Manila, Philippines, 24 July 1998, available at http://www.aseansec.org/3923.htm.

69. *Kyodo News Service*, "Thailand Calls for 'Flexible Engagement' in ASEAN," 26 June 1998. Surin Pitsuwan, opening statement by the Minister of Foreign Affairs of Thailand, at the Thirty-First ASEAN Ministerial Meeting, Manila, 24 July 1998.

Three key factors motivated Surin's proposal of flexible engagement.[70] First, at a time of severe economic crisis, Surin believed that accepting and espousing a more favorable attitude toward international human rights norms would help support his country's pleas for international assistance.[71] Moreover, Thailand was embroiled in a bitter fight with Burma—the main target of the Thai flexible engagement policy. Fighting between Burmese troops and its ethnic rebels led to a flood of refugees across the Thai border and ethnic groups supported by Burma had flooded Thailand with illegal drugs, which Bangkok saw as a threat to its national security. Flexible engagement was thus born out of Thai "frustration" with the Burma situation, and as a way of putting regional pressure on Burma to stem the flow of refugees and drugs.[72] "The promotion of human rights and the protection of our national interests are interlinked," said Thai deputy foreign minister Sukhumbhand Paribatra.[73]

Second, Surin's new Thai government was keen to prove its democratic credentials to the international community by distancing itself from ASEAN's non-interference-based support for Burma's repressive regime, and its lack of transparency and accountability.[74] In this respect, the legitimation of Thailand's new democratic polity was at stake. Surin would thus explain the flexible engagement policy as being rooted in "our commitment to freedom and democracy."[75] Thailand, he pointed out, "respects an open society, democracy and human rights." Hence "[o]ur membership in ASEAN and ASEAN's principle of non-interference should not hamper us from expressing our views on what we respect."[76]

Third, Surin believed that the new norm would help promote the efficiency, relevance, and prestige of ASEAN at a time of growing regional crisis: "ASEAN needed to put its house in order. It had lost its appeal and attraction, and its bargaining power waned as it lost its natural leader, Indonesia."[77] ASEAN's interests were also at stake as the European Union had refused to negotiate a new economic treaty with the Association over

70. Author's interviews with Pitsuwan, Bangkok, 30 January 2001, 10 May 2002, and 13 May 2002.

71. Author's interviews with Pitsuwan, Bangkok, 30 January 2001 and 13 May 2002.

72. "Surin Starts to Move the Mountain," *FT Asia Intelligence Wire*, 22 July 1998.

73. Cited in Roger Mitton, "ASEAN's Iconoclasts: Thailand Is Shaking up the Status Quo in Foreign Relations," *Asiaweek*, 14 August 1998.

74. Pitsuwan, opening statement delivered at the Thirty-First ASEAN Ministerial Meeting.

75. "The Role of Human Rights in Thailand's Foreign Policy." statement by Surin Pitsuwan at the Seminar on "Promotion and Protection of Human Rights by Human Rights Commissions," organized by the Friedrich Ebert Stiftung, 2 October 1998.

76. "Thailand Opposes ASEAN Non-Interference Policy," *The Nation*, 23 June 1998.

77. Author's interview with Surin Pitsuwan, Bangkok, 30 January 2001.

Burma's membership. ASEAN's Western dialogue partners—including Australia, Canada, the United States, and the European Union—had also criticized the Association's ineffectiveness in the Burma conflict. Flexible engagement within ASEAN had been designed to respond to broader intra-regional problems such as the economic and environmental crises of the late 1990s. Critics would argue that if ASEAN had been more relaxed on the issue of non-intervention, "friendly criticism" of Thailand by its neighbors of its domestic economic policies might have resulted in more timely Thai action to attend to its domestic troubles before it became a regional contagion. According to the *Economist*, "any persuasion from fellow ASEAN members [to Thailand] to set a new course was so discreet that it was easy to ignore."[78] The 1997 Indonesian forest fires highlighted the environmental challenge to ASEAN. That year, fires on the Indonesian islands of Sumatra and Kalimantan, according to some estimates, destroyed between 750,000 hectares to 1.7 million hectares of forest. Efforts to address forest fires through the ASEAN framework had not been successful, but it showed that ASEAN members expected better environmental management from fellow member states and needed to devise common responses that might involve compromise on the doctrine of non-intervention.

Surin argued that the economic crisis presented the region with "an opportune moment [for ASEAN members] to reassess their respective processes of economic and political development in the face of rapid and far-reaching changes in the global arena." Against this backdrop, "ASEAN members can perhaps no longer afford to adopt a non-committal stance and avoid passing judgment on events in a member country, simply on the grounds of non-interference. . . . If domestic events in one member's territory can impact another member's internal affairs, peace and prosperity, much can be said in favor of ASEAN members playing a more proactive role."[79] The *Nation*, a Thai newspaper sympathetic to Surin's stand, described the rationale for flexible engagement: "If you don't put out the fire in your house, it would very soon spread through the neighborhood—and if your friends came charging in with fire extinguishers and engines into your home, you can't really say he has 'interfered' in your domestic problem."[80]

78. "The Limits of Politeness," the *Economist*, 28 February 1998.
79. Surin Pitsuwan, "Currency in Turmoil in Southeast Asia: The Strategic Impact," speech delivered at the Twelfth Asia Pacific Roundtable, Kuala Lumpur, Malaysia, June 1998; and Pitsuwan, opening statement at the Thirty-First ASEAN Ministerial Meeting, Manila.
80. "Declare Victory and Retreat," *The Nation*, 23 July 1998.

Like Anwar's idea of constructive intervention, flexible engagement was intended to move ASEAN toward a more pro-active role. In Surin's words, it was "a matter of taking a more pro-active concern about one another and about being supportive of one another whenever needed."[81] Philippine foreign minister Domingo Siazon contrasted flexible engagement with ASEAN's approach of benign neglect of one another.[82] He argued that flexible engagement could be used as a means of improving regional transparency, provide early warning, and develop policy approaches to deal with transnational economic and social problems. With such approach, Siazon said, "we should be able to speak more freely on issues occurring in one member country that affect others, with a view to building more solid ground for regional action."[83]

Though much diluted from the idea of collective intervention, flexible engagement was nonetheless the most significant challenge to ASEAN's non-intervention norm. But Surin's intrusive regionalism was not backed by any prior regional tradition. ASEAN was founded as a grouping of illiberal regimes with no record in promoting human rights and democratic governance. The anti-apartheid movement in South Africa had succeeded partly because campaigners could link their struggle with the prior norm against racism. The campaign by human rights activists against Burma failed because advocacy of human rights and democratic governance had no place in ASEAN, which did not specify a democratic political system as a criterion for membership.

Instead, non-intervention was still enjoying a robust legitimacy among ASEAN's other leading members. As Singapore's foreign minister S. Jayakumar noted, "ASEAN countries' consistent adherence to this principle of non-interference" had been "the key reason why no military conflict ha[d] broken out between any two members countries since the founding of ASEAN."[84] He argued that "the surest and quickest way to ruin is for ASEAN countries to begin commenting on how each of us deals with these sensitive issues" like race, religion, language.[85] Although non-intervention was not synonymous with indifference to each other's well-being, "internal political

81. Pitsuwan, opening statement at the Thirty-First ASEAN Ministerial Meeting, Manila.
82. Lee Kim Chew, "ASEAN Unity Showing Signs of Fraying," the *Straits Times*, 23 July 1998.
83. Siazon, Jr., "Winning the Challenges of the 21st Century."
84. The *Straits Times*, 23 July 1998.
85. Lee, "ASEAN Unity Showing Signs of Fraying."

developments will remain a particularly sensitive area with the potential to set up centrifugal forces that can pull ASEAN apart."[86]

Indeed, with the exception of the Philippines, all other ASEAN members were far less receptive, some even openly hostile, to the concept of flexible engagement.[87] Surin was attacked for being a Western "stooge," although he vehemently denied this.[88] The contestation was played out most starkly at the annual ASEAN Foreign Ministers' Meeting held in Manila in July 1998. Attacking flexible engagement, Malaysian foreign minister Abdullah Badawi held that it would severely compromise ASEAN's practice of consensus and "quiet diplomacy." To abandon these principles, he argued, "would be to usher in a divided and fractious ASEAN and consequently an enfeebled ASEAN." Rejecting the notion that ASEAN's existing approach was deficient, Badawi urged members to refrain from criticizing each other "more loudly, posturing adversarially and grandstanding more loudly bring less results and does more harm than good."[89]

Flexible engagement offered no opportunity for enhancing ASEAN's appeal within the larger Asia-Pacific community. Instead, ASEAN members feared that such a policy would provoke vigorous Chinese opposition and undermine the ARF, the very brainchild of ASEAN. Indeed, the very survival of ASEAN would be at risk. Surin's critics within ASEAN argued that its existing mechanisms and processes were adequate for dealing with the new challenges. Badawi claimed that solving mutual problems had sometimes required ASEAN members to comment on each other's affairs, but they had done so "quietly, befitting a community of friends bonded in cooperation and ever mindful of the fact that fractious relations undermine the capacity of ASEAN to work together on issues critical to our collective well-being."[90]

Success in localization depends on the insider proponents being seen as upholders of local values and identity. But both Anwar and Surin were seen by their ASEAN peers as influenced by the West, pushing for the latter's agenda of

86. Cited in "ASEAN Ministers Urge Making All Members Prosperous," *Kyodo News Service*, 28 July 1997.

87. "Thais Retract Call for ASEAN Intervention," The *Straits Times* (Internet Edition), 27 June 1998.

88. Although influenced by the changing global norm of sovereignty, Surin Pitsuwan insists that he was not being coerced or pressured by the West even at the height of the economic downturn when international financial institutions could have been thought to have significant leverage on the crisis-hit nation. Author's interview with Surin Pitsuwan, Bangkok, 13 May 2002.

89. Opening Statement of Malaysia's minister of foreign affairs H.E. Dato Seri Abdullah Badawi at the Thirty-First ASEAN Ministerial Meeting, Manila, 24 July 1998.

90. Ibid.

human rights promotion and democratic assistance.[91] Though local in persona, they were insufficiently local in their inspiration and motivation.

Flexible engagement failed to produce any meaningful institutional change in ASEAN, at least at the time of its initial advocacy.[92] At the 1998 annual ASEAN Foreign Ministers' Meeting, Surin dropped the term.[93] ASEAN nominally adopted a new policy of "enhanced interaction" (although this was not reflected in any official statement) as a framework to deal with transnational issues.[94] Surin would later claim some successes of flexible engagement, including a brief discussion of Burma's internal affairs at an official ASEAN meeting in Singapore in 2000. This he saw as the "first ever talking about issues of internal nature in ASEAN."[95] However, it would be misleading to consider this to be a true agenda expansion, as ASEAN was still avoiding any discussion of, or approaches to, the protection of human rights or the provision of democratic assistance to fellow member states. Even the more modest proposals mooted by Anwar Ibrahim's constructive intervention idea, such as electoral assistance or promotion of civil society, remained outside of official ASEAN policy. In short, ASEAN did not depart from its non-intervention doctrine in any significant way.[96] Its reluctance and inability to send an intervention force to East Timor in 1999 despite pleas from the Indonesian President further attested to the continued salience of non-intervention.

91. Author's interview with Surin Pitsuwan, Bangkok, 13 May 2002.
92. The *Straits Times* (Internet Edition), 27 June 1998; the *Straits Times*, 25 July 1998, 23.
93. Pitsuwan, opening statement delivered at the Thirty-First ASEAN Ministerial Meeting, Manila.
94. *Asia Pulse*, "ASEAN Ministers Adopt Policy of 'Enhanced Interaction'"; author's interview with Surin Pitsuwan, Bangkok, 10 May 2002; author's interview with Ali Alatas, 4 June 2002; and author's interview with Termsak Chalermpalanupap, special assistant to the Secretary-General, ASEAN, Bangkok, 16 January 2001.
95. Author's interview with Surin Pitsuwan, Bangkok, 10 May 2002.
96. John Funston, "ASEAN: Out of Its Depth?" *Contemporary Southeast Asia* 20, no. 1 (1998): 22–37; Tobias Nischalke, "Insights from ASEAN's Foreign Policy Cooperation: The 'ASEAN Way,' a Real Spirit or a Phantom?" *Contemporary Southeast Asia* 22, no. 1: 89–112; Jürgen Haacke, *ASEAN's Diplomatic and Security Culture: Origins, Developments and Prospects* (London: Routledge Curzon, 2003). The end of the ASEAN Ministerial Meeting in Manila on 25 July 1998 saw the most intense debate over whether ASEAN should shift from non-interference to flexible engagement. Singapore's S. Jayakumar, the incoming Chairman of ASEAN's Standing Committee, flatly noted that this meeting had "began amidst some confusion and speculation as to whether there would be changes to ASEAN's fundamental principles. These controversies have been laid to rest. . . . The basic principles of non-intervention and decision-making by consensus would remain the cornerstones of ASEAN." S. Jayakumar's closing statement at the Thirty-First ASEAN Ministerial Meeting, Manila, Philippines, 25 July 1998, available at http://www.aseansec.org/3930.htm.

ASEAN created two new policy instruments as part of its "enhanced interaction" agenda. First, an ASEAN Surveillance Process (ASP) created in 1998 to monitor regional economic developments, provide early warning of macroeconomic instability, and encourage collective action to prevent another economic crisis.[97] The second was a ministerial troika to support regional political and security crisis prevention.[98] The ASP was officially described as "informal, simple and based on peer review process," without any threat of external audit or enforcement sanctions.[99] The Troika remained a paper instrument specified to "refrain from addressing issues that constitute the internal affairs of ASEAN member countries."[100]

## Comparison and Alternative Explanations

The foregoing discussion suggests a significant variation between the fate of common security and collective intervention. The localization of common security had three main effects on ASEAN: (1) its acceptance of security dialogues and cooperation as a formal task for ASEAN; (2) the displacement of the inward-looking ZOPFAN norm in favor of a more inclusive approach, which allowed ASEAN to play the role of midwife to the birth of a new Asia-wide security institution; and (3) the adoption by the new security institution (ARF) of new policy instruments, including CBMs, based on the ASEAN model. It is fair to say that the target norm of ZOPFAN was not just modified, but displaced. In contrast, the flexible engagement proposal underpinned by the collective intervention norm did not produce any meaningful institutional change in ASEAN. It continued to exclude human rights and democratic assistance tasks while the target norm, non-intervention, remained firmly in place. Although some new policy instruments were created, these remained weak and limited.

The variation can be explained in terms of the constitutive localization framework. Both norms challenged the cognitive prior of ASEAN: advocates of cooperative security targeted the ZOPFAN concept and those of flexible engagement targeted its non-intervention doctrine. But non-intervention was still enjoying a robust legitimacy, whereas the ZOPFAN idea had been discredited from within ASEAN. The cooperative security

97. Author's interview with Termsak Chalermpalanupap, special assistant to the Secretary-General, ASEAN, Bangkok, 16 January, 2001.
98. Ibid.
99. "Terms of Understanding on the Establishment of the ASEAN Surveillance Process," Washington DC, 4 October 1998, available at http://www.aseansec.org/739.htm.
100. Ibid.

**Table 5.1.** Cooperative Security and Collective Intervention

| External idea | Cognitive prior | Outcome |
|---|---|---|
| Common security (prelocalized version: cooperative security) | ZOPFAN | New institution: ASEAN Regional Forum |
| Collective intervention (prelocalized version: constructive intervention and flexible engagement) | Enhanced non-intervention | No new institution; "enhanced interaction": weak mechanisms for conflict management and cooperation |

norm had displaced ZOPFAN but did not override the doctrine of non-intervention in ASEAN, which was still enjoying considerable legitimacy and remained at the top of ASEAN's norm hierarchy. When non-intervention itself became the target norm, as in the case of flexible engagement, norm diffusion failed.

Both norms had insider proponents, but in the case of cooperative security, it was a transnational network: ASEAN-ISIS. The insider proponents in the second case were two individuals, Malaysia's Ibrahim and Thailand's Pitsuwan. This was clearly a factor in explaining the variation between the two cases.

The cooperative security norm could be grafted more easily into ASEAN thanks to the existence of two prior *receptive* norms in the ASEAN framework—the rejection of a balance of power approach to regional security involving multilateral military pacts, and the Indonesian concept of regional resilience. There were no such norms to host flexible engagement.

Finally, cooperative security offered greater scope for enhancing ASEAN's prestige. It enabled ASEAN to acquire a broader regional relevance and role. Flexible engagement had no such appeal. Instead, it threatened to undermine both ASEAN and the ARF.

Realists could explain the diffusion of cooperative security as a calculated move by some Asian governments to ensure the continued engagement of the United States in regional security affairs at a time of U.S. military retrenchment from the region.[101] However, this is at best a partial explanation for two reasons. First, such considerations applied to some countries (e.g., Singapore) more than to others (e.g., Indonesia). Second, the cognitive and institutional priors developed by weaker states that played a significant role in securing the engagement of far more powerful actors through the ARF would not fit easily

---

101. Paul Dibb, *Towards a New Balance of Power in Asia (Adelphi* Paper, No. 295) (New York: Oxford University Press); and Leifer, *The ASEAN Regional Forum.*

into realist and neo-realist explanations of norm diffusion privileging the power variable. Intra-regional power differentials also were not crucial, because the pattern of power distribution in ASEAN is not hierarchal. No ASEAN country was in a power position to impose its preferred norm over the others. Similarly, power alone cannot explain why the flexible engagement proposal fared badly, since it conformed more to the style of regional interactions preferred by powerful actors like the United States and the European Union, who were calling for sanctions against Burma.

Utility calculations from a neo-liberal perspective would have favored flexible engagement, especially after Surin had reframed it away from moral politics toward crisis management and efficacy gains for ASEAN. Flexible engagement offered more utility than cooperative security, whose utility potential was reduced by available balance of power mechanisms based on U.S. alliances in the region. But it remained underinstitutionalized because it conflicted with the deeply ingrained non-intervention norm of ASEAN, and it did not offer any real prospects for extending and enhancing the ASEAN model.

The goal here is not to dismiss realist and neo-liberal explanations of Asian regional institutionalization, but merely to point to their inadequacies and anomalies. To explain the variation between the two cases, one must consider the role of ideational forces and the process of their introduction and institutionalization in the region. And in so doing, one should not focus only on how the prescriptive ideas backed by outside advocates converted the norm-takers, but how the cognitive priors of the norm-takers influenced the reshaping and reception of these external ideas. This was not a matter of a simple or static fit, but a dynamic act of congruence-building through framing, grafting, localization, and legitimation.

Domestic politics (i.e., domestic political structures and regime preferences) may better explain why the cooperative security norm found greater acceptance than the flexible engagement concept. Those who backed a more interventionist ASEAN—Anwar Ibrahim, Surin Pirswuan, and Domingo Siazon—were representing its more democratic polities, whereas the opponents of the norm—the leaders of Vietnam, Burma, and Indonesia (under Suharto)—presided over illiberal regimes. A flexible engagement policy would have undercut their legitimacy. This consideration overrode whatever utility they could perceive from Surin's idea of making ASEAN more effective. Cooperative security did not pose a similar threat to these regimes, because it had no CSCE-like "human dimension" calling on the member states to offer greater protection for human rights.

But the domestic politics explanation strengthens, not weakens, the central argument that ASEAN's regional cognitive priors mattered in explaining its varied responses to cooperative security and flexible engagement. The authoritarian domestic politics in ASEAN was already incorporated into ASEAN's normative prior. The non-intervention norm in ASEAN was to a large extent geared toward authoritarian regime maintenance.[102] At the same time, a purely domestic politics variable delinked from the regional context is inadequate in explaining ASEAN's regional security strategy and preferences. Had domestic political structures could solely determine the responses of ASEAN members to flexible engagement, then Thailand (and to a lesser extent the Philippines) should have broken ranks with ASEAN after their reformist agenda was rejected. But loyalty to the Association prevailed over domestic preferences. Both Thailand and the Philippines stuck with the ASEAN consensus favoring non-intervention even though their preference, based on domestic politics, went against this outcome.

It may be argued that common security was a more malleable norm than collective intervention, hence the former could find acceptance whereas the latter failed. This is consistent with the claim of some norm scholars that malleable norms spread more easily than norms whose content is more specific and that make specific injunctions. This explanation, however, ignores the fact that collective intervention was also quite malleable, as it could be interpreted and framed as humanitarian intervention, flexible engagement, constructive intervention, and so on.

### The Future of Non-Intervention and Institutional Change

I have argued that the localization of flexible engagement failed in the 1997–99 period in terms of the criteria specified in the conceptual framework; that is, the degree and robustness of institutional change it generated. However, developments in Southeast Asia since then point in the direction of a more open attitude toward non-intervention and a greater willingness to institutionalize ASEAN. Three such developments stand out.

The first is ASEAN's growing impatience with Burma. In 2000, on the margins of the APEC summit, the Sultan of Brunei convened a meeting of ASEAN heads of governments and proposed that in the Association should discuss the Burma issue when it meets in Singapore the following week. This move had the blessing of prime ministers Mahathir Mohammed of Malaysia and Goh Chok Tong of Singapore. Goh, as host of the Singapore

102. This is true of most Third World regions. See Christopher Clapham, "Sovereignty and the Third World State," in *Sovereignty at the Millennium*, ed. Robert Jackson (Oxford: Blackwell, 1999).

meeting, set aside some time during which the leader of the Burmese Junta was asked to give a progress report on his country's political situation. The brief release of Aung San Suu Kyi from house arrest in May 2002 led Surin to insist that "everyone has tried to disown it [his idea of flexible engagement], but it has survived."[103] Indonesia's Alatas, one of the most vocal opponents of flexible engagement in 1998, would now say: "We have not dropped sovereignty, but we have made it more flexible." This "flexible view of sovereignty is being developed in practice, if not in theory."[104] A Singaporean Foreign Ministry official would say that Surin's "mistake" was to challenge the principle of non-interference "at the level of principle rather than at the level of practice."[105]

Since 2005, ASEAN countries have held talks with leaders of the military junta of Burma in order to persuade it to make good on its pledge of domestic reform, including the drafting of a constitution. Some ASEAN members, notably Malaysia, have even gone to the extent of speculating publicly about the expulsion of Burma from ASEAN if it did not change its ways.[106] ASEAN members went as far as expressing their "revulsion" at the junta's violent repression of the Buddhist monk-led uprising in Burma in August and September 2007.[107]

Second, ASEAN countries have cooperated more closely in dealing with a series of regional crises, including terrorism following the 9/11 attacks on the United States, the 2002 terrorist bombings in Bali, the outbreak of the Severe Acute Respiratory Syndrome (SARS) pandemic in 2003, and the Indian Ocean Tsunami in December 2004. These events have led to greater intelligence sharing against terrorists, coordination of national border control and quarantine policies, and creation of regional pandemic and early-warning tsunami systems. In 2003, partly in response to terrorist and SARS chal-

103. Author's interview with Surin Pitsuwan, Singapore, 27 September 2001.

104. Author's interview with Ali Alatas, Kuala Lumpur, 4 June 2002.

105. Author's interview with Bilahari Kaushikan, Permanent Secretary, Ministry of Foreign Affairs, Singapore, Paris, 11 March 2002.

106. Jim Gomez, "ASEAN Ministers Urge Myanmar Generals to Free Suu Kyi," *Associated Press*, 16 June 2003; "ASEAN's Myanmar Policy May Face Review—Philippines FM," *Agence France Presse*, 18 June 2003; "Myanmar Might Have to Be Expelled from ASEAN—Mahathir," *Agence France Presse*, 20 July 2003.

107. At a statement issued at the UN, ASEAN foreign ministers "expressed their revulsion to Myanmar foreign minister Nyan Win over reports that the demonstrations in Myanmar are being suppressed by violent force and that there has been a number of fatalities" and "strongly urged Burmese to exercise utmost restraint and seek a political solution." Moreover, "They called upon Myanmar to resume its efforts at national reconciliation with all parties concerned, and work towards a peaceful transition to democracy." "Southeast Asian Nations Express 'Revulsion' at Myanmar's Violent Repression of Demonstrations," Ottawa, Canada, 27 September 2007, available at http://www.indonesia-ottawa.org/information/details.php?type=news_copy&id=4765.

lenges, Indonesia proposed the creation of an "ASEAN Security Community." Its concept paper for the Community contained a number of bold measures, such as an ASEAN peacekeeping force and cooperation between its armed and security forces to combat threats such as terrorism. Moreover, it expressed an explicit commitment to human rights and democracy as the ideological basis of ASEAN.[108] In 2007, ASEAN ministers approved plans to set up an ASEAN human rights mechanism.

Third, in December 2007, ASEAN adopted a Charter, a constitutional document, whose objective is to give it a "legal personality" and strengthen its institutions. An Eminent Persons Group (EPG) appointed by ASEAN governments to make recommendations for the Charter called for significant changes to its institutional structure and decision-making procedures. The EPG called for ASEAN's organizational structure to be strengthened by giving its Secretary-General authority to sign agreements on behalf of ASEAN in non-sensitive areas, by adding to the number of senior level functionaries and professional staff, and turning the ASEAN heads of government meeting into an ASEAN Council. More important, it called for decision making by majority voting in areas excluding security and foreign policy. This was to be a departure from the traditional consensus principle. Most important, the EPG report recommended that compliance by members with ASEAN's objectives, principles, decisions, agreements, and timetables should be monitored and should any members be found to be in "serious breach," they could be penalized by being deprived of their membership rights and privileges, or, in extraordinary circumstances, even expulsion. Finally, it called for dispute settlement mechanisms in all areas of cooperation, especially economics and politics.[109] Previously, only the ASEAN Free Trade Area had its dispute settlement mechanism; although ASEAN's Treaty of Amity and Cooperation (1976) provides for a High Council to deal with disputes in political and security fields, it had never been used.

Do these developments constitute a shift away from non-intervention and imply acceptance of the flexible engagement concept? To some extent, they do. They also affirm the validity of the constitutive localization framework.

First, the shift from ASEAN's existing norms implied in these developments should not be overstated. In ASEAN's norm hierarchy, non-

108. "Deplu Paper on ASEAN Security Community," 2003, Ministry of Foreign Affairs, Indonesia. This document was tabled at the ASEAN Ministerial Meeting in Cambodia, 16–18 June 2003, 5. Deplu stands for Ministry of Foreign Affairs in Bahasa, Indonesia.
109. "Report of the Eminent Persons Group on the ASEAN Charter," December 2006, available at http://www.aseansec.org/19247.pdf. See also Amitav Acharya, "ASEAN at 40: Mid-Life Rejuvenation?" *Foreignaffairs.org*, 15 August 2007, available at http://www.foreignaf fairs.org/20070815faupdate86481/amitav-acharya/asean-at-40-mid-life-rejuvenation.html.

intervention and rejection of collective defense continue to trump collective intervention. ASEAN's criticism of Burma has not led to sanctions or suspension from the grouping.[110] Nor has its demand for political change in Burma been more than modest, focusing on the drafting of a new constitution providing for elections, which many in the international community regard as a sham. ASEAN has not objected to the fact that the constitution drafting process in Burma has been singularly unrepresentative, boycotted by the oppositional National League for Democracy, and that the new constitution would entrench the dominant role of the military by reserving for it a large proportion of seats in the legislature and the most important executive positions.[111] In the wake of the devastating cyclone of May 2007 in Burma, ASEAN countries were cautious about pressuring the Burmese regime to accept international aid, which it had been resisting because of the potential impact it might have on regime security. ASEAN's eventual decision to act as a conduit for international aid came as the result of Western pressure. However, such decisions are made on an ad hoc basis and ASEAN has resisted calls for creating a standing institution for emergency humanitarian assistance to disaster-hit areas.[112]

ASEAN cooperation against transnational threats remains limited to dialogue, information exchanges, and capacity-building initiatives, rather than multilateral operational measures. Even the much-talked cooperation among Malaysia, Singapore, and Indonesia to ensure the safety and security of the Malacca Straits from piracy and terrorist attacks, only led to coordinated patrols, rather than joint patrols that would involve intrusion into each other's territorial waters.

Fundamentally, the ASEAN Charter is a way of consolidating ASEAN's existing rules and institutional mechanisms, rather than creating genuinely

110. "ASEAN Should Keep Out of Myanmar's Affairs: Vietnam," *Agence France Presse,* 7 September 2000. On 29 June 2004. Indonesian foreign minister Hassan Wirayuda stated that "applying sanctions is not the issue here." He stressed that "it is not our approach to apply sanctions in order to get results, but to continue to talk with them as part of the ASEAN family." Indeed, Wirayuda acknowledged that "Myanmar is still as important as any other member of ASEAN," and that "on the situation in Myanmar, in particular, its implementation of the self-declared road-map to democracy, we continue to engage with them." "Hassan Claims There Is Progress in Myanmar," the *Jakarta Post,* 29 June 2004.

111. Amitav Acharya, "Democracy in Burma: Does Anyone Really Care?" *YaleGlobal-Online,* 1 September 2005, http://yaleglobal.yale.edu/display.article?id=6219.

112. As Singapore's foreign minister and the current chairman of ASEAN George Yeo stated, "It doesn't make sense for us to work on the basis of forcing aid on Myanmar because that would bring unnecessary complications and will lead to more suffering for the Myanmar people." "ASEAN to Coordinate Myanmar Aid Effort," 19 May 2008, available at http://www.reuters.com/article/worldNews/idUSBKK1919620080519?feedType=RSS&feedName=worldNews&pageNumber=4&virtualBrandChannel=0.

supranational and legalistic institutions. For example, there is no proposal to create an ASEAN court of justice. The terms of the proposed ASEAN human rights (not specified in the Charter but left to be decided later by the ASEAN foreign ministers) is more likely to be that of a monitoring and awareness-raising body, rather than one having the authority to hear complaints against, or impose penalties on, member states. The more drastic recommendations made by the non-official EPG report, especially the provisions for sanctions against members, were rejected by the governments and were not included in the official draft of the Charter.[113] The Charter actually entrenched the principle of non-interference by including it in this purportedly constitutional document aimed at taking ASEAN into a new era of transnational problem solving.[114] In the meantime, ASEAN's existing crisis-management and dispute-settlement mechanisms remain unused,[115] as do its formal agreements, such as the agreement on transboundary pollution (Indonesia's refusal to ratify this treaty is one of the reasons why it has been useless in combating the recurring haze problem caused by Indonesian forest fires).

Indonesia's ASEAN Security Community initiative attests to a similarly cautious approach to weaning itself from a strict adherence to non-interference. The document did not propose an ASEAN defense pact or suggest a democratic political system as the requirement for membership in ASEAN. Its original proposals met with resistance from among ASEAN members, and saw considerable dilution. The provisions for a regional peace-keeping force and the shared commitment to democracy were rejected.[116]

113. "Southeast Asian Leaders Adopt Charter," *USA Today*, 20 November 2007, available at http://www.usatoday.com/news/world/2007-11-20-asean-charter_N.htm. The final text of the ASEAN Charter is available at http://www.aseansec.org/21069.pdf.
114. Three principles of the Charter uphold the non-interference doctrine: principle (e)—"non-interference in the internal affairs of ASEAN Member States"; principle (f)—"respect for the right of every Member State to lead its national existence free from external interference, subversion and coercion; and principle (k)—"abstention from participation in any policy or activity, including the use of its territory, pursued by any ASEAN Member State or non-ASEAN State or any non-State actor, which threatens the sovereignty, territorial integrity or political and economic stability of ASEAN Member States." These principles mirror the principles and practices enunciated by ASEAN at different stages of its existence, thereby suggesting significant path dependency. By contrast, final action on unresolved intra-ASEAN disputes and any breach or non-compliance by member states are left to be decided by the ASEAN Summit, a political body of national leaders, rather than to professional and specialized judicial or administrative mechanisms. Charter of the Association of the Southeast Asian Nations, available at http://www.aseansec.org/21069.pdf.
115. Amitav Acharya, "Challenges for an ASEAN Charter," the *Straits Times*, 24 October 2005; Amitav Acharya and Jorge I. Dominguez, "How ASEAN Can Tackle Crises," the *Straits Times*, 19 July 2006.
116. "ASEAN Security Community Plan of Action," 15 June 2004, available at http://www.aseansec.org/16826.htm; "Peacekeeping Role Not for ASEAN for Now: Jaya," the *Straits*

ASEAN defense ministers have begun to meet on an annual basis, but this is far cry from an ASEAN defense pact, hence it does not constitute a break from ASEAN's stance against collective defense.[117]

Recent institutional changes in ASEAN are evolutionary, rather than a fundamental break from its extant institutions, suggesting the kind of path dependency and incrementalism that the constitutive localization framework suggests. The norm against collective defense survives and the framework of soft institutionalism is resilient. This is not to say that ASEAN will not move in the direction of further institutionalization. As chapter 2 suggests, localization is a dynamic process; it may occur if the conditions (see table 2.1) obstructing localization in a given period are to change over the longer term. A vital condition of localization is the quality and extent of local agency, including the nature and availability of insider proponents. It is noteworthy that recent initiatives that have fared better in inducing change in ASEAN have been led by actors from *within* ASEAN, rather than from external ones. Indonesia following its democratic transition has taken the lead in pushing for many of these changes, whereas Singapore—despite persisting authoritarian rule—has pushed for legalization and institutionalization, especially for an ASEAN Charter (this also suggests that domestic politics may not be as significant as regional normative compatibility and process politics in inducing localization). But greater local advocacy and support for initiatives for institutional change and stronger prospects for these initiatives enhancing ASEAN's international legitimacy must be present if the grouping's cognitive prior of enhanced non-intervention is to be overcome to pave the way for at least a limited acceptance of regionalist intervention. In other words, "a further dilution of the norm of non-intervention is possible if . . . [regional] crises bring to the fore new insider proponents and more effective framing and grafting discourses. But any such shift from non-intervention in ASEAN will be gradual and path dependent."[118]

THE post–Cold War institution-building experience in Southeast Asia suggests that changing power differentials, interdependence levels, and external normative conditions should not eclipse the importance of existing norma-

*Times*, 5 March 2004; Barry Wain, "Jakarta Jilted: Indonesia's Neighbours Are Not Very Supportive of Its Vision of a Regional Security Community," *Far Eastern Economic Review*, 10 June 2004.

117. "ASEAN Defence Ministers to Commit to Security Community," available at http://www.spacewar.com/reports/ASEAN_Defence_Ministers_To_Commit_To_Security_Community.html.

118. Amitav Acharya, "How Ideas Spread: Whose Norms Matter? Norm Localization and Institutional Change in Asian Regionalism," *International Organization* 58, no. 2 (Spring 2004): 264.

tive frameworks and social arrangements that generate a dynamic path dependency. It is therefore unrealistic for advocates of Asian regionalism to expect that these institutions will develop legalistic attributes similar to those of European regionalism in the near future. The dynamics of constitutive localization highlighted in this and previous chapters should serve as a cautionary tale to those who believe that ideas and institution-building models that are successful in one part of the world can be replicated elsewhere. This does not mean that Asian institution-building processes are doomed to failure. Throughout the region, there are signs of a progressive and evolutionary shift toward a broader and more cooperative approach to regional security brought about by the localization of Western multilateral concepts, without overwhelming regional identity norms and processes, which have been used as a building bloc. This trend represents a meaningful advance from the region's Cold War predicament.

# 6 Conclusions, Extensions, and Extrapolations

In the conclusion, I review the book's findings on the two puzzles about Asian regionalism identified at the outset: Why Asia did not develop a multilateral security institution in the immediate post-war period? and Why Asian regionalism remains underinstitutionalized? My broader goal is to link these findings with some general observations about the current state and future direction of Asian regionalism and the effects of the design features of Asian institutions on regional order. I then extend the argument to other issue areas and regions on the basis that the constitutive localization perspective has a theoretical and empirical relevance beyond Asian regionalism, capturing norm dynamics throughout the international system. Finally, I briefly explore how the approach of the book can be fruitful in bringing Asia into the domain of international relations theory.

## The Once and Future Trajectory of Asian Regionalism

My main concern in this book is to study and establish the impact of norms in shaping the trajectory of Asian regional institution-building. The two afore-mentioned questions about Asian regionalism cannot be answered by rationalist explanations that focus largely on power and interest or by a conventional constructivist explanation of norm diffusion. Although these explanations acknowledge the role of norms and identity, they offer little insight on the role of regional actors and processes. As such, they beg the question: if ideas played a role in shaping Asian regionalism, did the ideas and beliefs of regional actors and processes matter?

The second question determines the first: whether ideas shaped regional order depends on the local actors' attitudes, beliefs, and actions in building

144

congruence between outside ideas and the local context. One must identify and study such agency and processes in order to ascertain whether ideas matter.

In norm diffusion, local ideas and agents matter, and do so in a central way. The constitutive localization framework stresses a dynamic process of congruence building through which local actors accept foreign ideas in accordance with their "cognitive priors" or existing beliefs and conduct. Once in place, these cognitive priors shape future norm borrowing. In chapter 2, I identified the conditions that determine which ideas might be accepted by the local actors to develop new institutions and/or modify existing ones.

Using this framework, I traced the normative evolution of Asian regionalism in two historical phases of constitutive localization. The first centered on contestations in the early Cold War period, featuring the idea of collective defense and non-intervention against the backdrop of a regional cognitive prior formed by the anti-colonial and anti-power politics beliefs held by a section of the region's nationalist elite. The outcome of this was the acceptance of non-intervention and the rejection of collective defense. Subsequently, Asia developed a cognitive prior featuring the enhancement of non-intervention in the regional and global context, the emergence of certain elements of process diplomacy (soft institutionalism), the long-term avoidance of multilateral collective defense organizations, whether with external powers or within the region, and a multilateralism developed around ASEAN, which, while remaining open to limited political and economic engagement with outside powers, rejected EEC-style economic integration as well as the idea of a Pacific Community dominated by Western nations and Japan. These constituted a regional cognitive prior, a distinctive Asian construction of sovereignty that would shape the trajectory and design of its future regional institutions.

Norms that were foundational to Asian regionalism, such as non-intervention, did not originate within Asia nor were they simply borrowed from outside. The regionalist normative framework of Asia was the product of a dynamic interaction between the global norms of sovereignty and local normative aspirations and imperatives. Moreover, this regional normative framework strengthened the global sovereignty regime—an amplification effect, which is an important component of the constitutive localization framework. Once in place, the cognitive prior of regionalism without a sovereignty-eroding regional organization not only shaped Cold War Asian regional order, but also influenced the trajectory of Asian regionalism after the Cold War, including proposals for creating new institutions and reforming existing ones.

The second phase of constitutive localization in Asian regionalism featured contestation over the ideas of common security and collective intervention in the post-Cold War period. The outcome of this process was the localization and acceptance of the former and the rejection of the latter, even in its softer, truncated form. The institutional expression of this phase of constitutive localization was the creation of a new regional institution, the ARF, which continued the region's preference for non-legalistic cooperation and avoidance of defense multilateralism.

Overall, the two stages of constitutive localization suggest that normative change in Asian regionalism is evolutionary rather than revolutionary, path-dependent rather than path-breaking. The normative preferences of the regional actors that delegitimized collective defense and affirmed conflict resolution and avoidance through soft institutionalism also ensured that regional institutions created by weaker states would be deliberately and distinctively underinstitutionalized, despite shifts in the underlying material conditions and bargaining contexts, such as the Cold War and economic interdependence. The path dependency created by constitutive localization tells us much about the absence of European style regional institutions in Asia despite recent efforts at strengthening and legalizing their institutional framework to cope with new pressures.

## Normative Purpose and Regional Order

The dependent variable of this book is the purpose, trajectory, and design of Asian regional institutions. Constructivist scholarship on norms is heavily concerned with establishing that norms matter. In this book, I argue that norms matter because historically constructed regional norms have been resilient and influential in shaping the emergence, design, and purpose of Asian regional institutions, even more so than power and interest variables. But it can be argued that establishing the causal impact of norms would also require some appraisal of their contribution to international/regional order, defined in terms of the degree of conflict and stability in the region. In other words, norms shape institutional design, which in turn facilitates the creation and management of regional order. The question is: have the purpose, trajectory, and design of Asian regional institutions shaped peace and stability in the region?

Scholars of international institutions have paid increasing attention to studying what causes variations among them. But the emerging literature on institution design has paid less attention to how these variations affect the "nature" and "quality" of cooperation, or the prospects for international order.[1] The task of assessing the contribution of international institutions to order is complicated by the fact that order, as Alagappa notes, is a "slippery" concept in international relations. Not only can the concept be used in "multiple ways," but "[v]ery few define the concept or even clarify how it's used."[2] Recent literature on regional order offers help, however, by identifying three broad understandings. First, this literature revives Hedley Bull's classic formulation, which views international order as "a pattern of activity that sustains the elementary or primary goals of the society of states, or international society."[3] Bull identified these as the preservation of the state system, maintaining the sovereignty or independence of states, relative peace, or absence of war as the normal condition among states, the limitation of violence, keeping of promises, and the protection of property rights.[4] A second understanding, proposed by Lake and Morgan, takes regional order to mean something more than just the way regions are organized (e.g., "security complexes"); regional order includes "modes of conflict management" within regions, or "the way in which . . . states seek to manage their security relations."[5] Third, Alagappa argues that order implies "rule governed interaction," or "whether interstate interactions conform to accepted rules."[6] It is the third understanding that is especially important to employing the constitutive localization perspective to Asian regional order.

Although the dependent variable of this book is institution design and change, rather than order, it does offer some important insights into how Asian institutions have shaped regional order viewed in the above-mentioned terms. The main argument here is that the so-called underinstitutionalization and the incremental progress of regional institutions are not to be regarded as sure signs of the failure of regional institutions to shape regional order. Asian institutions may seem weak and ineffectual when judged against the performance criteria of their European counterparts, which have

1. See Barbara Koremenos, Charles Lipson, and Duncan Snidal, *The Rational Design of International Institutions* (Cambridge: Cambridge University Press, 2004). For a more direct attempt to link institution design with nature of cooperation, see Amitav Acharya and Alastair Iain Johnston, eds., *Crafting Cooperation: Regional International Institutions in Comparative Perspective* (Cambridge: Cambridge University Press).

2. Muthiah Alagappa, "The Study of International Order," in *Asian Security Order: Instrumental and Normative Features*, ed. Muthiah Alagappa (Stanford: Stanford University Press, 2003), 34.

3. Hedley Bull, *The Anarchical Society*, 2nd ed. (New York: Columbia University Press, 1977), 8.

4. Bull, *The Anarchical Society*, 16–19.

5. David A. Lake and Patrick M. Morgan, "The New Regionalism in Security Affairs," in *Regional Orders: Building Security in a New World*, ed. David A. Lake and Patrick M. Morgan (University Park: Pennsylvania University Press, 1997), 12.

6. Alagappa, "The Study of International Order," 39.

been stressed by the literature on international institutions. But if one resists the temptation to apply the European template of integrative regionalism to the Asian matrix, and adopts the broader conception of order mentioned above, several contributions of Asian regional institutions to regional order become evident.

Going by Alagappa's definition of order as principled behavior, a shared normative understanding of regional order has existed in Asia in the absence of European-style formal institutions. Friedberg compares Europe's "thick alphabet soup" of regional institutions with Asia's "thin gruel."[7] But Friedberg and others miss the extent to which this thin gruel has been a dietary preference, rather than a natural or cultural trait. The so-called lateness of regional institution-building in Asia does not mean the absence of shared regional norms.

The study of international institutionalization has long accepted the need to study both formal and informal associations.[8] Similarly, shared norms can matter in the absence of formal institutions. This is crucial in assessing the contribution of Asian regionalism to regional order. Donald Weatherbee characterized ASEAN regionalism as a phenomenon in which the "absence of explicit organizational arrangements and formally articulated regional structures becomes less important than the attitudinal underpinnings that support a recognized pattern of practice around which expectations converge."[9] Much the same can be said of other ASEAN-based regional institutions, including the ASEAN Regional Forum and ASEAN Plus Three.

Can the "thin gruel" of Asian regional institutions have substantial cooperative effects, as this book implies? I think it is fair to speak of " 'cooperation' to include sharing of norms that limit multilateral commitments," if these commitments threaten sovereignty whose preservation is a higher objective of regional groups in the Third World. Regionalism is effective if it delivers the "set goals" of institutions, which to an overwhelming degree in the Third World has been the preservation of sovereignty, even at the

---

7. Aaron Friedberg, "Ripe for Rivalry: Prospects for Peace in Multipolar Asia," *International Security* 18, no. 3 (Winter 1993–94): 22.

8. The idea of security regimes, for example, draws attention to "principles, rules and norms that permit nations to be restrained in their behavior in the belief that others will reciprocate." Robert Jervis, "Security Regimes," *International Organization* 36, no. 2 (Spring 1982): 357.

9. Donald Weatherbee, "ASEAN Regionalism: The Salient Dimension," in *ASEAN Security and Economic Development*, ed. Karl D. Jackson and M. Hadi Soesastro (Berkeley: University of California, Institute of East Asian Studies, 1984), 259–68.

expense of certain forms of collective action.[10] This has been the case with ASEAN ARF and APEC.

Asian regionalism has made important historical contributions to Asian regional order. Asian multilateral conferences and institutions helped to embed the Westphalian norms of sovereignty and non-interference within regional diplomatic and security practice. This conforms to both Bull's emphasis on the preservation of the state system and maintenance of the sovereignty or independence of states as the "elemental" functions of order, and Alagappa's view of order as rule-governed interaction. The "basic aim" of the Bandung Conference was not to set up a permanent regional organization, but to bring about an agreement on norms of inter-state relations. To restate the comments by the Bandung Conference Secretary-General Roselan Abdulghani, the conference was devoted to "the formulation and establishment of certain norms for the conduct of present-day international relations and the instruments for the practical application of these norms."[11] The Bandung Conference was "able to establish a substantial common denominator of anticolonialism, sufficient to provide the basis for a considerable latitude of joint effort."[12] Even the staunch anti-neutralist U.S. secretary of state John Foster Dulles acknowledged that the Bandung Conference "exerted a restraint on the Chinese communists in dealing with Taiwan."[13] ASEAN, ARF, and other institutions have concentrated on the same role of providing a platform for debating and defending the norms of sovereignty as applied to the regional context of conflict and cooperation. However outdated and pernicious non-intervention may seem today, its consolidation through Asian regional conferences and institutions helped to preserve territorial integrity and encouraged peaceful settlement of intra-regional disputes in Asia. Whereas European institutions sought to transcend the nation-state that had been implicated in two major catastrophic wars, Asian norms and institutions were created in the wake of decolonization with the explicit purpose of preserving the nation-state as a permanent feature of regional order. Hence, going by their original intention, and Bull's definition, Asian regional institutions have been order preserving.

What is the prospect that Asia's normative order will change? Will Asia develop stronger regional institutions, especially in the security arena? Asia's underinstitutionalization is proving incredibly resistant to change. Any

10. Acharya and Johnston, *Crafting Cooperation*.
11. Roselan Abdulghani, *The Bandung Spirit* (Jakarta: Prapantja, 1964), 103.
12. George McTurnan Kahin. *The Asian-African Conference, Bandung, Indonesia, April 1955* (Ithaca: Cornell University Press), 33.
13. "Hopeful Developments in Europe and in Asia," *Department of State Press Release*, no. 230, April 26, 1955.

change that has taken place has been incremental and path-dependent. Realists, who attribute Asia's lack of strong institutions to its dependence of the U.S. security umbrella, would probably argue that nothing would (or should) ever change: U.S. predominance will continue to constrain Asian institutionalization because some regional countries will see the U.S. military presence as a more reliable and desirable alternative to institutions.[14] However, this explanation is inadequate on two counts. First, most Asian countries, including Japan and Singapore, do not see contradictions between their ties with the United States and multilateralism. Likewise, not all countries that prefer an underinstitutionalized regionalism (e.g., Vietnam or China) maintain alliances with the United States. Second, power differentials are insufficient in predicting institution-building. Depending on which version of hegemonic stability theory one believes in, power asymmetries that produce security dependence on the part of the weaker states may or may not encourage institution-building. Thus, U.S. post-war hegemony produced a multilateral security institution in Europe, but not in Asia. Crone's attempt to explain this as a by-product of "extreme" U.S. hegemony in Asia is therefore not entirely satisfactory: contrary to his thesis, the relative decline of U.S. power in the 1980s could only produce weak institutionalization.[15] Therefore, something besides power is involved. Hemmer and Katzenstein hold that values and incongruent identities did matter in shaping the U.S. security approach to Asia,[16] while I have argued that the values and identities of Asian actors mattered even more.

Neoliberal perspectives provide another explanation for the slow and incremental institutionalization of Asia by focusing on the changing utility concerns of regional actors induced by growing regional economic interdependence. But they are too indeterminate. For example, Haggard argues that higher levels of interdependence in the Pacific do not necessarily translate into higher institutionalization and legalization of Asian regionalism.[17] Kahler, in another neoliberal analysis, predicts increased institutionalization and legalization precisely because of increased levels of economic interdependence in the region. The movement toward a more flexible view of sovereignty in

---

14. Michael Leifer, *The ASEAN Regional Forum (Adelphi Paper, No. 302)* (London: International Institute for Strategic Studies, 1996).

15. Donald Crone, "Does Hegemony Matter? The Reorganization of the Pacific Political Economy," *World Politics* 45, no. 4 (July 1993): 501–25.

16. Christopher Hemmer and Peter Katzenstein, "Why Is There No NATO in Asia: Collective Identity, Regionalism, and the Origins of Multilateralism," *International Organization* 56, no. 3 (Summer 2002): 575–607.

17. Stephen Haggard, "Regionalism in Asia and the Americas," in *Political Economy of Regionalism*, ed. Edward Mansfield and Helen Milner (New York: Columbia University Press, 1997), 46–47.

Southeast Asia since the 1997 regional economic crisis may be read as a function of Kahler's strategic interaction model, which posits a "legalized future" of Asian regionalism as a utilitarian and strategic response to the demands of growing economic interdependence.[18] Because the legalization of regional institutions involves the fundamental issue of state sovereignty, Kahler's perspective is important in understanding the recent move in Southeast Asia toward a more relaxed view of non-intervention. ASEAN's doctrine of enhanced interaction and its drafting of an ASEAN Charter can therefore be seen as a selective strategic response guided by utility considerations and subject to the logic of relative gains. Former Thai foreign minister Surin Pitsuwan, who became the Secretary-General of ASEAN in January 2008, advocated flexible engagement partly due to a need to respond more effectively to the demands of growing interdependence and shared vulnerability as demonstrated by the 1997 regional economic crisis.

I share Kahler's assessment of the overall trend toward greater institutionalization and legalization of Asian regionalism, although I view it as a much more limited phenomenon than he implies, and I am less convinced by the parsimony of his materialist and utilitarian explanation of this trend. The legalization of Asia-Pacific regionalism remains slow and heavily path-dependent. Even the 1997 financial crisis did not produce a mad rush toward institutionalization and legalization that would have broken the historical pattern of soft institutionalism in Asia. Moreover, the process is uneven—legalization in the security arena remains too scarce compared to that in the economic arena (e.g., ASEAN Free Trade Area [AFTA]) to support Kahler's thesis of a "legalized future" for Asian regionalism.

---

18. Rejecting cultural and domestic explanations for the levels of legalization, Kahler argues that legalization is contingent on choices that vary according to the instrumental and strategic concerns of regional actors. When actors see benefits of legalization outweighing its costs, such as in the sphere of economic integration and openness, they readily embrace it (an instrumental consideration). Moreover, the choice of legalization is shaped by "competing strategies and capabilities of other actors" (a strategic consideration). Miles Kahler, "Legalization as Strategy: The Asia-Pacific Case," *International Organization* 54, no. 3 (Sumer 2000): 549–71. See also Peter Drysdale, *International Economic Pluralism: Economic Policy in East Asia and the Pacific* (Sydney: Allen and Unwin, 1988); Peter Drysdale and Ross Garnut, "The Pacific: An Application of a General Theory of Economic Integration," in *Pacific Economic Dynamism and the International Economic System*, ed. C. Fred Bergsten and Marcus Nolan (Washington, DC: Institute for International Economics, 1993); Wendy Dobson and Lee Tsao Yuan, "APEC: Cooperation Amidst Diversity," *ASEAN Economic Bulletin* 10, no. 3 (1994): 231–44; Andrew Elek, "APEC Beyond Bogor: An Open Economic Association in the Asian-Pacific Region," *Asia-Pacific Economic Literature* 9, no. 1 (1995): 183–223; Miles Kahler, "Institution-building in the Pacific," in *Pacific Cooperation: Building Economic and Security Regimes in the Asia-Pacific Region*, ed. Andrew Mack and John Ravenhill (St. Leonards, NSW, Australia: Allen and Unwin, 1994); and Haggard, "Regionalism in Asia and the Americas."

In addition to functional and utilitarian motives that account for the increased legalization in Asia's economic regionalism, ASEAN is also motivated by the desire to signal to the international community that it is ready to formulate policies that conformed more closely, if not entirely, to international norms and practices.[19] This quest for legitimation is missing from neoliberal explanations, which also ignore or sidestep the importance of prior institutional choices—a different variable than "culture," which Kahler rightly dismisses—that continue to shape the mode and patterns of legalization in Asian regionalism. At most, the trend toward, and explanation for, Asia's growing but incremental institutionalization and legalization provides justification for viewing rationalism and constructivism as complimentary explanatory frameworks in norm dynamics.[20]

To sum up, institutional change in Asian regionalism cannot be explained as a product of material forces (e.g., the decline of U.S. power) or strategic bargaining spurred by growing regional economic interdependence. The so-called underinstitutionalization of Asian regionalism persisted even as the material conditions of institution-building significantly changed. A number of external shocks, such as the end of the Cold War, growing economic interdependence, and the Asian economic crisis failed to break the historical pattern of soft institutionalism in Asia, as expected and desired by the key norm entrepreneurs from Australia and Canada. Asian regional institutions, whether in the economic or security sphere, continue to remain closely tied to the soft and non-legalistic ASEAN Way, which itself reflected an earlier period of norm development in Asia. Changing material and external normative developments should not be emphasized at the expense of existing local normative frameworks and social arrangements generating deep but dynamic path dependency, which only permit an incremental and evolutionary process of institutional change in Asia.

## Extending the Argument: Asia-Pacific Economic Cooperation

The constitutive localization perspective can be extended beyond the security arena to explain the purpose and potential of regional economic institu-

---

19. This desire for conforming to international standards was implicit in Philippine foreign secretary Siazon's call for "An EU-Style ASEAN." The *Straits Times*, "EU-Style ASEAN Possible," 19 August 1998.

20. James Fearon and Alexander Wendt, "Rationalism vs Constructivism: A Skeptical View," in *Handbook of International Relations*, ed. W. Carlsnaes, T. Risse, and B.A. Simmons (London: Sage, 2002).

tions in Asia. The most prominent case in point is Asia-Pacific Economic Cooperation (APEC), established in Canberra in 1989. Its initial objectives were twofold. One was to offer regional support for trade liberalization in the global economy. The second was to promote cooperation among Asia-Pacific economies on trade, investment and other economic issues and manage the problems arising from growing regional economic interdependence.[21]

Although the ASEAN members participated in the founding of APEC, it was mainly seen as the initiative of Australia and Japan. Despite being an inter-governmental forum, APEC's roots lay in the PAFTAD and PECC processes that had been led by these two countries.[22] Similar to the earlier ideas about Pacific economic cooperation, APEC espoused the idea, albeit contested, of "open regionalism."[23] APEC's Australian inspiration was a major source of Malaysian displeasure, leading its prime minister Mahathir Mohamad to repeatedly question the organization's legitimacy. Although this was not an issue for others, especially Singapore, ASEAN's consensus-based approach meant that Malaysia's misgivings could undermine its level of support for APEC. In addition, the advent of APEC aroused ASEAN's misgivings not unlike those raised against the earlier Pacific Community idea. These concerns were twofold: a fear of marginalization within a larger grouping of more advanced and powerful Pacific nations, and the prospective formalism of rules-based trade liberalization, which APEC might encourage.

ASEAN's initial misgivings about APEC were assuaged by insider proponents—such as Singapore—which managed to frame the relationship between ASEAN and AP.EC as being that of "concentric circles," rather than being mutually exclusionary.[24] But before ASEAN would endorse APEC, it laid out four conditions: (1) APEC should not deal with political and security issues; (2) APEC should not lead to the formation of a trade bloc; (3) APEC's institutional arrangements should not reduce the importance and role of existing Asia-Pacific institutions for cooperation; and (4) ASEAN's machinery should be the center of APEC process.[25]

21. Andrew A. Faye, "APEC and the New Regionalism: GATT Compliance and Prescriptions for the WTO," *Law and Policy in International Business* 28, no. 1 (Fall 1996): 175–215.

22. Stuart Harris, "Policy Networks and Economic Cooperation: Policy Coordination in the Asia-Pacific Region," *Pacific Review* 7, no. 4 (1994): 381.

23. John Ravenhill, *APEC and the Construction of Pacific Rim Regionalism* (Cambridge: Cambridge University Press, 2001); C. Fred Bergsten, "Open Regionalism," *The World Economy* 20 (August 1997): 545–65.

24. *Far Eastern Economic Review*, 16 November 1989.

25. Noordin Sopiee, "Pan-Pacific Talks: ASEAN Is the Key," *International Herald Tribune*, 4–5 November 1989.

Conforming to the ASEAN Way of informal regionalism, APEC avoided legalistic mechanisms such as a proposed regional dispute-settlement mechanism akin to the legalistic procedures of the General Agreement on Tariffs and Trade/World Trade Organization (GATT/WTO). APEC also adopted ASEAN's consensus formula. The Osaka Action Plan on APEC in 1995 stated that a consensus approach would highlight the sense of "mutual respect" among all parties.[26] However, some improvisations were necessary: First, the idea of "flexible consensus," which "will allow those economies that are ready to move forward to do so and to allow other economies, which are not yet ready, to join later."[27] Second, the notion of "concerted unilateralism," which would see trade liberalization carried out not through time-bound formal treaties, but through "collective peer pressure of action plans implemented by each economy at its own pace."[28]

ASEAN's acceptance of APEC was not wholehearted. The Malaysian backlash against APEC came in the form of Mahathir's call for an East Asian Economic Grouping (EAEG; later renamed East Asian Economic Caucus [EAEC]) in December 1990, days before the collapse of the Uruguay Round Talks over agriculture subsidies. The EAEG excluded the key Western members of APEC—the United States, Canada, Australia, and New Zealand, with the leadership role clearly assigned to Japan.[29] EAEG recognized the new economic realities of the region with trade among East Asian countries expected to exceed trans-pacific trade in the 1990s, a sixfold increase in Japanese private investment in the region in the 1980s,[30] and the consolidation of a new intra-regional division of labor in East Asia due to Japanese, South Korean, and Taiwanese investment in Southeast Asia.

Despite being toned down to a Caucus to dampen fears of it being conceived as a formal trade bloc, the organization failed to take off. The most serious obstacle came from the Bush administration, which called the EAEG as "a very unwise direction to proceed."[31] In his memoirs, U.S. secretary of state James Baker confesses to having done his best to "kill" the proposal,

26. Asia-Pacific Economic Cooperation, *The Osaka Action Plan: Road Map to Realising the APEC Vision, Report of the Pacific Business Forum 1995* (Singapore: APEC Secretariat, 1995), 10.

27. Ibid., 10.

28. David Hulme, "Asia Takes Charge of the APEC Process," *Asian Business*, January 1996.

29. Later, in the wake of concerns regarding the exclusion of important regional actors, such as Australia, Malaysia was to insist that there was no "exclusion list" for EAEG and that Australia's participation would be possible at a subsequent stage.

30. *International Herald Tribune*, 8–9 December 1990.

31. The *Straits Times*, 22 December 1990.

"even though in public [he] took a moderate line."[32] U.S. pressure contributed to Japan's reluctance to assume leadership of the grouping, as Mahathir had envisaged.[33] The EAEC could get support only as a consultative forum within APEC to marshal the collective bargaining power of the regional states.[34]

As the EAEC proposal was being debated, APEC had taken a new turn by holding it first Leaders' Meeting in Seattle in 1993. The meeting, the idea for which originally came from Australian prime minister Paul Keating and which was enthusiastically taken up by the Clinton White House, signaled that the United States had found in APEC a useful medium to push for economic liberalization policies associated with the Washington Consensus. The U.S. motive included a desire to push the EU into making concessions on the issue of agricultural subsidies so as to bring closure to the Uruguay Round of GATT that had stalled over this issue. While the US was pushing APEC in the direction of trade liberalization, ASEAN as well as Japan were keen to use APEC as a vehicle for economic and technical cooperation (ECOTECH), which focused on human capacity building. This disagreement would cripple APEC.

Continued misgivings about APEC were part of the rationale behind ASEAN's effort to deepen its own economic cooperation in the form of AFTA. This took shape at the 1992 Singapore Summit of ASEAN leaders, the first such summit since APEC's creation. AFTA had the clear imprint of ASEAN's institutional model, including informality, non-adversarial bargaining, consensus building, and non-legalistic procedures for decision making. AFTA was to move forward at a "pace with which all governments felt comfortable." It offered at least a partial rejection of the trade and investment liberalization agenda pursued by APEC's Western members. One of AFTA's key underlying principles was ASEAN's "developmental regionalism" model.[35] This called for orienting regional free trade and investment in ways that would give domestic firms an expanded regional market at the same time giving them certain temporary protection or privileges so that they can survive increased competition and become internationally more competitive.[36] Such developmental regionalism was thus somewhat incon-

32. James A. Baker III and Thomas M. DeFrank, *The Politics of Diplomacy: Revolution, War, and Peace, 1989–1992* (New York: G.P. Putnam's Sons, 1995).

33. *Far Eastern Economic Review*, 31 January 1991, 32.

34. Rafidah Aziz, minister of international trade and industry of Malaysia, speech delivered at the Eighth Meeting of the Pacific Economic Cooperation Conference, Singapore, 20–22 May 1991.

35. Helen S. Nesadurai, *Globalization, Domestic Politics and Regionalism: The ASEAN Free Trade Area* (London: Routledge, 2003), 22, 41.

36. Nesadurai, *Globalization, Domestic Politics and Regionalism*, 41–42.

gruent with APEC's U.S.-backed ambitious trade and investment liberalization agenda.

The U.S. demand for reciprocity in trade liberalization policies contradicted ASEAN's preference for non-binding and consensual approach to institution-building and its (and Japan's) developmental approach to APEC. An ASEAN analyst would observe that the "American approach" to economic cooperation, which was to "start with legally binding commitments covering a wide range of issues," was something that "scares many people in Asia," because it conflicted with the Asian approach, which is "to agree on principles first, and then let things evolve and grow gradually."[37]

Countering the U.S. approach, ASEAN and other Asian members of APEC called for placing emphasis in APEC on economic and technical cooperation and trade facilitation, rather than trade liberalization. Specifically, Japan pushed for APEC to set up funds to promote capacity building in APEC's less developed members. And the 1997 Canadian leadership of APEC similarly created misgivings on the part of old APEC proponents of soft regionalism as the meeting seemed to be run "almost exclusively" by the APEC's "own bureaucracy," without involvement of outside actors, especially the track-II constituents—Pacific Basin Economic Council (PBEC), PAFTAD, PECC—which played such as important role in APEC's formation.[38] This would seem to be contrary to the tradition of informal and non-bureaucratic regionalism, which conformed to the ASEAN Way and which the track-II groups had respected.

It is commonplace to blame APEC's subsequent decline on the 1997 Asian economic crisis. This is only partly correct. The 1997 crisis did deal a fatal blow to APEC, which was not only incapable of responding to the crisis, because it had no mechanism for financial cooperation, but also because it simply endorsed the International Monetary Fund's(IMF's) controversial role in the crisis, which led to massive instability in Indonesia and aggravated the social and economic fallout of the crisis. The fact is that APEC had been weakened even before the 1997 economic crisis by the above-discussed normative tensions and disagreements about regional identity, especially those between the regional cognitive prior developed by ASEAN, which predisposed it toward a particular type of institutional

37. Hadi Soesastro, "APEC's Contribution to Regional Security: ASEAN and the APEC Process," paper presented at the Workshop on Development and Security in Southeast Asia, Manila, 13–16 December 1995, 8.

38. Hadi Soesastro, "APEC's Overall Goals and Objectives, Evolution and Current Status," in *Assessing APEC's Progress: Trade, Ecotech and Institutions*, ed. Richard E. Fineberg and Ye Zhao (Singapore: Institute of Southeast Asian Studies, 2001), 30.

mode and agenda, and the institutional and normative preferences of its Western members.

One result of the Asian crisis was the revival of the moribund East Asian regionalism. The crisis sparked regional disappointment and anger toward the United States, even among its allies, including Thailand and Japan. Washington's generous support for Mexico in dealing with the Peso crisis was contrasted with its relative apathy toward Thailand facing the Baht collapse. Moreover, the abrupt and total manner in which Washington rejected Japan's proposal for an Asian Monetary Fund as a bulwark against future crises "antagonized opinion leaders of the region."[39] The crisis spurred a new regional process, known as the ASEAN Plus Three (APT). The APT focused particularly on regional financial cooperation, which had not been undertaken within the APEC framework. At the behest of South Korean leader Kim Dae Jung, APT leaders set up an East Asia Vision Group (EAVG) to consider pathways toward regional cooperation. EAVG's report, released in 2001 and titled "Towards an East Asian Community: A Region of Peace, Prosperity and Progress' stressed the need for developing an East Asian, rather than Asian Pacific, regional identity and community. It also called for an East Asia Summit.[40] Whereas APEC had consciously avoided the language of community (an Australian bid to rename it Asia-Pacific Economic Community had been dropped due to opposition from ASEAN members), the EAVG championed the goal of "fostering the identity of an East Asian community" as well as "promotion of regional identity and consciousness."[41] Similarly, the East Asian Study Group (EASG), an inter-governmental panel, eloquently asserted that the need for "fostering a strong sense of East Asian identity and congeniality is essential for expediting genuine regional cooperation and, moreover, for helping reach the ultimate goal of East Asian integration."[42]

APEC has not been without accomplishments. It has served as a "regional forum for norm-setting by formulating and agreeing on a set of (non-binding)

39. Richard Stubbs, "ASEAN Plus Three: Emerging East Asian Regionalism?" *Asian Survey* 42, no. 3 (2002): 449.

40. "Towards an East Asian Community: Region of Peace, Prosperity and Progress," East Asia Vision Group Report, 2001, available at http://www.mofa.go.jp/region/asia-paci/report2001.pdf.

41. Ibid., 1–6.

42. "Final Report of the East Asia Study Group," ASEAN+3 Summit, Phnom Penh, 4 November 2002, 39, available at http://www.mofa.go.jp/region/asia-paci/asean/pmv0211/report.pdf.

competition principles."[43] But ASEAN's response to APEC reaffirms the importance of existing normative frameworks and collective identities in shaping the reception of new ideas and norms. This is as true of the economic arena as of the political-security arena. ASEAN's response to APEC harked back to many of the same arguments ASEAN had marshaled against the Pacific Community concept in the 1980s. Although ASEAN accepted APEC, thanks partly to the efforts at socialization undertaken by track-II fora, which comprised both Western and ASEAN policy intellectuals, its misgivings about APEC based on questions of regional identity and ASEAN's prior norms of developmental regionalism did not disappear. They not only shaped APEC's institutional structure and agenda, but when Western members of APEC appeared to deviate from them (e.g., the United States in pursuing its Early Voluntary Sectoral Liberalization [EVSL]), ASEAN's enthusiasm for APEC waned. In the meantime, ASEAN pursued normative and ideational alternatives to APEC, in the form of AFTA and EAEC. Thus, APEC had been weakened before the 1997 crisis, which can be regarded as the even main reason for its downfall. Later, the EAEC would form the basis for an identity-building framework that would guide East Asian regionalism leading to the first East Asia Summit in 2005. This normative and ideational delegitimation of APEC, especially the conception of APEC favored by the powerful actors led by the United States, must rank alongside the impact of the 1997 economic crisis in explaining APEC's downfall and the rise of East Asian regionalism.

### Extending the Argument beyond Asia

This book's empirical focus has been on Asia, but the framework of constitutive localization can be used to investigate norm diffusion in other parts of the world, including how ideas spread from global to regional levels and from region to region. Comparative research involving Asia and other regions could further enhance our understanding of how localization takes place under different social and normative environments, help identify and explain conditions that enable the local agents' private and public ideas to shape the process of norm diffusion, and the different types of localization that might result from these processes.

---

43. Soesastro, "APEC's Overall Goals and Objectives, Evolution and Current Status," 30. Vinod Aggarwal and Kun-Chin Lin, "APEC as an Institution," in *Assessing APEC's Progress: Trade, Ecotech and Institutions*, ed. Richard E. Fineberg and Ye Zhao (Singapore: Institute of Southeast Asian Studies, 2001), 178.

For example, the spread of norms about human rights and democracy can be seen in terms of the constitutive localization dynamic, in which prior and historically legitimate local normative frameworks play an important role in producing variations in their acceptance and institutionalization at different locations. Ignatieff's work on human rights notes the dangers of "overestimating [the West's] moral prestige" and ignoring the Third World's capacity for resistance, and suggests the possibility of using constitutive localization as a pathway for investigating the diffusion of human rights norms.[44] Appadurai's work on globalization illuminates three related processes of ideational change as a subset of cultural globalization: how local communities are "inflected" by global ideas, how global ideas are indigenized and the resulting local forms "repatriated" back to the outside world, and how local forms are globalized.[45]

In the sections below, I offer two examples from Latin America and Africa in order to illustrate the relevance of the localization framework beyond Asia: the Inter-American Democratic Charter (IADC) and the New Partnership for African Development (NEPAD). A brief comparative analysis of the norm dynamics behind these two regional initiatives leads us to predict contrasting possibilities of their success, in accordance with the theoretical argument of this book.

### Inter-American Democratic Charter

The Organization of American States (OAS) adopted the IADC on 11 September 2001 with the express "normative purpose" of providing a "collective right to democracy as opposed to the traditional defense of sovereignty."[46] The Charter was a response to the controversial 2000 elections in Peru, which the Fujimori regime was widely believed to have manipulated. Negotiations leading to the Charter have been described as a "bottom-up as opposed to top-down process."[47] The main initiative for the Charter came from South American states, especially Peru, rather than the dominant power, the United States, or the traditional "middle powers" like Canada, who are normally expected to provide leadership as morally cosmopolitan norm entrepreneurs. Peru was not a great power or a "middle

44. Michael Ignatieff, *The Warrior's Honour: Ethnic War and Modern Conscience* (Toronto: Penguin Books, 1998), 44.

45. Arjun Appadurai, *Modernity at Large: Cultural Dimensions of Globalization* (Minneapolis: University of Minnesota Press, 1996).

46. Andrew Cooper, "The Making of the Inter-American Democratic Charter: A Case of Complex Multilateralism," *International Studies Perspectives* 5, no. 1 (2004): 92.

47. Cooper, "The Making of the Inter-American Democratic Charter," 107.

power."[48] The individual local norm entrepreneurs were three key Peruvians—Manuel Rodriguez, then Peru's Permanent Representative to the OAS; Diego Garcia-Sayan, then Minister of Justice; and Javier Perez de Cuellar, former Secretary-General of the United Nations who was then the foreign minister of Peru. But these individuals did not act alone; they enjoyed and employed an extensive regional and international network built up by them.

The norm in question is the collective defense of democracy. The OAS had already accepted the norm of such intervention to deny membership to countries that have experienced coups. But it had not provided for "incumbent backsliding."[49] The IADC instituted such a provision, thereby facilitating significant normative change.

The U.S. response to the Peruvian crisis was to push for collective sanction against Peru. However, "despite its position as the dominant actor in the hemisphere, the United States could not impose its will on others."[50] This was partly because of the U.S. image as an "ambiguous (or even hypocritical) advocate of democracy in the Americas."[51] While Peru was the main advocate of the Charter, the opposition to the Charter came from Venezuela, one of the region's more authoritarian states. It is worth noting the similarity to the opposition by Burma and Vietnam to the idea of flexible engagement in Southeast Asia, which had been advocated by Thailand. Opposition to the IADC also came from the Caribbean states, attributing to the latter's "embedded support for the tenets of sovereignty and non-intervention," which result from their "own unique historical experiences."[52] These countries had not ratified the OAS 1997 Washington Protocol (OAS Resolution 1080), which had established the procedure for suspending member states whose regimes have entered office through a coup.

The adoption of the IADC is a case of progressive institutional change within the OAS. It modifies not just the norms of non-interference, but also enhances the "existing democratic solidarity paradigm" of the OAS, which had evolved after the Cold War, and had been institutionalized in Resolution 1080. The IADC (1) adds the right to democracy to the existing pro-democratic norms; (2) specifies a list of the essential elements of democ-

48. Cooper, "The Making of the Inter-American Democratic Charter," 92.

49. Thomas Legler, "The Inter-American Democratic Charter: From Peru to Venezuela and Beyond," paper presented at the Annual Conference of the International Studies Association, 25 February–1 March 2003, 9.

50. Cooper, "The Making of the Inter-American Democratic Charter," 101.

51. Cooper, "The Making of the Inter-American Democratic Charter," 100.

52. Cooper, "The Making of the Inter-American Democratic Charter," 102.

racy to be used as benchmarks against which the performance of the member countries could be assessed; (3) addresses both coups as well as antidemocratic and unconstitutional "backsliding," thereby extending Resolution 1080; and (4) provides for both preventive and proactive measures as well as punitive or reactive measures.[53] The preventive/proactive measures include "community watch" or collective vigilance for signs of democratic breakdowns or backsliding, and electoral assistance to countries undergoing democratic transition or restoration. The punitive actions include a rapid response provision, which is open-ended in the sense that it authorizes the OAS to take decisions and action on a case-by-case basis and as deemed appropriate. But because the Charter covers unconstitutional alterations to democratic government, collective action by the OAS under the IADC can be undertaken before a coup. The IADC also provides for mission diplomacy and third-party mediation measures. If these fail, it provides for punitive measures, including the suspension of membership of the concerned state from the OAS. The Charter also establishes a role for the OAS in strengthening democracy through a range of pro-active programs such as civic education of children and youth in democratic norms.[54]

But the IADC is not a case of fundamental change to the OAS institutions and normative framework. It also conformed to the established political framework and normative principles of OAS regionalism."[55] Although the civil society was consulted in the making of the Charter, the final product was marked by a high "degree of state-centrism." Preventive measures such as collective vigilance and mission diplomacy could be undertaken "by invitation only" or through prior consent.[56] The process leading to the creation of the Charter is thus described as a "hybrid"; "if much of the grip of the old has been lifted, this case demonstrates that the new has not been ushered in as a totality."[57] But this outcome represents a significant progress in OAS's approach to political instability in the region:

> In addition to offering a synthesis of the existing legal instruments at the regional level, the Democratic Charter marks a clear evolution of the nature of commitments of the American states to the collective defense of democracy. . . . Going well beyond formal mechanisms traditionally associated with the operation of a democratic order, the new definition of democracy comprises a

53. Legler, "The Inter-American Democratic Charter," 10.
54. Legler, "The Inter-American Democratic Charter," 9–10.
55. Cooper, "The Making of the Inter-American Democratic Charter," 108.
56. Legler, "The Inter-American Democratic Charter," 9.
57. Cooper, "The Making of the Inter-American Democratic Charter," 95.

number of original references to human rights, poverty, and development. Finally, the Charter institutionalizes the will of the American states to answer collectively in cases of "alteration" of the constitutional order vis-à-vis countries of the area, and to take the step of suspending nondemocratic states from the ambit of activities within the inter-American system.[58]

## The New Partnership for African Development

The origins of NEPAD can be traced to the Summit of the Organization of African Unity (OAU) in 1999, where Nigerian president Olusegun Obasanjo introduced a proposal on peace and security issues leading to a new initiative, the Conference on Security, Stability, Development and Cooperation in Africa (CSSDCA). This was perhaps modeled after the OSCE, with development being added to peace and security issues. At the G8 meeting in Okinawa in July 2000, a troika of African leaders—Abdelaziz Bouteflika of Algeria, Thabo Mbeki of South Africa, and Obasanjo of Nigeria—met with the G8 leaders and discussed debt relief for Africa. The outcome was the need for a "workable plan" for a "compact" between African leaders and the G8. As South Africa's foreign minister remarked, "We were pleasantly surprised at the convergence of views from both sides. . . . There seems to be emerging a very clear agenda and consensus around issues that we can build a strategic partnership on."[59] Following the Okinawa meeting, President Mbeki was given the task of developing a plan to institutionalize this partnership.

For its proponents such as South Africa, NEPAD is a response to Africa's economic ills, including poverty, underdevelopment, and the debt burden. It has been described as "the most ambitious project" for Africa's economic transformation,[60] which seeks to bring into Africa two globally prominent economic and political norms—"norms of free markets and democratic policies"[61] and "norms of good governance."[62] According to the proponents' view, these norms offer an answer to Africa's ills, including its "continued marginalization from globalization process"[63] and "economic decline

58. Cooper, "The Making of the Inter-American Democratic Charter," 95.

59. Cited in Jìmí O. Adésìnà, "NEPAD and the Challenge of Africa's Development: Towards a Political Economy of a Discourse," paper presented at for the Tenth General Assembly of the Council for the Development of Social Science Research in Africa, Kampala, Uganda, 8–12 December 2002, 7.

60. Yash Tandon, "NEPAD and FDIS: Symmetries and Contradictions," *Third World Network Africa*, 29 April 2002, 1.

61. International Peace Academy, "NEPAD: African Initiative, New Partnership?" *IPA Workshop Report* (New York: IPA, 2002), 4.

62. Ibid., 9.

63. Paragraph 2 of NEPAD, cited in Tandon, "NEPAD and FDIS," 2.

and poor governance."[64] For them, NEPAD is a "new framework of interaction with rest of the world."[65]

NEPAD's opponents, however, have sought to portray the ideology behind NEPAD as "a shorthand for privatization," imposed by the IMF and the World Bank.[66] It is seen as an extension of "the logic of the post-Washington Consensus," which is "profoundly neoliberal in mindset," combining a "belief in the moral necessity of market forces in the economy" and "entrepreneurs . . . as a good and necessary social group."[67] The normative contestation underlying NEPAD is well captured by a critic who opined that

> NEPAD is an instrument of contestation between Africans seeking self-determination in their development efforts and those forces that seek the continuation of the exploitation of the continent's resources upon which the accumulation of their wealth depends . . . NEPAD provides a good example for illustrating this historical contestation that continues to take place between these two forces.[68]

The debate over NEPAD contrasts new neoliberal norms with Africa's previous continental developmental norms and agendas.[69] NEPAD conflicts with several principles that have characterized the existing normative framework for Africa's development, including sovereignty and non-interference, African solutions to African problems, and the rejection of IMF-backed Structural Adjustment Programs (SAPs).

Viewed as such, NEPAD went against the essence of what Adebayo Adedeji has identified as four "imperatives" of Africa's existing "development paradigms"—"self-reliance, self-sustainment encompassing socio-economic transformation accompanied by the politics and policy of restitution, holistic human development and the democratization of the development process."[70] These principles, he contends, ran through earlier development plans for Africa—the Lagos Plan of Action (LPA 1980–2000) and the Final Act of Lagos (1980), the African Alternative Framework to Structural Adjustment Programme (AAF-SAP 1989), the African Charter for Popular

---

64. Cited in Tandon, "NEPAD and FDIS," 2.
65. Paragraph 60 of NEPAD, cited in Tandon, "NEPAD and FDIS," 3.
66. Adésínà, "NEPAD and the Challenge of Africa's Development," 4.
67. Adésínà, "NEPAD and the Challenge of Africa's Development," 3–4.
68. Dani W. Nabudere, "NEPAD: Historical Background and Its Prospects," paper presented at the African Forum for Envisioning Africa, Nairobi, Kenya, 26–29 April 2002, 3.
69. Adésínà, "NEPAD and the Challenge of Africa's Development," abstract.
70. Adebayo Adedeji, "From the Lagos Plan of Action to the New Partnership for African Development and from the Final Act of Lagos to the Constitutive Act: Whither Africa?" keynote address delivered at the African Forum for Envisioning Africa, Nairobi, Kenya, 26–29 April 2002, 10.

Participation for Development (1990), and the United Nations New Agenda for the Development of Africa in the 1990s. These strategies constituted "the continent's preferred development agenda" in the 1980s and 1990s.[71]

The very fact that NEPAD has had the strong backing of the Western donor countries forms the basis for much of the suspicion of the initiative from within Africa. The fact that it was at the Davos World Economic Forum meeting on 28 January 2001 that "the first formal briefing on the process in developing NEPAD" took place has added to this perception of NEPAD being an initiative imposed on Africa by Western donor nations.[72] Although proponents argue that NEPAD envisages more aid and trade flows to Africa, opponents see this as potentially leading Africa deeper into the debt trap. As Adedeji noted, "The protagonists of NEPAD should never forget that it was this model that exacerbated the dependency syndrome of the African economies and at the same time led to mass pauperization and deprivation of the African people."[73] Some suggested institutional features of NEPAD, such as the idea of a board of directors comprising debtor and creditor representatives, would "exacerbate neo-colonialism rather than advance the cause of economic decolonization."[74] One of the key institutional mechanisms of NEPAD is a "Peer Review Mechanism" for three core initiatives—peace and stability, democracy and political governance, and economic and corporate governance. That leaders found in violation of these norms were expected to undergo a process of "constructive dialogue" with their African peers to rectify the situation[75] has been criticized on the grounds that "[a]n African peer review mechanism (APRM) . . . will only work if its judgment always falls in line with that of the donors. Whenever it does not, the aid may stop flowing and the trade may become less free."[76]

The identity of the leading Africa proponent of NEPAD, South Africa, also mattered. The fact that the key NEPAD document was a "distinctly South African reading of the development challenges facing Africa,"[77] created the impression that the document was not "African" enough, leading

71. Ibid., 3–4.
72. Mbeki's speech at Davos, cited in Adésínà, "NEPAD and the Challenge of Africa's Development," 8.
73. Adedeji, "From the Lagos Plan of Action to the New Partnership for African Development and from the Final Act of Lagos to the Constitutive Act," 8.
74. Ibid.
75. International Peace Academy, "NEPAD," 9.
76. Adedeji, "From the Lagos Plan of Action to the New Partnership for African Development," 11.
77. Adésínà, "NEPAD and the Challenge of Africa's Development," 7.

to "identity concerns" about NEPAD.[78] Moreover, one of the sources of the South African plan for NEPAD was the official macroeconomic framework of South Africa, "Growth, Employment and Redistribution" (GEAR), which had been perceived to be "a profoundly neoliberal document."[79] Although attempts have been made by South Africa to "graft" the NEPAD principles onto some of the existing regional and continental developmental plans[80]—such as the Omega Plan of Abdoulaye Wade billed as "Africa's strategy for globalization"—[81] as well as the Millennium Partnership for the African Recovery Program (MAP), there have been misgivings and "identity concerns" about NEPAD's origins and implementation as an African project. The implementation of NEPAD seems to be delinked from the main regional institution, OAU (renamed African Union [AU]), thereby lacking in legitimacy as an indigenous initiative. According to one critic, "the origin of NEPAD lies . . . outside the OAU mechanism, and involves the troika taking 'matters into their own hands'."[82]

## Comparison

A comparative analysis of the Inter-American Democratic Charter and NEPAD suggests that the former was much more conducive to localization (see table 6.1). The manner of IADC's adoption was much more consistent with the requirements of localization than that of NEPAD. IADC's advocates were clearly not speaking to an outside audience, it was undertaken largely within the existing institutional apparatuses, and it was an extension of the OAS. On the contrary, NEPAD seems to conflict with the OAU mechanism, notwithstanding late attempts to integrate it with existing African plans and locate it within the OAU/AU. Furthermore, whereas the IADC was possible because of the discrediting of Latin America's prior norms, especially non-interference and the consequent tolerance for coups (thanks to democratic transitions), NEPAD was an initiative that clashed with norms such as non-interference and identity norms such as those embodied in previous African development plans. Hence, the prospects for NEPAD's success in inducing meaningful institutional change in the regional governance structure appears to be less bright than that of the IADC.

78. Adésínà, "NEPAD," 7.
79. Adésínà, "NEPAD," 8.
80. International Peace Academy, "NEPAD," 4.
81. Adésínà, "NEPAD," 8.
82. Adésínà, "NEPAD," 7.

**Table 6.1.** Inter-American Democratic Charter and the New Partnership for African Development

| | Inter-American Democratic Charter | New Partnership for African Development |
|---|---|---|
| Ideas | Democracy and human rights | "Norms of good governance"[a] and "Norms of free markets and democratic policies."[a] |
| Regional cognitive prior | Promotion of democracy and human rights. Diluted sovereignty and non-interference. | Sovereignty and non-interference; African solutions to African problems; rejection of Structural Adjustment Programs. |
| Local agents | Peru | Presidents of South Africa and Nigeria. |
| Contestation | Opposed by Venezuela (an authoritarian regime that disagreed over the definition of democracy) and the Caribbean countries (out of deference to non-interference, which remains strong in that sub-region). | Between Africans seeking self-determination in their development efforts and those forces that seek the continuation of the exploitation of the continent's resources. |
| Grafting norm | Non-recognition of regimes, which came into power through coups. | Some synergy on Omega Plan, Millennium Partnership for the African Recovery Program, and the New African Initiative. But these plans were themselves recent experiments by African leaders rather than affirmation of old development paradigms. |
| Role of dominant powers or middle powers | The United States and Canada were relatively passive supporters. | The United States and G8 pushing strongly for NEPAD. |
| Desired institutional outcome | Mechanisms that delegitimize not only regimes that come to power through coups, but also anti-democratic and unconstitutional "backsliding." Provides for both preventive and proactive measures as well as punitive or reactive measures. | "Peer Review Mechanism" for three core initiatives: peace and stability, democracy and political governance, and economic and corporate governance; "Under this mechanism, leaders found in violation of these norms will undergo a process of 'constructive dialogue' with their African peers to rectify the situation."[a] |
| Prospects | Probable success of norm diffusion. | Possible failure of norm diffusion. |

[a] International Peace Academy, "NEPAD: African Initiative, New Partnership?" *IPA Workshop Report* (New York: IPA, 2002).

## "Bringing Asia In"

In this book, I have tried to focus on the North-South divide in international relations (IR) theory. Katzenstein's warning against applying Eurocentric criteria to study Asian regionalism[83] underscores a larger point: IR theory remains heavily Eurocentric and Americanocentric. David Kang has criticized Western IR theorists for "getting Asia wrong."[84] My focus is on bringing Asia in.[85]

This book suggests two pathways through which international relations theory can be made less ethnocentric and more representative of non-Western, including Asian ideas and experiences.[86] The first may be termed the *universalization of local or locally derived knowledge*. This is done by showing that a conceptual framework for studying norm diffusion can be drawn from Asian historical experiences, especially Southeast Asian historiography, which highlights how local actors borrowed foreign ideas to seek legitimation. This could then be used to create a framework that could have broader applicability to both security and economic issues within Asia and beyond. Hence, the theoretically relevant insights about norm dynamics do not rest solely or mainly on Asia's cultural distinctiveness. Rather, the book generalizes from the Asian experiences to develop insights that have validity across cultures and time. Such an approach informs, enriches, and universalizes IR theory.

The constitutive localization perspective that underpins this book answers central questions about how ideas and norms spread through the international system and how they shape the design and performance of regional institutions. This perspective shows not only that ideas matter generally, but, more vitally, that they spread through local initiative and localization rather than hegemonic power or proselytization. Its generalizations about the norm dynamics in Asian regionalism, drawing on a classical pattern of interaction in Southeast Asia based on the flow of ideas from India to Southeast Asia, demonstrates that it is possible to develop theoretical explanations of world politics from local experiences, both historical and contemporary.

83. See chapter 2, n. 71 in this volume.
84. David Kang, "Getting Asia Wrong: The Need foe New Analytic Frameworks," *International Security* 27, no. 4 (Summer 2003): 57–85.
85. Amitav Acharya, "Identity without Exceptionalism: Challenges for Asian Political and International Studies," keynote address to the inaugural workshop of the Asian Political and International Studies Association, 1–2 November 2001, Kuala Lumpur, Malaysia.
86. For further discussion on ways to address the neglect of non-Western voices in IR theory, see Amitav Acharya and Barry Buzan, eds., "Why Is There no Non-Western International Relations Theory? Reflections on and from Asia," *International Relations of the Asia-Pacific* 7, no. 3 (September 2007; Special Issue).

A second pathway of addressing the absence of non-Western voices and experiences in IR theory may be termed the study of *local constructions or/ and contributions to global order*. Drawing extensively from previously unavailable or unused original documents of regional conferences from regional archives and sources shows how Asia played a major role in the construction of the global sovereignty regime, and that Asian actors were not simply passive recipients of international norms when it came to organizing the security architecture of their region. Conceptualizations of regionalism in world politics remain dominated by the European experience and Eurocentric criteria. Yet, major developments in norm diffusion in world politics both during and after the Cold War have taken place in Asian regional interactions, which need to be taken into account by IR theory.

I have shown how the early post-war Asian conferences localized and reconstructed non-intervention. The emergence and the normative and institutional features of ASEAN were not only the product of the localization of the non-intervention norm, but as a result of this local construction, the norm itself was strengthened at the global level. The ARF was the institutional product of the localization of the common/cooperative security norm, which originated in Europe. This localized norm of cooperative security has had a wider effect, helping not only to teach ASEAN principles and modalities to Northeast Asia and South Asia, but also providing the basis for conceptualizing possible security institutions in the Middle East.[87] Such developments have contributed to the *global* appeal of common/cooperative security as a framework for security cooperation alongside collective security and collective defense.

Viewed as such, the constitutive localization perspective has major implications for IR theory. It shifts the focus of the literature on norm diffusion from the question of whether ideas matter, to which and whose ideas matter. Although the first question dominates the debate between rationalists and constructivists, the second question is, or should be, a matter of debate within the constructivist school. Empirically, the debate can be presented by posing the following question: if ideational forces mattered in the construction of Asian regionalism, whose ideas mattered most?

---

87. There are some indications that the cooperative security norm, localized in Asia from its original European source, might be influencing international debates about how to promote cooperative security institutions in unstable regions, such as the Middle East. See for example, The Stanley Foundation, "The Future of Persian Gulf Security: Alternatives for the 21st Century," *Policy Dialogue Brief*, 3–5 September 2005; The Stanley Foundation, "The United States, Iran, and Saudi Arabia: Necessary Steps Toward a New Gulf Security Order," *Policy Dialogue Brief*, October 20–22, 2005; Joseph McMillan, Richard Sokolsky, and Andrew C. Winner, "Toward a New Regional Security Architecture," *Washington Quarterly* 26, no.3 (Summer 2003): 161–75.

To be sure, the roles of external normative currents and actors are important. Thus, the European/Westphalian norms of sovereignty in the early post–World War II period shaped the foreign policy and international relations of Third World states, including newly independent countries in Asia. Post–Cold War Asia saw both European and international (UN) norms (i.e., common security and collective intervention) shaping Asian regional multilateral security cooperation. But in addressing the "whose ideas matter" question, we shift constructivist norm scholarship from the current dominance of the "moral proselytism of transnational moral entrepreneurs," toward an analytic framework that stresses the adaptation and contextualization of relevant foreign ideas by local norm recipients. This framework builds a middle ground between sociological institutionalism, which emphasizes universal or universalizing moral standards and historical institutionalism, which emphasizes prior choices, frameworks, and path dependency. Ignoring historical institutionalism would lead to an incomplete explanation of transnational norm dynamics in world politics. Constructivists who explain why and how norms spread by looking primarily at the global normative environment (featuring such liberal norms as common security and collective intervention) and transnational norm entrepreneurship, would have difficulty telling us why Asia-Pacific regionalism remains underinstitutionalized with respect to these norms. After all, these norms have enjoyed global prominence and Western norm entrepreneurs have been earnestly committed to promoting them regionally. By focusing on receivership alongside the acknowledged role of transnational norm entrepreneurs, this book broadens the scope of our investigations into normative change in world politics.

The spread of ideas and norms is therefore not a one-way process in which local actors—individuals, epistemic communities, and regional institutions—act as passive learners to transnational norm entrepreneurs. This captures only a small part of norm diffusion. A more interactive understanding of the process is warranted, in which the initiative belongs also to local agents. Through local initiative, feedback, and reconstruction, the constitutive localization process stimulates norm diffusion and deserves to be recognized in any serious effort to understand normative change in global politics.

# Appendix
## KEY CONCEPTS, REGIONAL DEFINITION

## Key Concepts

### Norms

A *norm* is a "standard of appropriate behavior for actors with a given identity."[1] In this book, I use norms and ideas interchangeably although bearing in mind that ideas can be held privately, and may or may not have behavioral implications, whereas norms are always collective and behavioral.[2] Norms do not necessarily have a "moral" connotation or purpose. Some norms are undoubtedly moral, such as human rights norms. However, norms are about "appropriate" behavior, rather than "morally appropriate" behavior. Norms can be "amoral" or "morally neutral."[3] Constructivist

---

1. Martha Finnemore and Kathryn Sikkink, "International Norm Dynamics and Political Change," *International Organization* 52, no. 4 (Autumn 1998): 891.

2. Judith Goldstein, *Ideas, Interests, and American Trade Policy* (Ithaca: Cornell University Press, 1993).

3. Positivism's separability thesis holds that the legality of a norm does not necessarily depend on its substantive moral merits. Similarly, in order to have appeal and in order to be propagated, norms need not have moral content. Kenneth Einar Himma, "Incorporationism and the Objectivity of Moral Norms," *Legal Theory* 5 (1999): 415–34. Indeed, the literature on norms in sociology and psychology distinguishes between "moral norms" and "behavioral norms." Moral norms "refer to standards of conduct that are believed to be 'right,' 'just,' or 'ideal' forms of behavior." Behavioral norms are "standards of conduct that are deemed the 'real patterns,' i.e., what people actually do, irrespective of what they are ideally supposed to do, or what they themselves believe they should do" (M.D. Buffalo and Joseph W. Rodgers, "Behavioral Norms, Moral Norms, and Attachment: Problems of Deviance and Conformity," *Social Problems* 19, no.1 [Summer 1971]: 101–13). The distinction between moral and behavioral norms is borrowed from Lamar T. Empey, "Delinquency Theory and Recent Research," *Journal of Research in Crime and Delinquency* no. 4 (January 1967): 32–42. The standard of conduct and its appropriateness can be judged in terms other than what is "right, just or ideal," including some deeply held group values and cultural identities of actors. In addition, the moral content of norms may change over time, partly through processes of social construction and constitutive localization. Norms that are regarded as moral in a specific historical

literature has focused too much on the spread of moral norms at the expense of behavioral types. This limits the usefulness of constructivist perspectives on the role of ideas in world politics. In this book, I use norms in the broadest sense—they can be either, or combine both moral and behavioral elements.

Of the four concepts whose diffusion is studied in this book, nonintervention (at least in the early post-war period), common/cooperative security, and collective intervention can be regarded as having some moral content.[4] Collective defense in regional pacts can be regarded as a behavioral norm, because its advocacy and appeal rests on its supposed ability to respond to the "real" security needs of states. But as is discussed below, some proponents of collective defense do believe in its moral underpinnings, as well.

## Non-Intervention

*Non-intervention* (used in this book interchangeably with non-interference) is a central principle of state sovereignty alongside other principles such as recognition and equality of states. In essence, non-intervention connotes a proscription against action by a state or group of states to alter the domestic politics or some aspects thereof of another state. Two aspects of the doctrine of non-intervention are especially important to this study. First, although in its traditional sense non-intervention proscribes coercive action only, there is, however, some ambiguity on this point. Action undertaken with the consent of the target state is generally not regarded as a violation of non-intervention, but this has not prevented the *framing* of intervention to include supportive action. Hence the notion of *constructive intervention*.

---

context or time may be regarded as less desirable in other periods and contexts. This applies to the notion of non-intervention, which was a "moral" norm to leaders like Nehru in the early post-war period because of its association with neutralism and anti-colonialism, but became progressively "immoral" as the Cold War progressed because of its invocation to shield repressive regimes from human rights abuses. Similarly, the functional value of norms can change. Although norms of non-intervention and autonomy were, and continue to be, important in avoiding inter-state war in Southeast Asia, they have become functionally deficient in coping with transnational dangers such as financial volatility or terrorism. As I have noted elsewhere, "while norms do matter, they do not necessarily matter in a positive, progressive manner. Norms can matter negatively, by creating barriers and obstacles to change. The same stickiness that makes them important can also render them morally unappealing and functionally outdated. Yet, to say that norms arrest progress is not to dismiss their relevance; they are important in shaping both positive and negative outcomes" (Amitav Acharya, "Do Norms and Identity Matter? Community and Power in Southeast Asia's Regional Order," *Pacific Review* 18, no.1 [March 2005]: 102–3).

4. They can also be regarded as "prescriptive norms" that combine moral principles with considerations of efficiency and utility.

Second, non-intervention proscribes both military and non-military forms of interference, the latter including a range of actions, such as espionage; sanctuary and assistance to anti-regime groups; diplomatic action, including dialogue with a regime to alter its policies and raising the domestic political situation of a country in multilateral forums and economic and political sanctions.

## Collective Defense

*Collective defense* refers to a security arrangement geared toward deterring and defending against a commonly perceived threat external to a grouping. Unlike collective security, which involves agreement among a group of states to jointly deter and punish aggression committed by any one member of a group against any other, collective defense arrangements usually pre-designate the threat. Collective defense is not a moral concept, unlike, for example, human rights protection, although it may not, depending on the context, be entirely devoid of some moral purpose. European (especially British) proponents of balance of power in the seventeenth–nineteenth centuries viewed collective defense alliances—which were deemed necessary to maintain the balance—as morally desirable because they preserved the autonomy of states and prevented the state-system from turning into an empire. U.S. Secretary of State John Foster Dulles, the biggest proponent of collective defense in the early post-war period, famously (infamously to his critics) called non-alignment—which called for abstinence from collective defense pacts—"immoral," because it "did not take a stance between what the US considered right and wrong."[5] Dulles's non-aligned critics, especially India's Jawaharlal Nehru, for their part considered membership in collective defense pacts to be not only dangerous, because of the risk of provoking superpower rivalry and intervention they carried, but also found it entirely objectionable that the "great countries of Asia and Africa should come out

5. D.V. Venkatagiri, "The Transformation in Indo-US Relations: A SWOT Analysis," 27 July 2005, accessed 20 August 2007 from Manhattan International Development Corporation's website, now available as an 18 Oct 2008 Google snapshot of the page, at http://www.manhat tanidc.org/marketplace/news/details.cfm?QID=2693&ClientID=11002. For historical background, see Cecil Crabb, *The Elephants and the Grass: A Study of Non-Alignment* (New York: Praeger, 1967). Collective defense was part of Dulles's effort to legitimize (a core function of a norm) the global U.S. campaign to resist the advance of communism, which in his view posed a grave threat to U.S. values of freedom and justice. International relations scholars have recognized the "multilateral" (which implies inclusiveness) nature of collective defense institutions—such as NATO, which is seen to have fostered socialization and created the basis for a transatlantic security community. See for example, John G. Ruggie, "Multilateralism: The Anatomy of an Institution," in *Multilateralism Matters*, ed. John G. Ruggie (New York: Columbia University Press, 1993).

of bondage into freedom only to degrade themselves or humiliate themselves in this way."[6] The debate over collective defense pacts in the post–World War II period was thus couched, if not in strictly moral terms, then at least in terms of an argument over what constituted appropriate foreign policy and strategic behavior for the newly sovereign states; in other words, over "standard of appropriate behavior for actors with a given identity."[7]

### Common and Cooperative Security

*Common security* may be defined as a system of dialogue, confidence building, and transparency measures with the primary goal of reducing tensions and conflicts within a group of states. Common security is geared more toward intra-mural confidence-building and conflict avoidance than security against external threats. As such, common security is more inclusive than collective defense; it is often described as "security with" as opposed to "security against" one's enemy. Unlike collective security, common security carries no collective and formal military commitment against aggression from within a group of states. Instead, it relies on confidence building, preventive diplomacy, and conflict resolution to achieve intra-group understanding and stability. In post–Cold War Asia, common security was rendered into a doctrine of "cooperative security," to signify a less legalistic concept and process than the European (CSCE) notion of common security.

### Collective Intervention

*Collective intervention* is action—diplomatic, political, economic, and military—undertaken multilaterally to cope with transnational challenges facing a group of actors. This is different from the traditional definition of intervention. The latter implies action that an outside party undertakes to *affect or change the domestic institutions or politics of another state.* The concept of collective intervention is a broader notion that involves multilateral action to cope with issues that *may originate from within the physical boundaries of the state, but which have regional and international implications.* In other words, collective intervention is a framework for responding to domestic issues with transnational implications, issues that are neither strictly domestic nor strictly inter-state, but straddle both.

6. Speech by Jawaharlal Nehru to the Political Committee of the Bandung Conference, 23 April 1955, Proceedings of the Bandung Political Committee, UUOD.
7. Finnemore and Sikkink, "International Norm Dynamics and Political Change."

Like intervention generally, collective intervention can be military or non-military, the latter involving political and economic sanctions or threat of such sanctions, and other forms of pressure designed to induce change in the behavior of the target states. It can be undertaken for a variety of purposes, ranging from stopping genocide to promoting political change in, and providing humanitarian assistance to, states facing internal strife. In this respect, collective intervention differs from the more familiar notion of *humanitarian intervention*. Although the latter is an integral part of the collective intervention concept, in this book I have used collective intervention to underscore its broader nature. Humanitarian intervention connotes the primary purpose of intervention to be the protection of human rights from abuse, including genocide.

Collective intervention subsumes, but goes beyond, this definition. It may be directed at promoting political change, including regime change or political liberalization, or refer to collective action to deal with various transnational threats: financial volatility, refugees flows, human rights abuses, pandemics, terrorism, and environmental degradation. More important, whereas humanitarian intervention is often associated with the use of force, collective intervention includes political, diplomatic, and economic instruments.[8] Moreover, collective intervention is by definition a *multilateral* act, whereas humanitarian intervention may be undertaken unilaterally by a state or a group of states without having a multilateral basis. This is exemplified in controversies over U.S. and Belgian intervention in the Congo in 1964; India's intervention in East Pakistan in 1971, which resulted in the creation of Bangladesh; Belgium's intervention in Zaire in 1978; Tanzania's invasion of Uganda in 1979, which led to the overthrow of Idi Amin regime; and Vietnam's invasion of Kampuchea (Cambodia) in 1978. None of these interventions were spurred by the UN's approval.

My usage of the term collective intervention in this book is both broad and highly contextual. It is difficult to *name* the international norm that

---

8. Opinions differ as to whether humanitarian intervention must involve the use of military force. Sean Murphy sees humanitarian intervention as "*the threat or use of force* by a state, group of states, or international organization primarily for the purpose of protecting the nationals of the target state from widespread deprivations of internationally recognized human rights." Sean D. Murphy, *Humanitarian Intervention: The United Nations in an Evolving World Order* (University Park: University of Pennsylvania Press, 1996), 11–12 (emphasis added). On the contrary, Fernando Téson allows for non-military forms of humanitarian intervention. For him humanitarian intervention is "proportionate transboundary help, *including forcible help*, provided by governments to individuals in another state who are being denied basic human rights and who themselves would be rationally willing to revolt against their oppressive government." Fernando Téson, *Humanitarian Intervention: An Inquiry into Law and Morality*, 2nd ed. (New York: Transnational, 1997), 5 (emphasis added).

influenced ASEAN's deliberations about reforming itself in the 1990s in order to better respond to the human rights situation in Burma, the 1997 Asian financial crisis, and environmental challenges such as the Indonesian forest fires in the later half of the 1990s. As discussed in chapter 5, in proposing ideas such as "constructive intervention" (proposed by Malaysian deputy prime minister Anwar Ibrahim in 1997) and "flexible engagement" (mooted by Thai foreign minister Surin Pitsuwan in 1998), the advocates of collective intervention were conscious of the fact that the problems facing ASEAN were more than the humanitarian crisis in Cambodia or Burma. Their target was the sanctity of non-intervention, ASEAN's cognitive prior. But my interviews with the proponents of "flexible engagement" reveal that the international norm that came closest to influencing their thinking on taking ASEAN beyond non-intervention was *humanitarian intervention*. It was this norm that offered the most powerful challenge to the traditional notion of state sovereignty and non-intervention, which was at this time being blamed for ASEAN's weak response to the crises in Cambodia and Burma, as well as the Asian financial crisis. Moreover, it was this idea that was enjoying the greatest prominence in redefining attitudes toward sovereignty at the international level; hence, it offered the best chance of international legitimation and support of the proposals that the proponents of "flexible engagement" in ASEAN were clearly hoping to obtain. However, these proponents were not seeking the adoption of humanitarian intervention in the sense of advocating military intervention (although they did invoke the term "intervention") to alter the politics of weak states in their neighborhood. Rather they would frame it into a softer variant, which could then be presented to their ASEAN counterparts as a way of coping with a broad range of transnational challenges. This framing may be seen as a form of *prelocalization* (see table 2.1).

Collective defense and non-intervention were arguably two of the most powerful ideas of the Cold War international order. They reflected the advent of the Cold War in the East-West relationship, and the transition from colonialism to independence in the North-South domain, respectively. Similarly, common security and collective intervention were the two most globally prominent security norms of the post-Cold War era. They symbolized the transformation of the international security order following the end of the Cold War. Common security presaged the collapse of the Soviet bloc. Collective intervention indicated the transition from Westphalian sovereignty in the wake of the U.S.-led UN intervention in northern Iraq and Somalia. These two ideas were therefore core elements of the New World Order.

Aside from their global prominence, these four norms capture the security predicament of states in its internal and external dimensions. Non-intervention and collective intervention relate to international or transnational security challenges to states. Collective defense and common security are about the response of states to security threats from other states. Hence, these norms cover the broad range of the security behavior of states. By studying contestations and localization involving these four norms, one gets a comprehensive picture of the process of norm diffusion in Asian regionalism and its institutional outcomes—the primary purpose of this book—as well as the reception of these norms in world politics more generally.

## Southeast Asia

Although this is a book about Asian regionalism, Southeast Asia—defined here to include Burma, Thailand, Malaysia, Singapore, Indonesia, Vietnam, Brunei, Philippines, Cambodia, and Laos—occupies a central place in this study. This need not be surprising. Asian regionalism, in so far as institutions are concerned, has been quite Southeast Asian-centric. As Bernard Gordon, a perceptive observer of Asian regionalism, wrote in 1963:

> Indigenous interest in regional cooperation is not evenly spread throughout the whole of Asia . . . this interest very clearly centers on the subregion of Southeast Asia. Occasionally observers have suggested a considerably broader format for Asian regionalism; in particular, it has sometimes been proposed that India and Japan might take the lead in somehow bolstering the weak states of Southeast Asia . . . But present trends (and reasonable projections from them) do not support even that view, for it is only in Southeast Asia where cooperative patterns have begun to develop and where there is an increasing pace of "regional activity."[9]

This has proven to be prophetic. Following the failure of early post-war efforts, led by India and desired by China, to set up a permanent institution, it was in Southeast Asia that the first regional organization took shape in the form of ASEAN. Founded in 1967, ASEAN was presented by its founders as an Asian form of regionalism, stressing a distinctive Asian identity and cultural style. ASEAN also turned out to be arguably one of the most successful regional institutions outside Europe.[10] In the 1990s, ASEAN became the hub of a wider Asia-Pacific regionalism, hence we have the

9. Bernard Gordon, *Toward Disengagement in Asia: A Strategy for American Foreign Policy* (Englewood Cliffs, N.J.: Prentice-Hall, 1964), 92.
10. ASEAN's founding members—Indonesia, Malaysia, Thailand, the Philippines, and Singapore—were joined by Brunei (1984), Vietnam (1995), Laos and Burma (1997) and Cambodia (1999).

ASEAN Regional Forum (1994) and ASEAN Plus Three (1997). Even the region's economic institutions such as APEC have been based on the ASEAN model of decision making.

The definition of what constitutes Southeast Asia has varied, sometimes encompassing a wider area than what is recognized as its geographic scope today.[11] India, Pakistan and Sri Lanka, now considered to be part of South Asia, along with Indonesia and Burma were members of the Conference of South-East Asian Prime Ministers, which sponsored the 1955 Bandung Conference.[12] The historical study of Southeast Asian regionalism actually overlaps with the study of Asian regionalism. Southeast Asia is also important to the question of why a regional collective defense organization did not take hold in Asia. This is because SEATO constituted the most important post-war U.S. effort to organize a multilateral collective defense organization in Asia involving both Western and non-Western states.

11. Acharya, *The Quest for Identity: International Relations of Southeast Asia* (Singapore: Oxford University Press, 2000).
12. Colombo Conference Minutes, UUOD.

# Bibliography of Primary Sources

**Unpublished Documents**

Indian Council on World Affairs, New Delhi
ICWA ARC Files.

Library of Congress, Washington, DC
Deplu Paper on ASEAN Security Community, 2003.

Ministry of Foreign Affairs, Indonesia
John F. Dulles Papers.

Ministry of Foreign Affairs Archives, People's Republic of China
No. 207–00004–03
No. 207–00015–01

The National Archive, United Kingdom (TNA)

DEFE 13: Ministry of Defence: Private Office: Registered Files (all Ministers'), 1950–1979.
DO 35: Dominions Office and Commonwealth Relations Office: Original Correspondence, 1915–1971.
FCO 15: Foreign and Commonwealth Office: South East Asian Department: Registered Files (D and FA Series), 1967–1976.
FCO 24: Foreign and Commonwealth Office, Far East and Pacific Department and Foreign and Commonwealth Office, South West Pacific Department: Registered Files (H and FW Series), 1967–1976.
FO 371: Foreign Office: Political Departments: General Correspondence, 1906–1966.

Unarchived unpublished official documents (UUOD)

Bogor Conference Minutes: Conference of the Prime Ministers of the Five Colombo Countries, Bogor, 28–29 December 1954—Minutes of Meetings and Documents of the Conference.
Colombo Conference Minutes: Southeast Asia Prime Ministers' Conference, Colombo, 28 April–1 May 1954, Minutes of Meetings and Documents of the Conference.

Proceedings of the Bandung Conference Political Committee: Proceedings of the Political Committee of the Asian-African Conference, Bandung, 20–24 April 1955.

## Published Documents

Asia-Pacific Economic Cooperation (APEC). 1995. "The Osaka Action Agenda: Implementation of the Bogor Declaration," in *Selected APEC Documents, 1995*. Singapore: APEC Secretariat.

———. 1995. The Osaka Action Plan: Road Map to Realising the APEC Vision: Report of the Pacific Business Forum 1995. Singapore: APEC Secretariat.

Association of Southeast Asian Nations (ASEAN). 1976. "The Treaty of Amity and Cooperation in Southeast Asia and the Declaration of ASEAN Concord." 24 February. Available at http://www.aseansec.org/1217.htm and http://www.aseansec.org/1216. htm.

———. 1988. *ASEAN Documents Series, 1967–1988*. 3rd ed. Jakarta: ASEAN Secretariat.

———. 1992. "Singapore Declaration, ASEAN Heads of Government Meeting." 27–28 January. Available at http://www.aseansec.org/1396.htm.

———. 1995. *The ASEAN Regional Forum: A Concept Paper*. Jakarta: ASEAN Secretariat.

———. 1998. "Terms of Understanding on the Establishment of the ASEAN Surveillance Process." Washington DC, 4 October. Available at http://www.aseansec.org/739.htm.

———. 2000. *The ASEAN Troika*. Jakarta: ASEAN Secretariat. Available at http://www .aseansec.org/3637.htm.

———. 2004. "ASEAN Security Community Plan of Action." 15 June. Available at http:// www.aseansec.org/16826.htm.

———. 2006. "Report of the Eminent Persons Group on the ASEAN Charter." December. Available at http://www.aseansec.org/19247.pdf.

———. 2007. "Charter of the Association of Southeast Asian Nations." Available at http:// www.aseansec.org/21069.pdf.

ASEAN-ISIS. 1993. "Confidence Building Measures in Southeast Asia," *Memorandum*, no. 5, December.

*Asia Africa Speaks from Bandung*. 1955. Jakarta: Department of Foreign Affairs.

Asian Relations: Proceedings of the Asian Relations Conference. 1948. New Delhi: Indian Council of World Affairs.

*The Conference on Indonesia, Proceedings*, January 20–3, 1949. New Delhi: Ministry of Information and Broadcasting.

Department of External Affairs, Canada. 1995. *Documents on Canadian External Relations*, vol. 21. Available at http://dfait-maeci.gc.ca/department/history/dcer/details-en. asp?intRefid=1308.

"Final Report of the East Asia Study Group." 2002. ASEAN+3 Summit, Phnom Penh. 4 November. Available at http://www.mofa.go.jp/region/asia-paci/asean/pmv0211/report .pdf.

Leland M. Goodrich and Edvard Hambro. 1946. *Charter of the United Nations: Commentary and Documents*. Boston: World Peace Foundation.

Ministry of Foreign Affairs, Thailand. 1998. "Thailand's Non-Paper on The Flexible Engagement Approach." Press Release no. 743/254127, 27 July 998. Available at http:// www.thaiembdc.org/pressctr/pr/pr743.htm.

The Report of the Arab League on the Bandung Conference. 1955. Cairo: League of Arab States.

*Speeches of Jawaharlal Nehru, 1953–67.* 1957. New Delhi: Government of India.

"Towards an East Asian Community: Region of Peace, Prosperity and Progress." 2001. East Asia Vision Group Report. Available at http://www.mofa.go.jp/region/asia-paci/report2001.pdf.

United Nations. 1945. Documents of the United Nations Conference on International Organization, San Francisco, 1945, vol. 6 New York: United Nations Information Organizations.

U.S. Department of State. 1955. "Hopeful Developments in Europe and in Asia." Press Release no. 230. 26 April.

——. 1981. Foreign Relations of United States, 1952–1954, vol. 16, The Geneva Conference: Korea and Indochina. Washington, DC: Government Printing Office.

——. 1984. Foreign Relations of United States, 1952–1954, vol. 12, East Asia and Pacific, part 1. Washington, DC: Government Printing Office.

——. 1989. Foreign Relations of United States, 1955–57, vol. 22, Southeast Asia. Washington, DC: Government Printing Office.

——. 2000. Foreign Relations of United States, 1964–1968, vol. 27, Mainland Southeast Asia; Regional Affairs. Washington, DC: Government Printing Office.

### Author's Interviews

Adnan Abdul Rahman, Bangkok, 23 August 1997.

Ali Alatas, Jakarta, 27 September 2000; Kuala Lumpur, 4 June 2002.

Bilahari Kaushikan, Paris, 11 March 2002.

Dewi Fortuna Anwar, Bangkok, 10 May 2002.

Geoffrey Wiseman, New Orleans, 24 March 2002.

Jusuf Wanandi, Kuala Lumpur, 4 June 2002.

Kwa Chong Guan, Singapore, 21 May 2003.

Richard Solomon, Kuala Lumpur, 4 June 2002.

Surin Pitsuwan, Bangkok, 30 January 2001; Singapore, 27 September 2001; Bangkok, 10 May 2002; Bangkok, 13 May 2002.

Termsak Chalermpalanupap, Bangkok, 16 January 2001.

Yukio Satoh, Singapore, 1 June 2002.

### Statements and Speeches

Abdullah Badawi. 1998. Opening statement delivered at the Thirty-First ASEAN Ministerial Meeting, Manila, 24 July.

Ali Alatas. 1992. "The Emerging Security Architecture in East Asia and the Pacific—An ASEAN Perspective." Lecture delivered at the National University of Singapore Society, Singapore, 28 October.

Baker, James A. 1991. "The U.S. and Japan: Global Partners in a Pacific Community." Speech delivered in Tokyo, 11 November.

Clark, Joe. 1990. "Canada and Asia Pacific in the 1990s." Speech delivered to the Victoria Chamber of Commerce, Victoria, British Columbia, 17 July.

——. 1990. Speech delivered at the Foreign Correspondents' Club of Japan, Tokyo, 24 July.

——. 1990. Speech delivered at the Indonesia-Canada Business Council and the Canada Business Association, Jakarta, 26 July.

Clinton, Bill. 1993. "Fundamentals of Security for a New Pacific Community." Speech delivered to the National Assembly of the Republic of Korea. Reproduced in *Dispatch* (U.S. Department of State) 4, no. 29 (10 July).

Jayakumar, S. 1998. Closing statement delivered at the Thirty-First ASEAN Ministerial Meeting, Manila, Philippines, 25 July. Available at www.aseansec.org/3930.htm.

Mohammed Najib Tun Razak. 1992. "Regional Security: Towards Cooperative Security and Regional Stability." Speech delivered at the Chief of the General Staff Conference, Darwin, Australia, 9 April.

Pitsuwan, Surin. 1998. "Currency in Turmoil in Southeast Asia: The Strategic Impact." Speech delivered at the Twelfth Asia Pacific Roundtable, Kuala Lumpur, Malaysia, June.

——. 1998. Opening statement delivered at the Thirty-First ASEAN Ministerial Meeting, Manila, 24 July.

——. 1998. "The Role of Human Rights in Thailand's Foreign Policy." Statement presented at the Seminar on Promotion and Protection of Human Rights by Human Rights Commissions, organized by the Friedrich Ebert Stiftung, 2 October.

Rafidah Aziz. 1991. Speech delivered at the Eighth Meeting of the Pacific Economic Co-operation Conference, Singapore, 20–22 May.

Siazon Jr., Domingo. 1998. "Winning the Challenges of the 21st Century." Address of the chairman of the Thirty-First ASEAN Ministerial Meeting, Manila, 24 July. Available at http://www.aseansec.org/3923.htm.

Solomon, Richard. 1990. "Asian Security in the 1990s: Integration in Economics: Diversity in Defence." Speech delivered at the University of San Diego, 30 October. Available at http://findarticles.com/p/articles/mi_m1584/is_n10_v1/ai_9290222.

——. 1991. "U.S. Relations with East Asia and the Pacific: A New Era." Statement delivered on 17 May 1991. Reproduced in *Dispatch* (U.S. Department of State) 2, no. 21 (27 May). Available at http://findarticles.com/p/articles/mi_m1584/is_n21_v2/ai_1149804.

Syed Hamid Bin Syed Jaafar Albar. 1999. "The Malaysian Human Rights Commission—Aims and Objectives." Speech at the Bar Council Auditorium, Kuala Lumpur, Malaysia, 28 October.

Zoellick, Robert. 1991. "U.S. Engagement with Asia." Statement delivered at the opening of the ASEAN 6+7 Post-Ministerial Conference, Kuala Lumpur, Malaysia, 22 July. Reprinted in *United States Foreign Policy: Current Documents 1991* (Washington, DC: U.S. Department of State, 1994): 669–72.

# Index